Hollywood Goes Latin

Spanish-Language Cinema in Los Angeles

Edited by María Elena de las Carreras and Jan-Christopher Horak

Table of Contents

Laurel and Hardy with their accent coach, Robert O'Connor, in *La vida nocturna* (1930, dir. James Parrott).

Introduction

María Elena de las Carreras and Jan-Christopher Horak

In the early 20th century, Los Angeles enjoyed a buoyant homegrown Spanish-language culture comprised of local and itinerant Mexican stock companies that produced zarzuelas, stage plays and variety acts. After the introduction of sound films, Spanish-language cinema thrived in the city's downtown theatres, screening throughout the 1930s, 1940s, and 1950s in venues such as the Teatro Eléctrico, the California, the Roosevelt, the Mason, the Azteca, the Million Dollar, and the Mayan Theater, among others. Through the Mexican-owned distribution company, Azteca Films, Inc., Spanish-language films were distributed to hundreds of theatres in the United States. With the emergence and growth of Mexican and Argentine sound cinema in the early to mid-1930s, downtown Los Angeles quickly became the undisputed capital of Latin American cinema culture in the United States.

Meanwhile, the advent of talkies in 1930 resulted in the Hollywood studios hiring local and international talent from Spain and Latin America, including Mexico, Argentina, and Cuba, for the production of films in Spanish. Parallel to these productions, a series of Spanish-language films was financed by independent producers who utilized Hollywood rental studios. Both Hollywood and independents contributed to the foundation of a Spanish-language film culture. By the mid-1930s, local producers and Latin American film companies supplied the growing local Spanish exhibition market in Los Angeles, while distributors sent films throughout the United States and Latin America. As a result, Los Angeles can be viewed as the most important hub in the United States for the production, distribution, and exhibition of films made in Spanish for Latin American audiences.

Given the level of film production in Spanish, it is not surprising to learn that in the 1930s, the Hollywood film studios also trained Hispanic filmmakers and technicians for its "Cine Hispano" productions. Once production ended, many of them returned to their native countries and contributed significantly to the establishment of national cinemas in Latin America. Others left when the Spanish Civil War (1936-39) broke out and then had an impact on the Spanish film industry, once the war ended. The demand for Spanish-speaking actors to work in the "Cine Hispano" productions attracted Hispanic Hollywood talent, local stage performers and international actors who collaborated in the making of a very diverse American cinema that showcased the idiosyncrasies, traditions and cultures of Latin America and Spain. Among key figures were Mexican actors José Mojica, Ramón Novarro, Dolores del Río, Tito Guízar, Lupita Tovar and Lupe Vélez; Spanish writers, actors and directors included Edgar Neville, Conchita Montenegro, Juan Torena, José López Rubio, Miguel de Zárraga and Gregorio Martínez Sierra; and South American actors and directors Carlos Gardel, Mona Maris, Barry Norton, José Bohr, Carlos Borcosque and Tito Davison. Their work presented an on-screen reflection of Hispanic identity that has not been equaled since the advent of film talkies. Hollywood's "Cine Hispano" was exhibited in U.S. theaters and distributed to the mass market of Spanish-speaking countries where it competed with the emergence of national film productions.

For decades, the Spanish-language productions of Hollywood have been ignored by film historians, because nationalist Latin American film critics mercilessly attacked the films, even while some titles were embraced by local audiences. The arguments made against Hispano Hollywood focused on two issues that continue to inform discussions even today, namely, that Hollywood Anglos had been completely tone deaf when it came to employing Spanish-speaking actors from different countries with strongly identifiable regional accents. Secondly, Hollywood producers were indifferent to cultural differences between various Latin American countries, often mixing conflicting musical or cultural heritages. In the following pages, these criticisms come up repeatedly. At the same time, even nationalists have understood that despite its sometimes wrong-headed attempts at producing films for Spanish-speaking audiences, the industry trained a whole generation of film technicians who founded film industries that eventually competed against Hollywood.

In 2013, the UCLA Film & Television Archive received a grant from the Getty Foundation to stage "Recuerdos de un cine en español: Latin American Cinema in Los Angeles, 1930-1960," as a part of their citywide exhibition, *Pacific Standard Time: LA/LA (Latin America/Los Angeles)*. That exhibition of nearly forty classic films from Mexico, Cuba, Argentina, and Hollywood took place from 23 September to 10 December 2017. A curatorial committee, consisting of Colin Gunckel, María Elena de las Carreras, Alejandra Espasande Bouza and Jan-Christopher Horak, was responsible for programming the series, with many films preserved specifically for the program by the UCLA Film & Television Archive. Apart from the film program, screened at the Archive's Billy Wilder Theatre, as well as at the Downtown Independent, formerly the Azteca Theatre, the project produced a catalogue and a book, *Cinema Between Latin America and Los Angeles. Origins to 1960* (2019, Rutgers University Press), edited by Gunckel, Lisa Jarvinen, and Horak.

As a prelude to the Fall series, and in conjunction with the 73rd FIAF Congress in Los Angeles, the UCLA Film & Television Archive and the Academy of Motion Picture Arts and Sciences organized a symposium from 29 April to 3 May 2017 on the production of Spanish-language cinema during the "golden age" of the Hollywood studio system. "Hollywood Goes Latin: Spanish-language Cinema in Los Angeles" brought together scholars and film archivists from all over Latin America, Spain and the United States to discuss the many issues surrounding the creation of Hollywood's "Cine Hispano." The goal of the symposium was to explore the making of Spanish-language films by the Hollywood studios and U.S. and Mexican independent producers, seeking to capitalize on the Spanish-language market of the Americas and Spain. The symposium discussed filmmakers, stars, crafts people, exhibitors and distributors involved in production and circulation of U.S.-made Spanish-language films. Many of the papers were presented in Spanish with simultaneous English translations, while English speakers were translated into Spanish. The contributions presented at this two-day symposium are collected and partially revised here. In some cases, manuscripts have been rewritten for publication, in others, the authors chose to publish their symposium texts, albeit translated into English. The essays have been organized slightly differently than the presentations at the FIAF Conference. The volume is broken into two sections: "Exhibition, Distribution, Reception" and "Production."

The book begins properly with a study of the Los Angeles exhibition market for Spanish language cinema in the 1930s and 1940s. Acknowledging the pioneering work of Colin Gunckel, Horak presents a history of the rise and fall of Mexican cinema theatres in L.A.'s now razed Mexican neighborhoods around downtown Main Street. Until the late 1940s, the fortunes of these cinemas were connected to the work of Frank Fouce, the Azteca Film Company, and the Calderón Brothers, producer/distributor/exhibitors from El Paso and Chihuahua. Together, they created a system of production, distribution and exhibition which was completely out of the control of the Hollywood majors, despite being headquartered in its backyard, and can be viewed as constituting a major minority cinema.

In contrast to Horak who focuses on exhibition in Los Angeles, Peruvian film researcher Violeta Núñez Gorriti analyzes distribution and exhibition of Hollywood's Spanish-language films in four key Latin American markets, namely in Lima (Peru), Buenos Aires (Argentina), Montevideo (Uruguay), and Mexico City (Mexico). Núñez Gorriti looks at how local distributors, who had previously had monopolies on all exhibitions, were supplanted by a system of first- and second-run cinemas, which screened both Hollywood Spanish and English films. The absence of systematic information for other Latin American countries precludes incorporating other cities into this study. As a result, the findings here are provisional, until more data allows for a broader and more accurate understanding of the market, but it seems evident that Hollywood's Spanish-language features were not rejected out of hand by local audiences.

Catalan archivist and film historian Esteve Riambau looks at a different aspect of the reception of Hollywood Spanish-language cinema by analyzing reviews and comments in the well-known Spanish-language film magazine *Cinelandia* (1927-1936). Published in Los Angeles by the Spanish-American Publishing Co., the magazine addressed a largely female audience, while promoting American cinema in all Spanish-speaking markets. In contrast to the first two essays in this volume which attempt to relativize the alleged lack of popular success for Hollywood's Hispanic productions, Riambau demonstrates that journalists usually led the charge against these films, undergirding the Hollywood Hispano project's reputation as being an abject failure.

The reception of a given film often has long-term consequences for the ultimate survival and preservation of a title. Given the oft-repeated negative reputation of Hollywood's Hispano cinema, as well as extremely high mortality rates for all films produced in Hollywood in the early 1930s, it is not surprising to learn that the great majority of these films have been lost. Roberto Green Quintana looks at the challenges for film preservationists when dealing with Spanish-language film productions from this period. He discusses the work by the UCLA Film & Television Archive and others to preserve and make available films for the Fall 2017 film program, "Recuerdos de un cine en español: Latin American Cinema in Los Angeles," while noting some of the film technical issues when working with this material.

The book's second section, highlighting Spanish-language film production, begins with a key text, as demonstrated in the number of citations in this volume. Juan B. Heinink and Robert G. Dickson's monograph, *Cita en Hollywood* (1990), is indeed the *urtext* for the history of Hollywood Hispanic cinema. In it, the authors document and briefly discuss every Spanish-language film made between 1929 and 1939, whether by the major Hollywood studios or by independent producers. Their Spanish-language essay in that volume is translated into English here for the first time and revised specifically for this publication, making this groundbreaking text available to non-Spanish speakers for the first time.

Following these broad-based studies, the volume continues with essays on individual filmmakers and actors who played significant roles in the production of Spanish-language films in Hollywood in the 1930s, and then often returned to their native countries (or elsewhere), to help establish domestic film industries in Latin America. María Elena de las Carreras, for example, looks at the amazing career of the Chilean film director Carlos Borcosque, who after receiving training in Hollywood in the 1930s, cutting his teeth on Spanish-language films at Metro-Goldwyn-Mayer, went on to become one of Argentina's most prolific and successful film directors of the studio era, completing over thirty feature films between 1939 and 1966. As in the case of almost all Latino directors, Borcosque earned a living and learned a craft, but had little possibility to develop his artistic persona, until he began making films in Argentina.

The Director of the Cinemateca de Cuba in Havana, Luciano Castillo, on the other hand, looks at the Hollywood career of film director Ramón Peón, who directed Cuba's most well known silent film, *La Virgen de la Caridad* (1930), before moving to Hollywood, and then establishing himself as a major force in the Mexican film industry of the 1940s and 1950s. In Hollywood, however, Castillo demonstrates that Peón, despite his previous accomplishments in Cuba, suffered long periods of unemployment at the margins of the industry, sometimes working as an assistant director, but also having to earn his keep as a street performer.

Next, María Esperanza Vázquez Bernal and Xóchitl Fernández analyze the film career of Gabriel García Moreno, a Mexican film director who moved to Hollywood in the late 1920s after completing several silent films in Mexico. Once there, García Moreno became involved in the invention of motion picture technology, e.g., the Moreno-Snyder sound film camera, which he tried unsuccessfully to market. He next worked on inventing a low-cost color film process, but ultimately returned to Mexico City, where he designed and built a modern sound film studio for the Calderón Brothers in 1937, thus helping to create the infrastructure for a Mexican film industry.

Among the Spanish-speaking actors who populated Hollywood's Hispanic features in the early 1930s was the Spanish actor Romualdo Tirado. According to Alejandra Espasande Bouza, a film archivist at the Academy Film Archive and one of the co-curators of "Recuerdos de un cine en español: Latin American Cinema in Los Angeles, 1930-1960," Tirado began his career as a child actor in Spain, but soon relocated to Mexico, later becoming a fixture in the Los Angeles Mexican theatre scene, while commuting regularly in the 1920s between the two cities. With the advent of Hispanic Hollywood features, Tirado advanced to a reliable character actor in literally dozens of Spanish-language films.

Next, César Fratantoni looks at the case of Carlos Gardel, the Argentine tango singer, who may have had the most unique career in Spanish Hollywood. Cases of autonomy under the umbrella of a major studio are extremely rare in the Golden Age of Hollywood, the period ranging from the 1920s to the 1950s. Yet, in 1934 Carlos Gardel arrived in New York City and managed to control the production of four very successful Spanish-language films, using Paramount's production facilities and distribution network. Thanks to newly discovered documentation, and the survival of many of his letters, we have a rare look at the challenges a Hispanic producer would face, if he tried to do business with one of the Big Five.

One of the earliest independent Mexican producers working in Los Angeles at the beginning of the 1930s was the actor-director Guillermo Calles. Rogelio Agrasánchez Jr.'s essay on the Native American film star, who began his career in Hollywood before World War I, is adapted from his book, *Guillermo Calles: A Biography of the Actor and Mexican Cinema Pioneer* (2010). In his contribution, Agrasánchez theorizes that the actor suffered descrimination as an actor and director, due to his ethnic origins, and, despite several successful films as director, could not find appropriate work in Hollywood.

Rosario Vidal Bonifaz, from the University of Guadalajara, discusses the amazing career of Mexican opera star José Mojica, certainly the most prolific and successful of the Latin stars in Hollywood. A native from Jalisco, José Mojica became one of the most important tenors of his time, and a star at the Fox Film Corporation between 1930 and 1934, when the company attempted to capture the Hispanic markets through popular musicals. The author reviews the short, yet sparkling, film career of Mojica and its impact on some Latin American markets (Mexico, Peru, Uruguay and Spain). Vidal Bonifaz concludes with a short analysis of *La cruz y la espada* (1934), one of the few Spanish-language films that has survived in its full-length version; the film is also considered by some to be the reason why, years later, its leading man decided to quit Hollywood and withdraw to a Peruvian monastery.

Catalan professor and film scholar Núria Bou's presentation analyzes the acting style of Conchita Montenegro in *La femme et le pantin* (1929, Jacques de Baroncelli) and her Hollywood films (1930-1935). The author postulates that *La femme et le pantin* and her American films were more erotic and risqué than any films she made in Hollywood for Spanish-speaking audiences. Through textual and comparative analysis, the essay demonstrates how the "American performance style" influenced her subsequent film work, and the impact that this approach also had on the reception of her films in Spain.

According to Spanish journalist and historian Mar Díaz Martínez, Antonio Moreno's story is one that should not be forgotten: he embodied the American dream, like very few in the silent era, but his life and career were changed dramatically after the arrival of sound, not because of his voice, but because of his American-accented Spanish. His filmography, starting with D.W. Griffith and ending with John Ford, is a fascinating trip through classic Hollywood cinema, a master class in demonstrating how unfair film history can be to stars who don't become legends. But Antonio Moreno deserves to become a legend, once his story has been properly told.

Eduardo de la Vega Alfaro's essay relates the previously unknown history of the production of *Contrabando* (1932), shot by Mexicans in Tijuana and Baja California at the moment when Hispanic cinema made in Hollywood had reached its apex. Financed by the politician, soldier, and revolutionary Agustín Olachea Avilés, the film visualizes the rebellion of a group conspirators opposing the elected government, after the murder of General Álvaro Obregón Salido. Produced both in Spanish and English versions, the film was an early attempt to utilize conventions developed in the "Mecca of Film," in order to create a nationalist cinema, while also competing directly with the most powerful film industry in the world.

Finally, Mexican film studies professor Bernd Hausberger offers a fascinating footnote on the aborted career of Celia Villa, a daughter of the Mexican revolutionary politician Pancho Villa. Capitalizing on the notoriety of her father, especially in the United States, Celia Villa attempted to parlay her connections into a Hollywood film career, especially after she was hired for the publicity tour of Metro-Goldwyn-Mayer's *Viva Villa!* (1934, Jack Conway). However, as Hausberger notes, Celia Villa was also represented in the press as an exotic "other," her public persona formed by ethnic- and gender-inflected stereotypes, which mitigated her career.

The volume closes with a complete bibliography of all sources, and a list of the Spanish-language films produced between 1929 and 1939, as well as short biographies of the contributors to this volume. It is hoped that the historical research presented here will contribute to an expansion of historical interest in the long-neglected Spanish cinema of Hollywood in the 1930s.

I
Exhibition, Distribution, Reception

Creating a Minority Cinema: Spanish-Language Film Exhibition in Downtown Los Angeles before World War II

Jan-Christopher Horak

SPANISH-LANGUAGE CINEMA IN LOS ANGELES

On May 20, 1932, the Teatro California on Main Street in downtown Los Angeles presented the local premiere of Mexico's first "National" sound feature fiction film, *Santa* (1932), directed by Antonio Moreno and starring Lupita Tovar, both of whom had substantial careers in Hollywood. The film had previously premiered in Mexico City (30 March) and El Paso, Texas (16 May), at a hugely successful midnight screening, but it seems clear from the publicity push that the L.A. premiere was to introduce Mexican cinema to a worldwide audience. Only Los Angeles could boast an international corps of film journalists who could potentially carry the news of the Mexican achievement to the rest of the globe. According to an article in *La Opinión*, *Santa* was coproduced by José and Rafael Calderón, who brought the film to Los Angeles and probably financed the premiere, which drew an A-list of Hollywood personalities, including Tovar, José Mojica, Mona Maris, Laurel and Hardy, Barry Norton, Ramón Pereda, Julio Peña, Juan Torena, Paul Ellis and Carlos Villarías. Mojica and the Mexican Consul, Mr. Joaquín Terrazas, were named official hosts.[1] The movie pre-show featured local artists, including the popular baritone Rodolfo Hoyos, the tenor Manuel Maytorena and the Pasadas Sisters, directed by Ernesto González Jiménez. The theatre was decorated with huge portraits of the film's stars, Tovar, Moreno and Carlos Orellana, and the crowds jockeyed to see and talk to their favorite Spanish-speaking actors,[2] while critics in the next morning's papers praised the film for its realism and its melodrama. As *La Opinión* wrote:

1 Premiere announcement in *La Opinión*, 20 May 1932, 6; see also *La Opinión*, 29 May 1932, 4.
2 Rogelio Agrasánchez Jr., *Mexican Movies in the United States. A History of the Film Theaters and Audiences 1920-1960* (Jefferson, N.C.: McFarland & Company, 2006), 50ff.

We are positive that the Mexican community, almost in its entirety, will attend the California Theater. We know that Mexicans want to see the movie not only for its merits, but also because it's the first one, because it tells a touching story, and, mainly, because it's a Mexican film.[3]

The L.A. premiere of *Santa* embodies an early moment in the history of a vibrant cinema culture that has all but disappeared in Los Angeles, namely Spanish-language cinema in downtown's first- and second-run theatres on Main Street. Spanish-language films were in fact screened at numerous cinemas throughout the 1930s, 1940s and 1950s, with the great majority of these films originating from Mexico, followed by Argentina, Spain, Los Angeles and Cuba, all of which maintained indigenous film industries. With ticket prices rarely exceeding ten and fifteen cents, going to the cinema was a family affair for Mexican-American audiences, who flocked there with children and grandparents in tow to see images from home and hear their mother tongue. In these cinemas, Latinos/Latinas became producers of spaces for dialogue, which were unique and separate from the institutionalized culture and politics of Anglo-America.

The cinemas of Mexico and Argentina in the classic studio period 1930-1960 are no longer the *terra incognita* they once were, thanks to the work of a number of younger film scholars who have freed themselves the prejudicial notion that all Latin American cinema before the Cuban Revolution was nothing more than pale imitations of Hollywood in Spanish.[4] Nevertheless, there is still much work to be done, both in terms of analyzing the surviving films as cultural products in an international market, and, especially, in terms of the history of distribution and exhibition of these films within and outside Latin America. Thanks to the groundbreaking work of such scholars as Rogelio Agrasánchez Jr., Colin Gunckel and Lisa Jarvinen, we now know that the Los Angeles film market was of some significance to Mexican-Americans in Southern California and Texas.[5] And from Agrasánchez we also learn that nearly five hundred cinemas in the United States showed Spanish-language films at least occasionally in this time period.[6] However, it was while conducting research for the Getty Foundation-funded film program, "Recuerdos de un cine en español: Latin American Cinema in Los Angeles, 1930-1960," as a part of *Pacific Standard Time: LA / LA*, that I became aware of just how extensive the penetration of Latin American cinema into the American market had been. In point of fact, it is almost shocking to realize that virtually 100% of Mexico's film production received play dates in the Los Angeles film market in the 1930s and 1940s. As a result, Los Angeles was not only the most important showcase for Spanish-language films in the United States, but also provided a window to Latin America and the world on Mexican and Argentine cinema. Indeed, through Latin American film

3 "El estreno de Santa en el T. California," in *La Opinión*, 22 May 1932, 4.

4 Those scholars include Colin Gunckel, Lisa Jarvinen, Jacqueline Avila, Paulina Suárez-Hesketh, Desirée J. García, Sergio de la Mora, Elissa J. Rashkin, Mathew B. Karush, Fernando Mino Gracia, Graciela Montaldo, Nina Hoechtl, and Alejandra Espasande.

5 See Colin Gunckel, *Mexico on Main Street. Transnational Film Culture in Los Angeles before World War II* (New Brunswick, N.J.: Rutgers University Press, 2015); Lisa Jarvinen, *The Rise of Spanish-Language Filmmaking. Out from Hollywood's Shadow, 1929-1939.* (New Brunswick, N.J.: Rutgers University Press, 2012).

6 Agrasánchez, 2006. In an appendix, Agrasánchez lists all of L.A. Spanish-language theatres, but misses the Arrow, which in 1940 was renamed Teatro Azteca.

journalists working in Los Angeles and covering the American film scene, it is likely that national film distributors and exhibitors in Latin America would have been well-informed about which films were successful in the belly of the beast.

Furthermore, Los Angeles was not only a center of Spanish-language film exhibition, but also a not-insignificant producer of Spanish-language films in the 1930s, both studio-contracted and independent film productions. Furthermore, Vermont Street in Los Angeles became the headquarters for the two major distributors of Latin American films in the United States: Azteca Films, Inc., and Clasa-Mohme, Inc. Functioning efficiently at the level of production, distribution and exhibition, L.A.'s Spanish-language cinema thus reveals the contours of a completely intact minority cinema in the United States, which operated independently of the American studio majors, who supposedly had a monopoly at all levels of the film industry. To my knowledge, such a concept of a minority cinema in the United States has previously only been discussed in the literature in terms of African-American cinema in the so-called "race film era," while Spanish-language cinema has been perceived as existing only in the margins, and not as a functioning system. In fact, though under-capitalized and subject to economic intrusions, this cinema was able to survive for more than three decades outside the institutional infrastructure of mainstream American cinema, i.e., Hollywood.

Just how was it possible to create an intact and generally stable infrastructure for the production, distribution, and exhibition of Spanish-language features in Los Angeles, largely outside Hollywood's centripetal power? Obviously, a demand for Spanish-language culture, whether film, theatre or press, manifested itself in the empirical presence of Spanish-speaking audiences, hungry for films in their native tongue.[7] Such an audience already existed when audiences flocked to Main Street theatres to see Spanish-language versions of American films, and more importantly, Spanish-language popular theatre.[8] Once American interest in Spanish version productions waned, the Mexican film industry and some U.S. independents increasingly met the growing demand for Latin American cinema. The start was slow, even after the worldwide success of *Santa*. But by the late 1930s, the number of community cinemas had increased from zero to five. At the same time, Argentina's film industry made huge inroads into the Spanish L.A. market, without Mexican film producers losing ground, because audience demand had supported a growing number of Spanish-language cinemas. Moving all these foreign language productions into the American film market involved a distribution system, which grew ever larger from the 1930s to the 1940s.

Finally, reliable screening spaces had to be available. While there were a number of cinemas screening Spanish-language films in the early 1930s, the exhibition market did not stabilize until after 1933, when the Depression's grip on the film industry slowly weak-

---

7 See oral history with Lilia Guízar, the daughter of Tito Guízar, and her husband Ramón Inclán, a film critic in the 1950s for *La Opinión*. See also oral history with Mexican-American residents Ricardo Ponce and his wife María Elena, who first met at the California Theatre in Los Angeles. See Getty Foundation's "LA / LA" Oral History, UCLA Library.

8 Sánchez notes that in the 1920s the Mexican community in Los Angeles was larger than any other except Mexico City, and in the 1920s supported no less than five regular theatres and half a dozen other occasional theatrical spaces. See George J. Sánchez, *Becoming Mexican American. Ethnicity, Culture, and Identity in Chicano Los Angeles, 1900-1945.* (New York: Oxford University Press, 1993), 179.

ened. It was with the reestablishment of the Teatro California as a first-run house that Frank Fouce entered into L.A.'s exhibition market. His empire would by the end of the thirties grow to five theatres, then begin shrinking again in the post-war period, but remain a vibrant part of the community until the 1960s, when television and other external factors upended most Spanish-language film theatres.

This essay, then, will first address the existence of a Spanish-language cinema culture in Los Angeles in the 1930s and 1940s, then discuss the distribution of Spanish-language films in North America, and close with a statistical analysis of national cinemas and trends for exhibition in the local theatrical market of Los Angeles. As was the case with Hollywood, Spanish-language cinema in Los Angeles was above all a popular cinema, encompassing many different genres and stars, the latter moving freely between film studios in Mexico City, Hollywood, Buenos Aires, and even Madrid. Unlike some Mexican film historians who remain narrowly focused on a handful of films from Mexico's Golden Age, I have analyzed all advertisements and short "reviews" in *La Opinión* for the years 1930-1942 to ascertain not only which Spanish- language films premiered and were reprised, but also to ascertain that audiences were grateful for all kinds of films in Spanish, even those "version films" produced in Hollywood at the beginning of the sound era. I thereby modify the established wisdom promulgated by nationalist film critics and intellectuals that such films were deeply unpopular with audiences. Utilizing empirical data from advertisements allows us to define the contours of Spanish-language cinema in the United States as a minority cinema, catering to the needs of recent immigrants from Latin America, as well as Spanish-speaking Americans. I have limited my research to the pre-World War II period, as a matter of convenience, but also because structural changes in the Mexican community after World War II, connected to urban renewal and the expulsion of Mexicans from the city center, changed the terms of this minority cinema. After World War II, Los Angeles city fathers approved the destruction of downtown Mexican neighborhoods, and with them several Mexican theatres, so that the city could project an Anglo-Saxon image that would attract immigrants from the mid-western United Sates. As a result, the cultural spaces for community dialogue moved to other real and virtual sites, including new Spanish-language television networks.

EMPRESA FOUCE

The Los Angeles Spanish-language theatre market cannot be separated from the name of Francisco ("Frank") Fouce. Born in Honolulu, Hawaii, of Spanish parents on 26 October 1899, Fouce immigrated with them to Los Angeles in 1902.[9] Growing up in Los Angeles, Fouce began working in the film industry as a child actor, according to family sources.[10] When he was fourteen, his dad, Antonio Fouce, died, only forty-eight years old,[11] possibly forcing Frank's mother to run a boarding house with furnished rooms just blocks from

9 An obituary for Fouce's mother, 'Loyisa' (sic) Fouce, actually Luisa, states she "moved to California thirty-eight years ago." See *Los Angeles Times,* 25 August 1938, 36.

10 His *Los Angeles Times* obituary states that he was a silent film actor at one time, but probably only as an extra or bit player, since no actual credits could be found. See Fouce obituary, *Los Angeles Times,* 13 January 1962.

11 California Death Certificate, 14 January 1914, Los Angeles, CA (Ancestry.com). Antonio Fouce applied for citizenship in October 1905 and affirmed he had entered the United States via San Francisco on 22 March 1902. U.S. Naturalization Records, 1840-1957 (Ancestry.com).

the old Plaza. The 1920 U.S. census lists Fouce as living at home with his mother Luisa, his brother Manuel, his sister Dolores, and her two children, with Fouce's occupation given as motion picture timer in a lab. He married Anna Rosen that same year on New Year's Eve.[12] City directories list Frank as living at home until 1926, his occupation variously listed as machinist (1917), clerk (1921) and manager of the Gay Theatre (1925) on N. Main St.[13] According to some sources, he became manager of the Teatro Alegría on Main Street in 1925.[14] In 1927, Fouce is listed as a motion picture director, living on N. Plymouth Blvd. in Hollywood. A year later he moved back to downtown L.A. (408 ½ Boylston St.) and was working in a film lab (1929). He next managed the Teatro Estella (1930), a legitimate Spanish-language stage. While his address in the City Directory was listed as Boylston St., a 1930 census document notes that Fouce and his wife were again living with his mother and he was unemployed.[15] By 1932, Fouce and his wife Anna had moved back to Hollywood (Lodi Place), right in the shadow of Columbia's Gower Studios, indicating an improvement in his financial situation. When the Calderóns opened *Santa* in May 1932, Fouce was working for Columbia, possibly in their Spanish-language film production unit, and it is probable he had helped negotiate the deal with the California, since *Carne de cabaret* (1931, Christy Cabanne) and two other Spanish Columbia features had been screened at the California in 1931. Sometime after the *Santa* premiere, Fouce established his own distribution company, Spanish International Pictures (SIP), which continued to operate at least on paper until 1936.[16] Prior to acquiring the California in 1933, Fouce purchased local distribution rights to *La voluntad del muerto* (1930, George Melford), *Drácula* (1931, George Melford), *Resurrección* (1931, Edwin Carewe), *Don Juan diplomático* (1931, George Melford), and *Contrabando* (1932, Alberto Méndez Bernal, Raymond Wells). Once he acquired the California, Fouce initially only showed films for which he had purchased local rights. Like *Santa* and *La Llorona* (1933, Ramón Peón) many SIP films were also distributed by Azteca.[17]

I've dwelt on Frank Fouce's biography in some detail, because it demonstrates that Fouce moved at the fringes of the film industry, and, given changing jobs, was not in an economically secure position, at least through his twenties and early thirties. The question then becomes, how was Fouce able to build up a theatrical empire in a few short years and during the depths of the Depression? Fouce must have received loans or financing from someone. As will be demonstrated below, I'm relatively certain that it was the Calderón Brothers who helped Fouce, better said that Fouce may have initially been a representative for the Calderón family operations, whose goal it was to create a theatrical market for Mexican films in Los Angeles.

Fouce leased the California in August 1933, and three months later the Teatro Eléctrico. In November 1934, he added the Hidalgo as a second-run space. By 1938, he had become the most important Spanish-language exhibitor in the city, operating the Cal-

---

12 See 1920 United States Federal Census, and California County Birth, Death, Marriage Records, 1849-1940 (Ancestry.com).

13 Los Angeles City Directories are available online at the Los Angeles Public Library, http://rescarta.lapl.org/ResCarta-Web/jsp/RcWebBrowse.jsp .

14 Information sheet on Fouce, courtesy of the Agrasánchez Film Archive.

15 Ibid.

16 "Don Rubén Calderón Habla Sobre los Proyectos de la Azteca Films Dist. Co.", *La Opinión* 8, No. 234, 7 May 1939, 4.

17 Letter, Frank Fouce to Gregorio del Amo, 10 March 1938. See Del Amo Estate Company Collection, Archives & Special Collections, CSU Dominguez Hills.

ifornia, the Teatro Roosevelt, and the Teatro Eléctrico on Main Street, and the Mason on Broadway. The California usually ran as a first-run house, the Mason presented live theatrical shows, while the other two theatres functioned as second-run, although Fouce would often open a big film in all three Main Street cinemas at once, as he did when on 9 February 1938 he opened *Bajo el cielo de México* (1937), Fernando de Fuentes's sequel to *Allá en el rancho grande* (1936).[18] Fouce also still occasionally utilized the Teatro México, on South Main Street, which he had leased in 1935, programming, e.g., Tito Guízar's *Mis dos amores* (1938, Nick Grinde) there in June 1939.[19] The Arrow/Azteca opened in late March 1939 and was utilized as both a first- and second-run theatre, putting the Roosevelt out of commission at least for a few years.[20] In 1944, Fouce purchased the Liberty Theatre at 136 S. Main St., while leasing the Mayan on South Hill St., and purchasing the Mason in 1946, which he had previously leased.[21] In March 1949, Fouce purchased the Mayan and a year later he leased the Million Dollar Theatre from the Harry Popkin Organization, while continuing to operate the California and Mason. By the time he died on 11 January 1962, Frank Fouce had also branched out into Spanish-language broadcasting, owning KXETV in San Diego and numerous other stations that became a part of Univision.

L.A.'S MAIN STREET SPANISH-LANGUAGE CINEMAS

When the California Theatre opened its doors at 810 S. Main Street on Christmas Eve 1918 with a screening of Douglas Fairbanks' *The Americano* (1918, John Emerson), it had a seating capacity of 1900, making it one of the largest cinemas in the city.[22] Owner Fred Miller and manager Harry Leonhardt immediately received praise for their elaborate stage and film presentations and the orchestral music of Carli Elinor,[23] making it a direct competitor to Sid Grauman's only recently opened movie palace, the Million Dollar. In October 1919, Samuel Goldwyn, looking for a first-run theatre in Los Angeles, leased the California and installed Samuel ("Roxy") Rothafel, who reopened the theatre on 7 November 1919 with Goldwyn's *Flame of the Desert* (1919, Reginald Barker). But Rothafel's tenure was short-lived: in January 1920, he moved on to Chicago, although the California remained a Goldwyn house under Fred Miller's direction, as an advertisement from 1922 documents.[24] By 1925, though, diminishing profits forced Miller to close the theatre, while he managed others, like the Alhambra, Figueroa, and, beginning in 1927, the Carthay Circle.

Then in May 1930, Miller decided to reopen the California, initially showing American films. However, within four months, Miller had changed the name to the California International[25] and apparently signed contracts with some of the major studios to release their Spanish-language versions, since it then became a first-run theatre in October and

18 *La Opinión*, 9 February 1938, 4.
19 Agrasánchez, 53; *La Opinión*, 25 June 1939, 4.
20 *La Opinión*, 21, 23 March 1939, 4.
21 *Los Angeles Times*, 4 January 1946, 13.
22 Elena Boland, "Pioneer Theatre Man Reenters Field," *Los Angeles Times*, 18 May 1930, B9.
23 Ross Melnick, *American Showman. Samuel 'Roxy' Rothafel and the Birth of the Entertainment Industry*. (New York: Columbia University Press, 2012), 180.
24 See webpage "Historic Los Angeles Theatres—Downtown," which provides images and some history of the cinema, https://sites.google.com/site/downtownlosangelestheatres/california.
25 "Algo sobre el Teatro Internacional," *La Opinión*, 1 Aug. 1930, 6.

remained as such until early 1932, hosting no less than sixteen Spanish-language world premieres, including *Drácula, El presidio* (1930, Ward Wing), *Las luces de Buenos Aires* (1931, Adelqui Millar) and *La gran jornada* (1931, David Howard). After the world premiere in February 1932 of Columbia's *Hombres en mi vida,* (1932, David Selman), starring Lupe Vélez and Gilbert Roland, the California went dark. In March the theatre was leased to Albert E. Finger, who opened the Yiddish-language feature, *His Wife's Lover* (1931, Sidney M. Goldin) on 7 March; a short-lived endeavor.[26] What had happened?

The fact that only four studio-produced Spanish-language features opened in the first five months of 1932 meant the production pipeline had dried up. This fact is in accordance with previous research on Hollywood's production of Spanish-version films, which has noted the cessation of most version production after 1931. The closing of the California may have also had something to do with the worsening Depression, which left huge numbers of Mexican-Americans unemployed and destitute. According to statistics, wholly one-third of L.A.'s Spanish-speaking audience of 150,000 was deported by zealous Federal authorities, working ironically in conjunction with the Mexican Consulate, which endeavored to repatriate citizens.[27] This was not the first intrusion into the Mexican-American community and would certainly not be the last. Main Street's film culture would physically disappear in the next wave of anti-Mexican, anti-immigrant policy. In the post-World War II period, the Los Angeles city fathers in cooperation with the federal government accelerated urban renewal in the Bunker Hill and North Main Street Mexican area, "clearing out neighborhoods and literally splitting communities with freeways;" urban renewal in L.A. meant Mexican removal.[28]

In Spring 1932, Rafael Calderón was initially unable to find a screen to show *Santa*, because the California, the only acceptable theatre in the community, was closed. The California was subsequently procured through the intervention of Frank Fouce. Supposedly, the California's manager, Mr. Finger, who had leased the theatre in March from its owner, Fred Miller, was not interested in showing Mexican films, but only Yiddish-language films, which he had a hand in distributing.[29] This narrative may be partially apocryphal, since Finger literally only programmed one film at the California in March, but as *La Opinión* noted about the *Santa* premiere: "A foreign company is in charge of the opening of the film. This company is run by a man named Finger, who has shown Jewish films at the California before."[30] The question remains, to what degree Frank Fouce was involved in the premiere, beyond helping broker the rental, and if his association with the Calderóns began at that time or had begun earlier.

26 *His Wife's Lover* was announced for a two-week run, but may have only played a week. The presentation included two Yiddish shorts and a stage show. No other screenings could be documented. Finger was not a film man, but a salesman, who may have lost his shirt. He apparently still had a lease on the California when *Santa* premiered, and therefore handled the theatre logistics for the premiere, according to press reports.

27 Sánchez, 123.

28 Liette Gilbert, *Decolonizing the City: The Construction of Social and Spatial Consciousness of Mexicans in Los Angeles*, M.A. Thesis, UCLA, 1995, 44.

29 "Don Rubén...", *La Opinión,* 7 May 1939, 4. See also *La Opinión,* 1 May 1932, 7.

30 *La Opinión,* 1 May 1932, 7.

In the Summer of '32, many in the Mexican community hoped that *Santa's* two-week run, followed by the first run of Guillermo Calles's *Regeneración* (1930, Guillermo Calles), would lead to a revival of the California as a Spanish-language house; it was not to be. The California would remain, except for a brief run of revivals in early 1933, dark until August, when Frank Fouce finally acquired the theatre. The California reopened on 14 September 1933 with another Calderón distributed property, *La Llorona* (1933, Ramón Peón). Just as *Santa* had been a Calderón distributed "national production," so too was *La Llorona* advertised as a national production. After purchasing the theatre from Fred Miller, Fouce installed new projectors, a Western Electric sound system, and renovated the whole theatre, including new paintings, new drapes, upholstery, and new carpets. In announcing the reopening of the California, Fouce stated: "The California will be totally renovated for the new season. No expense has been spared, as we believe that it's our duty to give the Mexican community a venue worthy of their culture and their finesse."[31] Interestingly, despite the fact that there were no regular screenings of Spanish-language films at the time, *La Opinión* pushed back on Fouce even before *La Llorona*'s premiere: "Unfortunately, there are class divisions. As a result, middle-class and upper-class audiences will attend the California, while Mexican working classes will attend the Hidalgo Theatre, because of its location and the nature of its shows."[32] As in the case of the *Santa* premiere, *La Llorona*'s premiere was preceded by a live stage show. Fouce followed up with a premiere on 28 September of *La sombra de Pancho Villa* (1932, Miguel Contreras Torres), a patriotic film about the Mexican revolution, and with a biopic of the famous Mexican composer Juventino Rosas, *Sobre las olas* (1933, Miguel Zacarías), on Columbus Day; all three films were distributed by Fouce's Spanish International Pictures. The California would continue as a flagship theatre of the Empresa Fouce until January 1, 1949.[33] Two days later, the Broder Association of Detroit (Jack Broder) opened the theatre with the reprise of a Jorge Negrete film and continued Spanish-language programming through the 1950s.[34] The theatre was then purchased by Bruce Corwin and the Metropolitan Theatre chain, programming Mexican films into the 1970s, according to Colin Gunckel, who also dates the cinema's demise in 1987, after a final stint as a Pussycat Theatre.[35]

Less than three months after opening the California, Fouce took over the management of the Teatro Eléctrico, with programming commencing on 30 November 1933 with *La Llorona*. The cinema first appears in the 1913 Los Angeles City Directory as the Electric Theatre, located at 212 N. Main Street, M.M. Hurwitz proprietor.[36] It would change hands several times over the next decade, until Harry Ewing acquired it in 1922.[37] Ewing, who also owned the Estella Theatre and after 1930, the Hidalgo, programmed the Electric with popular Mexican theatre, including zarzuelas, and occasionally films. The cinema was wired for sound in 1930, advertising itself as "El Teatro de sonido perfecto," reprising *Sombras de gloria* (1930, Andrew L. Stone) in September, but programming of

31 *La Opinión,* 24 August 1933, 4.
32 *La Opinión,* 6 September 1933, 4.
33 Frank Fouce, "Nuestro Adiós al Antiguo Teatro California," in: *La Opinión,* 1 January 1949, 4.
34 "El Circuito Broder ha rentado el Teatro California," *La Opinión,* 7 January 1949, 4.
35 Colin Gunckel, Notes, "Spanish-language theaters, 1910-1990," no date.
36 City Directory, Los Angeles 1913, 636, http://rescarta.lapl.org/ResCarta-Web/jsp/RcWebImageViewer.jsp?doc_id=040428be-8b21-4de1-9b1e-3421068c0f1c/cl000000/20150518/00000008
37 According to Los Angeles City Directories, the Electric was managed by Hurwitz (1913), Abraham Shapiro, Mrs. Sophia Hurwitz (1915), P.T. Davidson and C.W. Blake (1917), H.A. Levin (1920), and Harry E. Ewing (1922).

The Mason Theatre, "Home of Mexican Films," in Los Angeles. Courtesy of the Los Angeles Public Library.

films remained extremely irregular, often going dark between second-run screenings of Spanish and American films. In November 1933, Fouce took over, renaming it Teatro Eléctrico. As it seated only 345 patrons, Fouce ran the same sequence of films at the Eléctrico that he had previously opened at the California, at least until February 1935 when Fouce premiered *Juárez y Maximiliano* (1933, Miguel Contreras Torres, Raphael J. Sevilla) at all three Fouce houses simultaneously, which by then included the Hidalgo. Sometimes, the Eléctrico would double bill a Spanish feature with an American film, as it did in September 1936 when *Celos* (1935, Arcady Boytler) was paired with *Times Square Playboy* (1936, William McGann). The Eléctrico would continue as second-run for the California and co-premiere house with the California and Hidalgo, until the theatre was renamed the Roosevelt in April 1940.

The Teatro Hidalgo was the oldest and possibly most ragged theatre in the Mexican community. Located at 373 North Main, where the 101 Freeway now intersects the street, its urban Mexican neighborhood North and South of the Hidalgo long demolished. A photo taken on 25-26 November 1931 of the Hidalgo—those are the dates that José Mojica's *Cuando el amor ríe* (1930, David Howard, William J. Scully) was reprised there—shows the theatre sandwiched between a mom and pop grocery store and a dancing hall. Most of the buildings on the block are two-story, with a larger three-story structure just South of the theatre, housing a Mexican dentist, the Farmacia Hidalgo at 363 N. Main (which regularly advertised in *La Opinión*) and a hotel. The large windows above the marquee are dark and curtainless. The marquee, with its single ring of lights around Teatro Hidalgo in relief, looks like it could date from the nickelodeon era. The dark entrance leads into a theatre space that accommodated 750 patrons.

It is unclear when the Hidalgo was built, but it starts making an appearance in 1914 in City Directories. It was from the start a legitimate theatre for Mexican folk productions, but also presented films regularly. At the dawn of the sound era, the theatre changed hands several times. In July 1930, Meyer Tallis, who had owned the theatre since April 1925, sold it to a consortium, including Romualdo Tirado, Ernesto González Jiménez and Arturo Pallais Jr., all well-known theatrical figures in the Mexican-American community through their management of the Teatro México. Five months later, in November 1930, the owner of the Estella and Electric, Mr. Harry E. Ewing, bought the Hidalgo, renovated it, and installed new Western Electric sound film projectors. The first sound film to be shown there was *Sombras de gloria* in April 1930. But film screenings remained irregular until after the 27 November 1930 reopening with a reprise of Paramount's *El cuerpo del delito* (1930, Cyril Gardner, A. Washington Pezet), becoming a reliable second-run house and even occasionally premiering films, like Benito Perojo's *El embrujo de Sevilla* (1931), a Spanish film produced in Germany. By March 1932, Carlos Emanuel had purchased the theatre, showing Spanish-language films until he sold the Hidalgo to Frank Fouce in August 1934. Fouce continued to utilize the Hidalgo as a second-run, but abandoned the space in May 1936, with Ramón Peón's *Padre querido* (1935) being the last film screened. It was demolished that same year.

In early 1937, Frank Fouce acquired the Roosevelt Theatre, a space seating 800 persons. Located at 842 S. Main Street, the theatre had been built in 1913 and was called the Miller Theatre after its owner Fred Miller. He leased the theatre to others for several years in the later teens, then sold it in 1924, although it continued to be called the Miller until 1926. From 1929 to 1932, it was called the Triangle Theatre and managed by Samuel H. Human. In 1932, a Main Theatre at that address briefly advertised in *La Opinión* as "El cine de las familas," but showing second-run American titles.[38] In January 1937, *La Opinión* featured an advertisement, noting that the Roosevelt Theatre would soon present "2 grandes películas" and would be a family theatre, but it was not until May that the Roosevelt is listed as an Empresa Fouce cinema. It began screening films on 2 July 1937 when *¡Ora Ponciano!* (1936, Gabriel Soria) premiered there, as well as at the California and Eléctrico.[39] Fouce closed the theatre in April 1939 after *México lindo* (1938, Ramón Pereda) had premiered there. Almost exactly a year later, on 3 April 1940, the Roosevelt moved to a new location at 212 N. Main Street, the space previously occupied by the Eléctrico. Like its former namesake, the Roosevelt continued to operate as a first- and second-run house throughout the 1940s, although it was only a fraction of the size. Fouce shuttered the theatre on 31 October 1949 and it was demolished in 1960.

Beginning in September 1938, the Mason Opera House was listed as an Empresa Frank Fouce theatre. However, it wasn't until three years later, 11 September 1941, that Fouce inaugurated regular programming of Spanish features with a reprise of Cantinflas's *Ni sangre, ni arena* (1941, Alejandro Galindo), renaming the house the Teatro Mason. Located at 127 S. Broadway, the Mason Opera House had been built in 1903 with more than 1500 seats and was operated for more than two decades by the A.L. Erlanger organization, hosting many of this country's most famous legitimate stage actors. Sold in 1928, the Opera House was managed by Chester N. Sutton in the early 1930s. In the early 1940s, Fouce programmed mostly older features as reprises, but by 1943 it had become a first-run house with films premiering there and at the California or at the Liberty. In January 1946, Fouce purchased the theatre from Louisa B. and H.V. Hoffman, after having leased it for eight years;[40] he also added a new marquee "Home of Mexican Films," allowing the theatre to stand out from the other small businesses on the block. Once Fouce gave up the California and opened the Mayan in March 1949, the Mason again became a second-run space, and remained so after Fouce purchased the Million Dollar in 1950. Fouce closed the Mason in December 1954. It was demolished the next year.[41]

Frank Fouce's final acquisition in the 1930s was the Arrow Theatre, which he purchased in March 1939. Opened as a legitimate theatre in 1925, the 550-seat house was located at 251 N. Main St. It was operated by a variety of individuals in the late 1920s, but in 1930, Carl H. Drane became manager; the Arrow reprised *Sombras de gloria* in November and *Así es la vida* (1930, George J. Crone) in December, but these were one-offs. Between March and September 1936, the Arrow under the management of Walter and John Menard attempted some reprises of older Spanish-language films, but regular programming did not begin again until Fouce inaugurated the theatre on 22 March 1939 with the Spanish version of *Snow White, Blanca Nieves* (1937, Walt Disney), followed by

38 *La Opinión,* 18 September 1932, 7. No other documentation could be found in City Directories for either the Main or Roosevelt theatres prior to 1934, when it was listed as the Main.
39 *La Opinión,* 8 January 1937, 4; See advertisement in *La Opinión,* 23 May 1937, 11, and 2 July 1937, 4.
40 *Los Angeles Times,* 4 January 1946, 13.
41 Gunckel, Notes, no date.

a reprise of *Águila o sol* (1937, Arcady Boytler). Fouce operated the Arrow, which he renamed the Azteca in March 1940, as a second-run theatre until May 1941, when he abandoned the space. The new name reflected his wish to identify the theatre as embedded in the Mexican community, but may have also been a nod to his distributor and probable financial partner, Azteca Films.

The only competition to the Empresa Francisco Fouce were the cinemas of James C. Quinn, who operated the Monterey on Whittier Blvd. in East Los Angeles, the Unique on 1st Street in Boyle Heights, and, beginning in December 1940, the Teatro Vernon on Vernon Street, just South of Downtown in Huntington Park; all were suburban theatres that offered split-week American-Spanish programming.[42] The Unique began programming Mexican films in August 1939, while the Monterey opened on 24 September 1939, both of them functioning as third- and fourth-run theatres.[43] While the Vernon's Spanish-language programs closed after only a year, in December 1941, the other two theatres remained neighborhood third-run Spanish houses through the end of the 1950s.

AZTECA FILM DISTRIBUTION

Thus, in the period under question, from 1930 to 1942, the Spanish-language film market expanded in Los Angeles from at times zero cinemas to seven screens at the end of the decade. This incredible growth of Mexican-American screens was only possible because there was a significant audience of native speakers. Amazingly, new films from Mexico could not alone satisfy that growing market. According to Agrasánchez, the demand for Mexican films was so great because contract laborers and other immigrants again began flooding into the United States, thanks to the subsiding effects of the Depression.[44] Frank Fouce and other community theater owners increasing turned to screening older films, which had proved themselves popular in the past. The L.A. theatrical market for Spanish-language films thus functioned both as a site of discovery for new Latin American and Spanish feature films, and for the remembering of classic hits from the past. Both acts of reception functioned directly on the local level, on the national level through the distribution of *La Opinión* and its reportage of the cine scene, and on the international level via the reports of Latin American correspondents, all of which benefited distributors of Spanish-language film "product."

The creation of a Spanish-speaking exhibition market would not have been possible without a functioning distribution system. While *La Opinión* advertisements in many cases did not list distributors, it is clear that Azteca Films had a virtual monopoly on distribution of Mexican films to the United States.[45] In point of fact, just as the Hollywood majors con-

42 *La Opinión*, 22 December 1949, sec. 2, 3.

43 Agrasánchez, 58; *La Opinión*, 22 August 1939, 4, 24 September 1939, sec 2, 3.

44 Agrasánchez, 12.

45 Azteca titles were identified through advertisements, correspondence, and the Calderón Brothers spreadsheet, which listed all films produced by the company, when the national government in Mexico forcibly nationalized the distribution company in 1956. See "Azteca Films, Inc. Recapitulation of Picture Costs, 1944-1953," Calderón Estate Collection, Permanencia Voluntaria. See also *Motion Picture Production Encyclopedia 1952* (Los Angeles: Hollywood Reporter, 1952), 966. IMDb.com. lists Cinexport Distributing Company as a major distributor of many Mexican titles. However, no listing or address could be found in either the *Motion Picture Almanac* or the *Film Daily Yearbook*. According to an article in *Variety*, Cinexport was based in New York, where company head José Guerrero also owned the Teatro Hispano, at 136th St. and 5th Avenue, and attempted to organize a Spanish-language theatre circuit in New York City. See *Variety*, 29 June 1938.

trolled film exhibition in the United States through vertically structured companies that included production and distribution, so, too, did Mexican-Americans monopolize the Los Angeles Spanish-language theatrical film market through control of theatres, distribution, and, increasingly, production.[46] The key to understanding that system is the relationship between Frank Fouce and the Calderón Brothers, which began some time before the premiere of the first Mexican sound film in Los Angeles, *Santa* (1932).

Even before the premiere of *Santa,* the Calderón Brothers had been active in film exhibition and distribution in the United States. José and Rafael Calderón had started out as exhibitors in Chihuahua, Mexico, in the 1920s, then expanded across the border to El Paso and San Antonio, Texas.[47] By the 1930s, they had moved into production with José's son, Pedro A. Calderón, producing films, like *La Zandunga* (1938, Fernando de Fuentes), and into owning their own studios and laboratories in Mexico City.[48] With capital from the Calderón Brothers, Frank Fouce was probably able to purchase the California; the Empresa Fouce expanded with the acquisition of the Hidalgo, the Electric and México, while Fouce apparently kept his hand in distribution. His letterhead in 1938 not only included the names of his theatres, but also "Spanish International Pictures. Motion Picture Producers, Brokers, & Distributors;" the film titles listed on the letter's left margins being titles also distributed by Azteca, indicating that in fact Fouce's company and the Calderón Brothers' operations were economically linked, if not identical.[49]

The Calderón family connections to Los Angeles ran deep. An older brother of José Calderón, Mauricio, had moved to the city prior to World War I and operated a music store on North Main Street with a music publishing business, Repertorio Musical Mexicano, which soon became a hub for Mexican musicians working in the recording industry.[50] Knowledge of that business probably encouraged the Calderóns to produce films with popular music, once sound came in, but also allowed them to gauge prospects in the growing film industry. Azteca Film Inc. was founded in 1931 by José and Rafael Calderón, along with Alberto Salas Porras, in El Paso, Texas, with a Los Angeles office located at 1906 Vermont Avenue. Rubén Antonio Calderón, Rafael's son, was named Manager, and Gustavo Acosta, another blood relative, as Booker for the L.A. Exchange. Acosta later worked for Columbia's Latin American distribution office, and was probably responsible for brokering a deal for Columbia to distribute many of the Calderón films in Mexico in 1947. Interestingly, the Azteca logo on film advertisements listed El Paso as its headquarters, possibly because Rafael Calderón was still identified as President in trade address books, although he primarily directed the mother ship, the Calderón exhibition operations: the Circuito Alcazar. It is likely that the distribution business for both North

46 See "Lo que ha dado; lo que dará « Azteca Films »," in *La Opinión,* 2 January 1938, sec. 2, 3, which notes that Azteca had the concession for all premieres of "our national cinema" in Los Angeles since 1935.

47 A spreadsheet from 1957 for *Los Chiflados del Rock and Roll* shows that the Calderóns owned twenty-five theatres in Mexico at that time. Calderón Estate Collection, Permanencia Voluntaria.

48 In an interview with *La Opinión,* Rafael Calderón announced the purchase of the National Studios in Mexico City, and that Azteca Films would distribute new Mexican films to the American Southwest. See "Del cine en México", *La Opinión,* 18 March 1934, sec. 2, 3. The Calderón family remained in the film-producing business until the late 1980s, and were responsible for producing literally hundreds of films, many in later years exploitation titles.

49 Compare letter from Frank Fouce to Gregorio del Amo, 10 March 1938, and "Azteca Films, Inc. Recapitulation of Picture Costs, 1944-1953."

50 See Viviana García Besné and Alistair Tremps, "Please Sing to Me: The Immigrant Nostalgia that Sparked the Mexican Film Industry," in Colin Gunckel, Jan-Christopher Horak, Lisa Jarvinen (eds.), *Cinema between Latin America and Los Angeles. Origins to 1960* (New Brunswick, N.J.: Rutgers University Press, forthcoming). See also Sánchez, 183.

America and Mexico was based in Los Angeles.[51] A photo from 1939 taken at Azteca's L.A offices shows Acosta and Rubén Calderón with posters of their films on the walls. Azteca Films then "began boosting the film industry in Mexico, buying as many films as it could," as well as distribution offices in San Antonio, Denver, Chicago, and New York. Azteca's work was clearly perceived as promoting the interests of Mexican culture.[52] In 1939, the Los Angeles exchange was sending out an average of twenty films a day to cinemas in California, Arizona and Nevada. In 1944, ownership of the L.A. office of Azteca was transferred to Rubén and his brother, Guillermo Calderón (with Porras), including a catalog of 136 films, a significant number yet to be released.[53] Azteca had a virtual monopoly on Argentine films through a deal with Argentina Sono Film. When Azteca was nationalized by the Mexican government in 1954, the Cinematográfica Mexicana Exportadora (CIMEX) underpaid $ 1.7 million for the distribution company; at the time, Azteca owned more than 600 titles from Mexico. As Agrasánchez notes, "Azteca operated practically without competition from 1932 until 1942..."[54] In 1942, Clasa-Mohme, a distributor founded by Gustav Mohme and Clasa Films, opened a distribution office on Vermont Avenue in Los Angeles, and was soon competing successfully against Azteca, inaugurating a new phase in the American Spanish-language film market.

While the premiere of *Santa* led to the Mexicanization of the L.A. Spanish-language film market, beginning in late 1933, that market first formed with the production of Spanish-language films by the American majors. Three distinct phases thus mark the development of that exhibition market in the 1930s: (1) 1930-33, when Hollywood produced and distributed Spanish "talkers" and theatres were still owned by Anglo-Americans; (2) 1934-37, when films produced in Mexico began to dominate the market and Mexican-Americans acquired their own theatres; (3) 1938-1942, when the market became increasingly diverse with productions from Argentina, Cuba, Mexico, Spain, and local independently produced films vying for attention.

HOLLYWOOD VERSION PRODUCTION

Except for 1930, when less than thirty Spanish-language films were screened in Los Angeles, some of them still silent, the number of sound films screened per year averaged between fifty and sixty until 1935. Through 1933, the great majority of these films were supplied by the Hollywood majors, who initially premiered Spanish films in their own first-run theatres, but quickly switched to the Mexican theatres on Main Street. However, independent producers, often working with local Mexican directors, also supplied films to that market. Hollywood stopped producing Spanish versions of their English-language films by 1932, except Fox, which had set up a Spanish-language film unit to produce original films in Spanish, and Paramount's Paris and Astoria operations, where Spanish "talkers" continued to be produced until at least 1935. In 1934, as studio production

51 See "Salió a Texas el señor Calderón," in *La Opinión,* 2 December 1939, 4. See also *Film Daily Yearbook 1941 (*Los Angeles: Film Daily, 1940), 566; *Motion Picture Almanac 1940-41* (New York: Quigley Publishing Co., 1940), 755.

52 "Don Rubén" 4. A shipping label in the Calderón Collection of the Pemanencia Voluntaria for Azteca Films, Inc. (1970) names Los Angeles, San Antonio, Chicago and New York as branches.

53 Contract between Azteca Film Distributing Company and Azteca Film Distributing Company of California, 30 September 1944, Calderón Estate, Permanencia Voluntaria.

54 Agrasánchez, 46, 161.

plummeted, Mexican films filled the void, but until the California opened in September 1933 available screens remained a problem. Thus, while Los Angeles had seen thirty-eight films from Hollywood in 1933, thirteen films from Mexico and two from Spain, 1934 brought thirty-one Mexican films, twenty-one American-produced Spanish films, and one from Spain/Germany to the city. Given the lack of screening opportunities described above, it is not surprising that many Hollywood Spanish-language films only played for two or three runs. However, there were also major hits: *Sombras de gloria*, independently produced by Sono-Art Productions at the Metropolitan Studios, opened at the Fox Criterion in January 1930, and was then reprised at least fifteen times that same year, including runs at the Hidalgo, México, Eléctrico and Arrow. Almost as successful with ten runs was *Así es la vida*, also independently produced at Metropolitan by Sono-Art, and *El vuelo de la muerte* (1933), Guillermo Calles' independent Mexican-American production, with eight runs. Only a few studio films reached that last bar, and they were mostly Fox films starring Mexican opera and recording star José Mojica: *El precio de un beso* (1930, James Tinling, Marcel Silver), Fox's Spanish version of *One Mad Kiss* (1930, Marcel Silver, James Tinling), *La ley del harem* (1931, Lewis Seiler), *Melodía prohibida* (1933, Frank Strayer) and *La cruz y la espada* (1934, Frank Strayer). Also moderately successful were *Carne de cabaret* (1931), Columbia's Spanish version of *Ten Cents a Dance* (1931, Lionel Barrymore) and Metro-Goldwyn-Mayer's *La Mujer X* (1931), the Spanish version of *Madame X* (1929, Lionel Barrymore) directed by Carlos F. Borcosque, the Chilean director who would help build the Argentine film industry a few years later. Thus, of the 176 American films produced and screened in Los Angeles before 1934, only the handful mentioned above enjoyed very successful runs. On the other hand, only 11% of Hollywood-produced films tanked completely in their first run. Obviously, the income generated from the Mexican community (and apparently from Latin America) was insufficient for the accountants in the major studios, but the numbers suggest we must modify slightly the established wisdom that Latin American audiences in general, and Mexican-American Angelenos in particular, completely failed to embrace Hollywood's efforts. It should also be noted that unlike early Mexican films, e.g., *Santa* and *La Llorona,* Hollywood's product was seldom reprised in later years, but that may have had more to do with Azteca as monopoly distributor than their lack of popularity.

THE RISE OF MEXICAN CINEMA IN LOS ANGELES

The period 1934-1937 saw both the establishment of the first Mexican-American owned cinemas through Frank Fouce and a major uptick in film production in Mexico after the runaway success of *Allá en el Rancho Grande*. Fouce began operating the Hidalgo and the California, then expanded to include the Eléctrico, the Arrow, and occasionally the México during this period. As a result, the number of Spanish-language films screened increased from 54 films in 1934 to 67 films in 1937. At the same time, the percentage of Mexican films increased from 54% in 1934 to 83% in 1937, while independent American films replaced studio product, remaining steady at around 35% until 1937, when it dropped to 13%.

The first major hit in the L.A. market was Gabriel Soria's *Chucho el roto* (1934), which opened at the Hidalgo in April 1934, and then was reprised ten times by 1938 and another ten times through 1942. A year later, in October 1935, *Madre querida* (1935, Juan Orol) premiered at the California and was then reprised fourteen times through 1942. *Allá en el*

Rancho Grande (1936) opened at the California and Eléctrico simultaneously in February 1937 and was reprised twenty-three times. Only slightly less successful was another Gabriel Soria film, ¡*Ora Ponciano!* (1936), which opened simultaneously at the California, Eléctrico, and Roosevelt in July 1937 and was reprised fourteen times. Other hits included Fernando de Fuentes' *Bajo el cielo de México* (1937) with fifteen runs, *Jalisco nunca pierde* (1937, Chano Urueta) and *Amapola del camino* (1937, Juan Bustillo Oro), both with thirteen runs. At the same time, Mexican films were not uniformly successful, with as many as thirty-two films during this period screening less than twice after their initial L.A. premiere. Meanwhile, except for Miguel Contreras Torres' independently produced American feature, *No matarás* (1935), with eight runs, American films continued to underperform, usually not reaching more than three or four reprises. Thus, it seems clear that Latino audiences in Los Angeles preferred films with folkloric themes that emphasized *Mexicanidad* and were popular entertainments, rather than art films. For example, classics of the Golden Age, like Arcady Boytlers' *La mujer del puerto* (1935), Fuentes' *El fantasma del convento* (1934) and *Vámonos con Pancho Villa* (1935) underperformed, compared to more popular fare. Overall, about 12% of Mexican films released failed to garner more than a few runs, which still seems an acceptable failure rate, given the intense competition.

ARGENTINA RISES

With an increase in the number of screens in the immediate pre-World War II period, the overall number of Latin American films screened in the local Los Angeles market increased significantly, including not only films from Mexico but also from Argentina, Spain, Cuba and Latino producers in Los Angeles. The number of available screens expanded in part due to new Spanish-language programming at the three suburban theatres owned by James C. Quinn, but also because Fouce's cinemas were running at full capacity for the first time. As a result of this rise in capacity, the number of Spanish-language films screened in Los Angeles jumped from 85 to 197 films between 1938 and 1942, with the number of playdates exploding from 184 to 520. While the number of Los Angeles premieres only increased slightly from 46 in 1938 to 71 in 1942, the number of reprises increased geometrically from 138 to 449. That increase was possible because of Quinn's second- and third-run theatres, but also because Azteca made many more older films available. Thus, a popular film, like Chano Urueta's *Jalisco nunca pierde* (1937), which opened in September 1937 at the California, Roosevelt and Eléctrico, and was reprised in all three theatres during the course of 1938, enjoyed further runs at the Arrow in 1939, at the California and Roosevelt in 1941, and at the Unique and Monterey in 1941. Other very popular Mexican films in this period, garnering more than ten playdates, were: *Mientras México duerme* (1938, Alejandro Galindo), *La casa del ogro* (1938, Fernando de Fuentes), *Diablillos de arrabal* (1938, Adela Sequeyro), *El capitán aventurero* (1938, Arcady Boytler), *Mi madrecita* (1940, Francisco Elías), *Cuando los hijos se van* (1941, Juan Bustillo Oro) and *El gendarme desconocido* (1941, Miguel M. Delgado). Including a comedy with Cantinflas, a musical with Mojica, and a crime drama with Arturo de Córdova, this list reveals a broadening of audience tastes over previous years, when the *comedias rancheras* predominated.

In the same time period, the percentage of films from Mexico decreased from 87% in 1938 to 58% in 1942, a significant drop, due both to a cut in production in Mexico, but also because of increased demand for Spanish-language cinema, which Azteca met by distributing new films from Cuba and, most importantly, Argentina. The real drop in the percentage of Mexican films occurred in 1940, when the number of Argentine films jumped from an average of five to nine films in the years 1935-39 to twenty-nine in 1940, fifty-eight in 1941 and fifty-seven in 1942. This is somewhat surprising, given that Argentine films performed on average significantly less well than Mexican films. Except for *La ley que olvidaron* (1938, José A. Ferreyra), which opened at the California in July 1940 and was reprised more than nine times until 1942, many Argentine films averaged only two or three reprises and some less, thus failing at the box-office. Unlike Mexican films, which often premiered in Los Angeles only weeks after their Mexican openings, Argentine films were often released with a two- or three-year delay, which may account for a drop in their success. Thus, Manuel Romero's *Fuera de la ley* (1937) opened at the California in March 1941, while *Melodías porteñas* (1937, Luis Moglia Barth) premiered in June at the same theatre. On the other hand, Luis César Amadori's *El pobre* Pérez (1937) opened in April 1940 and went on to six reprises before the end of 1942. Other successful Argentine films included *La vida es un tango* (1939, Manuel Romero) with seven play dates, *Caminito de gloria* (1939. Luis César Amadori) with six dates, *Puerta cerrada* (1939, Luis Saslavsky) with seven, *Doce mujeres* (1939, Luis Moglia Barth) with seven, and *El matrero* (1940, Orestes Caviglia) with six in 1941-42. Except for *Doce mujeres,* all these films seem to feature specifically Argentine subjects (tango, the pampas), which may account for their popularity. As noted, the box-office numbers for popular Argentine films lagged by half behind the numbers of the most popular Mexican films.

In 1939, films from Spain also had a brief boost in popularity. Whereas only two to five Spanish films screened per year in the 1930s, eleven films opened in Los Angeles from Spain in 1939, possibly the result of the end of the Spanish Civil War, which made international commerce feasible again. Since the number again dropped in 1940, one can assume that interest may have peaked for local audiences. Mostly directed by Florián Rey or Benito Perojo, titles from Spain performed less strongly than Argentine titles. Only two films achieved box-office numbers equal to Mexican films, namely *La hermana San Sulpicio* (1934), a religious film, and *Nobleza baturra* (1935), both starring international star Imperio Argentina and directed by Florián Rey.

Independently produced American Spanish-language films enjoyed a second vogue in 1940, with no less than eighteen titles premiering that year. As Lisa Jarvinen and others have noted, these films produced between 1938 and 1940 proved to be the last gasp of American-made Spanish-language films. In contrast to the early 1930s, when Hollywood's Spanish-language films were only marginally successful or flops, most of the films from the later period managed to achieve at least results similar to the Argentines. The following titles, including three films starring Tito Guízar, had at least seven runs in L.A. until the end of 1942: *Verbena trágica* (1939, Charles Lamont), *Mis dos amores* (1939, Nick Grinde), *Papá soltero* (1939, Richard Harlan), and *El otro soy yo* (1939, Richard Harlan). *El milagro de la Calle Mayor* (1939, Steve Sekely), and *Odio* (1940, William Rowland) achieved at least ten playdates, equaling some of the most successful Mexican films. The evidence indicates that these independent American films performed better than their reputation in the literature. The last-named title, *Odio,* was distributed in L.A. as a Mexican film, marking a future trend whereby American capital shifted to Mexican film production in the 1940s and 1950s.

1940-41 also saw the distribution of at least eleven Cuban films, although almost 50% apparently flopped. One can assume that given the low level of capitalization in the film industry of Havana, low production values may have played a role in these box-office duds. The remainder, however, were modest successes with four to six runs, including *Ahora seremos felices* (1938, Fred Bain, William L. Nolte), *La canción del regreso* (1939, Max Tosquella, Sergio Miro), *Estampas habaneras* (1939, Jaime Salvador), *Cancionero cubano* (1940, Jaime Salvador). All of the films were comedy romances with lots of Afro-Cuban music, while *Estampas* was screened at the California in July 1940 under the title *Chaflán en La Habana*, as it was in Mexico, to cash in on Mexican star Carlos ("Chaflán") López's minor role in the film.[55] Nevertheless, the very fact that Cuban films were distributed in the L.A. market belies previous historical givens, and bolsters the argument of Luciano Castillo that there was a foreign reception of pre-revolutionary Cuban films. In the 1950s, Mexican producers would increasingly invest in Cuban film productions, including *Yambaó* (1957, Alfredo B. Crevenna), produced by Rubén Calderón, and *Santo contra el cerebro del mal* (1961, Joselito Rodríguez), produced by Rubén's cousin, Jorge García Besné.

CONCLUSION

In this essay, I have endeavored to document the exhibition of Spanish-language cinema in a specific locale, namely Los Angeles, produced in Mexico, Spain, Argentina, Cuba and the United States in the pre-World War II sound period. I have documented the history of Mexican film theatres on and off Main Street in downtown Los Angeles, operated by Frank Fouce, but probably financed by José Calderón, a Texas and Chihuahua-based film exhibitor, hoping to create a market in America for Mexican films. As a result, L.A.'s mostly Mexican audiences viewed virtually 100% of Mexico's film production in the 1930s, but also representative stars and popular film genres from five Spanish-speaking countries; this reception space therefore can be considered a transnational space, embedded in the larger Anglo-American space of Hollywood mainstream cinema. I have further demonstrated that Azteca Films, the distribution arm of the Calderón Brothers' empire, dominated the American market for Latin American films, at least until 1942. In outlining the contours of an intact and functioning Spanish-language film industry, consisting of film exhibition, distribution and production, and based in Los Angeles, I demonstrate that the Hollywood majors did not have an absolute monopoly on film production and reception. Rather, what we are viewing must be understood as a vibrant minority cinema, established literally in the backyard of Hollywood.

55 See advertisement for *Chaflán en la Habana* in *La Opinión,* Vol. 14, No. 310, 21 July 1940, sec. 2, 3.

Hollywood's Spanish-Language Movies in Buenos Aires, Lima, Montevideo, and Mexico City

Violeta Núñez Gorritti

METHODOLOGICAL APPROACH

This paper is a first attempt to analyze the distribution-exhibition process in four cities in Latin America of Spanish-language films produced by Hollywood. Three are located in South America: Lima, Buenos Aires, Montevideo, while Mexico City is in North America. The absence of systematic information from other cities prevents us, for the moment, to realize a broader, more accurate understanding of the process and reach final conclusions.

The rise of talking pictures in the late 1920s brought with it a number of problems that had to be solved. One was language. Not everyone understood English. The need to make films intelligible for foreign audiences caused Hollywood producers to film the same film in different languages. Between 1929 and 1939, about 175 feature films and a significant number of shorts were made in Spanish and distributed throughout the Americas and Spain. In many cases, the Spanish versions were exhibited before the original version was released. To define the Spanish talking pictures made by Hollywood studios, we used *Cita en Hollywood,* published by Juan B. Heinink and Robert G. Dickson. In order to undertake a comparative study of distribution and exhibition, we consulted Mexican, Peruvian and Uruguayan "Billboard cinematographic" information, but, unfortunately, found only partial information for Argentina.

Film distribution in the silent period was generally organized via "Cinematographic Programs" that were substantially modified when talking pictures started. The Programs, amalgamated by distributors, procured films from different companies and countries, creating an extensive distribution-exhibition circuit. The most important and famous in South America was Max Glücksmann's Program from Argentina, which had an influence on Chile, Peru and Uruguay. After the rise of talking pictures, older distributors no longer had access to Hollywood films, because American companies opened exchanges in almost every country. In many cases the Programs were subsumed under Mexican and Argentine film distribution, while in others, they disappeared. The distribution circuit was maintained, but was reorganized to meet new needs imposed from Hollywood. As

Carlos Gardel and Rosita Moreno, *El día que me quieras* (1935, John Reinhardt).

a general premise, we will theorize that the distribution-exhibition of Hollywood Spanish-language films contributed to redefining the interests of "the Mecca of Cinema." To better explain the process of change we will take as an example the city of Lima, Peru.

DISTRIBUTION-EXHIBITION IN LIMA

As in many Latin American countries, the projection of moving images arrived in Lima in 1897, shortly after their introduction. Film exhibition was initially organized after 1900 by theatrical entrepreneurs. In 1908, with the opening of urban spaces for theatrical film exhibition, promoted and financed by native capital, the arrangement was permanently formalized. Foreign distribution began to influence the Lima market in 1911. In September, Pathé signed a contract with the General Cinematographic Society SGC of Buenos Aires. A determining factor in the configuration of the market was the exclusivity of cinematographic programs.

The emergence of the Cinema Theater Company, the International Film Company, and the entrance into the local market of Argentina's General Cinematographic Society resulted in a reordering of the market that was steadily growing. In 1915, the Empresa del Cinema Teatro and the Compañía Internacional Cinematográfica were founded; both extended their market reach to Ecuador, Bolivia and Chile, where they opened branches. In 1917, Universal Pictures announced a direct deal for cinemas in the newspaper *El Comercio*. Soon, Max Glücksmann's Free Program and the Sociedad Anónima Cinematográfica Sud Americana, both from Argentina, settled in Lima.

The distribution companies offered theater owners a program of films from different countries and companies, especially from Hollywood. In order to receive it, the cinemas had to work exclusively with that company, and also had to save a place in the exhibition circuit. In advertising, the smaller cinemas announced that the program "was the same" as projected in the main theaters. The cinemas paid distributors for the program, either through a daily rent or a percentage of the box-office. The distributor offered a feature film, plus short films and newsreels to complete the program.

The film market in Lima between 1897-1929, corresponding to the silent period, was complex. It was organized according to the category of the theater, the origin and prestige of the production company (Metro, First National, Universal, etc.), the economic performance of the hall, and the genre of the film. The top-tiered movies were premiered in a circuit of five first-class theaters, located in the city center, called "circuit head," giving rise to a particular name for that circuit, for example the "Excelsior Circuit." The cinemas needed to offer a varied and attractive bill and were required to change programming daily. For matinees, films for children and young ladies were projected, reserving vermouth and evenings for premieres, or for events focusing on a specific audience, e.g., "for males only".

Each first-class theater premiered a minimum of two films a week. The premieres on Tuesdays and Thursdays included vermouth. After the first premiere, the film went to a main hall in a neighborhood for a second premiere, and was then programmed in other smaller theaters, until it completed a circuit that could be extended for a period of one month to more than fifty movie theaters. Previous feature releases were programmed again in the following weeks, as second-run. Perhaps this system was influenced by the theater tradition where each troupe that arrived in a city brought a new repertoire but released the previous season's hits. Other films from previous seasons were reprised, given their original success. Finally, due to these successes, there were annual releases of films.

From the silent period 1897-1929, Lima inherited approximately fifty-three movie theaters, built in its main urban centers; twenty-one of these premises were opened in the early years of the 1910s. By the end of the 1930s, there would be eighty cinema theaters. Talking pictures first opened in December 1929. The adaptation to new sound cinema systems was a gradual process. The investment required to purchase new equipment involved costs that exhibitors initially rejected. The reluctance to accept talking pictures was thus strengthened by the economic crisis that occurred as a result of the 1929 Wall Street Crash, and the political instability caused by the fall of the Leguía regime in Peru. Furthermore, there was major resistance to new film lease conditions, motivating the creation of the Association of Cinematographic Exhibitors in 1931, in defense of their interests. Many theaters preferred to program silent films from the old programs before submitting to the new norms; such was the case of the Sala San Martín, which became a faithful defender of silent films. Also, the musicians of the Lima Society demanded the stop of talking pictures, because sound films eliminated the need for their services. In spite of these facts, all theaters in Lima had sound equipment by the end of 1933.

AUDIENCES AND CINEMATOGRAPHIC INFRASTRUCTURE

In 1930, Lima had 350,000 inhabitants, but by the end of the decade it had 500,000. It had sixty-five urban cinemas, which expanded to eighty locations in 1940. In 1930, the population of Mexico City was 1,230,000 inhabitants, which grew to 1,758,000 by 1940. Cinemas in the urban centers increased from twenty to forty-two locations between 1930 and 1939. The population of Buenos Aires was 1,575,000 inhabitants by the end of the 1920s, rising to 2,415,142 in the next decade. Over five hundred movie theaters dotted the province of Buenos Aires. The population of Montevideo in 1930 was 481,725 inhabitants with eighty theaters. By 1940, the population had risen to 708,852 inhabitants, while the number of cinemas remained the same.

Between 1930-1939, 3,698 feature films were released in Lima, 3,142 in Montevideo and 3,141 in Mexico City. Hollywood dominated 75% of all distribution, leaving little margin for competitors, including native producers who were in the process of expanding. We note that Lima, despite having a lower population, exhibited more films than its Latin American peers.

Feature films released in Lima, Montevideo and Mexico City 1930-1939

Year	Lima	Montevideo	**México City**
1930	287	176	244
1931	238	228	244
1932	263	246	278
1933	321	294	275
1934	372	287	348
1935	415	307	286
1936	452	304	389
1937	459	396	388
1938	456	428	284
1939	435	376	405
Total	3698	3142	3141

Latin American-produced talking pictures entered the market in 1933. In the 1930s, Lima exhibited 167 Mexican, 112 Argentine, and 41 Peruvian films. Montevideo screened 121 Argentine and 15 Mexican films. Mexico City offered 160 domestic titles and 19 Argentine films. These numbers were substantially modified in the next decade.

Between 1936-1940, a total of 27,367,888 tickets were sold in movie theaters nationwide in Peru. In Montevideo in the 1930s, tickets sold amounted to more than 46 million; in both cases we do not know gross ticket sales, nor have we found similar information for Buenos Aires or Mexico City.

SPANISH-LANGUAGE HOLLYWOOD CINEMA: FIGURES AND CONSTANTS

As is known, Hollywood companies made around 175 Spanish-talking feature films between 1930 and 1939. We have found that 154 of these films were distributed in Buenos Aires, Mexico City, Lima and Montevideo; specifically, 137 were released in Lima, 115 in Montevideo, and 97 in Mexico City. The numbers for Buenos Aires were too incomplete to allow for a figure.

The Spanish-language films of Hollywood were premiered in Lima as an "exclusive" with the same sumptuousness and publicity as English-language American product. The first Spanish-talking feature, produced by Paramount, *El cuerpo del delito* (1930, Cyril Gardner, A. Washington Pezet) opened on August 12, 1930 at the Teatro Princesa, an exclusive first-run Paramount cinema. It was followed by *Charros, gauchos y manolas* (1930, Xavier Cugat), *Amor audaz* (1929, Louis J. Gasnier), *Cascarrabias* (1929, Cyril Gardner), *Drácula* (1931, George Melford), *El proceso de Mary Dugan* (1931, Marcel De Sano) and *Nada más que una mujer* (1934, Harry Lachman). Lima cinemagoers could hear comedians Stan Laurel and Oliver Hardy say in Spanish "to the races" in *La vida nocturna* (1930, James Parrott) and *Una noche de duendes* (1930, James Parrott), and hear Buster Keaton in Spanish in

Estrellados (1930, Edward Sedgwick) and *¡De frente, marchen!* (1930, Edward Sedgwick). They could hear and *see* Carlos Gardel in his films, which made his Lima fans even more delirious since they already knew him through his records.

The premieres of Spanish-talking pictures followed similar pre-existing patterns. Metro, Warner, and Universal features premiered at the Teatro Colón and Cine Teatro Excelsior, and Paramount films at the Teatro Princesa. Given the reluctance of cinema owners to adapt new technical sound systems and the new rules of the game, many Lima cinemas did not exhibit these films until later, after they adapted to sound. In the early years of the decade the premiere of the films were featured as "exclusives" in a single theater with all the pomp and pageantry necessary. When Hollywood reduced its interest in the production of films in Spanish they stopped such elaborate treatment and premieres were scheduled in theaters of less importance, similar to Mexican and Argentine films, leaving the largest cinemas in each city reserved for English-language Hollywood features.

In Mexico City, the first Spanish sound film to premiere was *Sombras de gloria* (1929, Andrew L. Stone), on January 30, 1930. In the case of Montevideo, it was *El cuerpo del delito* (1930, Cyril Gardner, A. Washington Pezet), which premiered on June 20. Columbia, Fox, Metro, Paramount, Universal and Warner contributed 135 films, representing 88.23% of the total distributed. We note that only twenty-seven modified the exhibition title.

Films according to Production Company distributed 1930-1942

Company	Features	%
Fox	45	29.41
Paramount	38	24.83
Metro	27	17.64
Universal	12	7.84
Columbia	7	4.54
Warner	6	3.92
Others	18	11.76
Total	154	100.00

Between the years 1930-1936, 118 films were distributed and exhibited, 81% of the total. The year of greatest exhibition was 1931.

Distribution of films in Mexico, Lima and Montevideo 1930-1942

Year	México City	Lima	**Montevideo**
1930	14	9	10
1931	31	39	28
1932	10	22	29
1933	5	13	12

1934	10	9	10
1935	7	14	12
1936	6	12	6
1937	3	2	1
1938	1	4	1
1939	2	8	6
1940	-	1	5
1941	-	2	1
1942	-	1	-
Total	97	137	117

We should point out that the original versions were rarely released in the cities under study, with significantly fewer found cases in which two versions were released.[1]

Changes of titles of exhibition by country 1930-1942

Original title	Buenos Aires	México City	Lima	Montevideo
Carne de cabaret	El triunfo del amor	*	*	El triunfo del amor
Castillos en el aire	-	*	Despertar de una ilusión	-
La ciudad de cartón	-	-	*	*
Contra la corriente	-	*	Esposas frívolas	-
Cuando canta la ley	-	*	*	*
De bote en bote	-	Los presidiarios	*	*
De la sartén al fuego	-	La legión extranjera	*	*
Del infierno al cielo	-	*	*	*

1 In Lima both versions were shown of *Dracula* (1931) / Drácula, 8 May 1932 and 6 February 1931, respectively; *Min and Bill / La fruta amarga*, 12 May 1932 and 26 January 1933; *The Man Who Came Back* (1931) / *El ángel de la calle*, 7 August 1931 and 15 June 1933; *The Trial of Mary Dugan* (1931) / *La legión de honor*, 31 January1930 and 24 December 1931.
In Mexico City, both versions of *The Big House* (1930) / *El presidio*.
In Lima, only the original version was screened of *Beau Hunks* (1931) / *Politiquerías; Doughboys /¡De frente marchen!*, 1 January 1931; *Paramount on Parade* (1930) / *Galas de la Paramount* , 13 November 1930; *Honey* (1930) / *¡Sal de la cocina!*, 25 July 1930; *Mystery Woman*, 25 April 1930; *Pardon Us* (1931) / *Haciendo de las suyas*, 15 October 1931.
In Montevideo both versions were shown of *The Cat Creeps* (1930) / *El tenebroso*, 28 August 1931 and 16 October 1931, respectively; *The Criminal Code* (1931) / *El código del crimen*, 10 May 1932; 16 May 1931; *The Doctor's Secret* (1929) / *El secreto del doctor*, 9 August 1930; *Honey / ¡Salga de la cocina!*, 19 January 1932 and 18 December 1931.
Original versions only were shown in Montevideo of *Half Way to Heaven / Sombras del circo*, 23 December 1930; *The Letter* (1931) / *La carta*, 13 December 1930; *Paramount on Parade / Galas de la Paramount*, 26 September 1930.

El Diablo del mar	-	-	Corazones que esperan	-
Dos noches	-	*	*	-
El otro soy yo	-	-	*	*
Entre noche y día	*	-	*	En manos de los tahúres
Las Fronteras del amor	-	¡Viva mi tierra!	-	*
La fruta amarga	-	*	Fruta prohibida	*
Galas de la Paramount	Paramount de gala	-	*	*
El Impostor	-	*	*	*
La Incorregible	-	La homicida	*	*
La melodía prohibida	-	*	La melodía perdida	Melodía prohibida
El milagro de la Calle Mayorl	*	*	*	*
¡Salga de la cocina!	-	-	*	*
El secreto del doctor	Media hora	*	*	*
Tango Bar	*	*	En tango bar	*
El trovador de la radio	-	-	El trovador	*
Un hombre de suerte	-	*	Un hombre con suerte	*
El valiente	-	El patíbulo	*	*
La vida bohemia	-	-	*	*
La voluntad del muerto	La heredera de Mr. West	*	*	*

DISTRIBUTION CIRCUIT FOR HOLLYWOOD SPANISH-LANGUAGE FILMS

It is impossible to explain the distribution circuit for each of these films, so we have chosen selected titles, like *Drácula* and the Carlos Gardel, José Mojica and Tito Guízar films.

The Spanish *Drácula* was first shown in Mexico City on April 4, 1931. On May 5, it premiered in Lima, June 12 in Buenos Aires, and in Montevideo in September 1932. The original version directed by Tod Browning was premiered in Lima in August 1932, almost a year and a half after the Spanish version, and was not screened in Montevideo until February 1945. The original version was not released in Mexico, and we have no clue of its premiere in Buenos Aires.

Dracula in Buenos Aires, Lima, Mexico and Montevideo 1930-1939

Title	Company	México		Lima		Buenos Aires		Montevideo	
Drácula	Universal-1931	1931	04/04	1931	05/02	1931	05/12	1932	09/14

Carlos Gardel[2] made eight Spanish-language films, all released by Paramount Pictures. While all of them premiered in Buenos Aires, seven opened in Lima /Montevideo and five in Mexico City. Only *La casa es seria* (1933, Julien Jaquelux) premiered in Buenos Aires. *Las luces de Buenos Aires* (1931, Adelqui Millar) and *Espérame* (1933, Louis J. Gasnier) opened in 1931, first in Buenos Aires, then in Montevideo and Lima, while in Mexico City they were released in 1932 and 1933, respectively. Perhaps, due to the success of the earlier titles, *Melodía de arrabal* (1933, Louis J. Gasnier) screened simultaneously on May 18, 1933 in Lima and Montevideo. *El tango en Broadway* (1934, Louis J. Gasnier) first premiered in Lima and two months later in Montevideo. *Cuesta abajo* (1934, Louis Gasnier) opened first in Montevideo in September 1934, next on October 3 in Mexico, and on October 11 in Lima. *El día que me quieras* (1935, John Reinhardt) was first screened in Lima in June 1935, in July in Montevideo and in August in Mexico. Finally, *Tango Bar* (1935, John Reinhardt) opened first in Mexico in July 1935, in Montevideo in September and in Lima in October.

Carlos Gardel Films exhibited 1930-1939

Title	Company	Lima		México City		Buenos Aires		Montevideo	
Las luces de Buenos Aires	Paramount -1931	1931	12/24	1932	01/27	1931	09/23	1931	10/02
Espérame	Paramount -1933	1933	12/21	1933	03/02	NI	-	1933	10/14
Melodía de arrabal	Paramount -1933	1933	05/18	-	-	1933	04/05	1933	05/18

2 Carlos Gardel (born Charles Romuald Gardès; 11 December 1890—24 June 1935) was a French-Argentine singer, songwriter, composer and actor, and the most prominent figure in the history of tango.

La casa es seria	Paramount -1933	-	-	-	-	1933	05/19	-	-
El tango en Broadway	Paramount -1934	1935	01/18	-	-	1935	-	1935	03/12
Cuesta abajo	Paramount -1934	1934	10/11	1934	10/03	NI	-	1934	09/27
El día que me quieras	Paramount -1935	1935	06/28	1935	08/29	1935	07	1935	07/11
Tango Bar	Paramount -1935	1935	10/29	1935	07/18	1935	-	1935	09/05

The famous Mexican tenor and actor, José Mojica,[3] made eleven films for Fox. Buenos Aires was the first to premiere *El precio de un beso* (1930, James Tinling, Marcel Silver) in August 1930; Montevideo at the end of the same month; Mexico City in September and Lima in March 1932. The films *Cuando el amor ríe* (1930, David Howard, William J. Scully), *Hay que casar al príncipe* (1931, Lewis Seiler), *La ley del harem* (1931, Lewis Seiler) and *Mi último amor* (1931, Lewis Seiler) were presented first in Montevideo, then in Lima, but weren't released in Mexico. *El caballero de la noche* (1932, James Tinling) was only released in Montevideo. *El rey de los gitanos* (1933, Frank Strayer) was screened in March 1934 in Mexico, in July in Montevideo, and in Lima in July 1935. *La melodía prohibida* (1933, Frank Strayer) premiered first in Montevideo in March 1934, in June in Mexico, and in Lima in September 1935. *La cruz y la espada* (1933, Frank Strayer) was screened first in May 1934 in Mexico City and a day apart in Montevideo and Lima in May 1935. *Un capitán de cosacos* (1934, James Tinling) was released in February 1935 in Mexico City, and in March in Montevideo; it did not premiere in Lima. *Las Fronteras del amor* (1934, John Reinhardt) opened in June 1935 in Montevideo and then in Mexico City in August; it was not exhibited in Lima. We believe that the delay in the exhibition of Mojica's films in Lima was due to the fact that Fox opened a subsidiary as early as 1933, so Fox films still maintained the pattern established by the "cinematographic program."

José Mojica Films Exhibited 1930-1939

Original title	Company	Lima		México Mexico		**Buenos Aires**		**Montevideo**	
El precio de un beso	Fox-1930	1932	03/26	1931	09/04	1930	08/14	1930	08/30
Cuando el amor ríe	Fox-1930	1933	09/27	-	-	NI	-	1931	03/21
Hay que casar al príncipe	Fox-1931	1932	11/10	-	-	NI	-	1931	09/09

3 Fray José de Guadalupe Mojica (September 14, 1895—September 20, 1974) was a Mexican Franciscan friar and former tenor and film actor. He was known in the music and film fields as José Mojica. He was among the few Mexicans who made history in the early years of Hollywood.

La ley del harem	Fox-1931	1933	11/30	-	-	NI	-	1932	05/11
Mi último amor	Fox-1931	1934	05/05	-	-	NI	-	1932	11/23
El caballero de la noche	Fox-1933	-	-	-	-	NI	-	1933	03 23
El rey de los gitanos	Fox-1933	1935	07/13	1934	03/03	NI	-	1933	07/21
La melodía prohibida	Fox-1933	1935	09/10	1934	06/23	NI	-	1934	03 14
La cruz y la espada	Fox-1933	1935	05/04	1934	05/03	NI	-	1934	05 04
Un capitán de cosacos	Fox-1935	-	-	1935	02/07	NI	-	1935	03/29
Las Fronteras del amor	Fox-1934	-	-	1935	08/15	NI	-	1935	06/13

Considered the first singer actor, "charro cantor" of Mexican cinema, Tito Guízar[4] was first known for his films *Allá en el Rancho Grande* (Fernando de Fuentes, 1936) and *Amapola del camino* (1937, Juan Bustillo Oro), both Mexican productions, distributed in Lima and Montevideo, before his Hollywood movies. Tito Guízar made six Spanish-talking films, distributed by Paramount, all of which premiered in Lima, with five opening in Montevideo. *Cuando canta la ley* (1939, Richard Harlan) premiered first in Montevideo, while his other Paramount films opened first in Lima. Curiously, only two premiered in Mexico City: *Mis dos amores* (1938, Nick Grinde) and *Papá soltero* (1939, Richard Harlan).

Tito Guízar films exhibited 1930-1939

Original Title	**Company**	**Lima**		México **City**		**Montevideo**	
Milagroso Hollywood	Royal Films	1935	12/21	-	-	-	-
Mis dos amores	Paramount-1938	1938	12/08	1938	10/29	1939	01/20
El trovador de la radio	Paramount-1938	1939	04/04	-	-	1939	08/09
Papá soltero	Paramount-1939	1939	07/29	1941	09/27	1939	12/05
Cuando canta la ley	Paramount-1939	1939	11/25	-	-	1940	11/06
El otro soy yo	Paramount-1939	1940	02/22	-	-	1940	11/20

According to the production company, the distribution circuit was as follows: Fox films were distributed in a circuit, Buenos Aires-Montevideo-Mexico-Lima. Paramount films were shown first in Buenos Aires; then Lima, Montevideo and Mexico City competed for the second site. On the other hand, Mexico City and Montevideo competed for first spot

4 Federico Arturo Guízar Tolentino (April 8, 1908—December 24, 1999) was a Mexican-born singer and actor. Born in Guadalajara, Jalisco, he performed under the name of Tito Guízar. Together with Dolores del Río, José Mojica, Ramón Novarro, and Lupe Vélez, Guízar was among the few successful Mexican actors in Hollywood.

in the Metro circuit, which then moved on to Lima. Conversely, Mexico and Lima competed for first opening in Universal's circuit, before moving to Buenos Aires and Montevideo. Warner Bros. movies traveled from Mexico to Lima, and then to Montevideo.

CONCLUSION

Studying the distribution of Hollywood's Spanish-language films in Buenos Aires, Lima, Mexico City and Montevideo allows us to discover screening patterns in Latin America. These distribution circuits afforded Latin American audiences the ability to share the same songs, specific new words, and fashions, among other aspects, which influenced people's daily lives in each country. When it's noted that we share a common history, the distribution routes of cultural products like cinema help us to understand the origin and implications of that phenomenon.

The transition from silent to talking pictures presupposed a new deal for the exhibition-distribution market. Hollywood dismissed its local intermediaries, namely local programmers, opening branches in each country, but still continuing to utilize silent distribution circuits. Direct distribution of its films allowed Hollywood companies to strengthen its dominance of local Latin American markets. Hollywood's progressively weakening interest in producing Spanish-language films therefore cannot be attributed to their supposed commercial failure. On the contrary, most were well received by the public in different Latin American countries, which produced a not-insignificant economic benefit, despite film critics considering them to be of lesser value than the original versions. It is more probable that once these versions fulfilled their mission of helping through the transition to sound, it made little sense to continue production, since dubbing allowed them to intervene directly in Latin American markets.

The competition among cinemas was intense to maintain an attractive and varied slate of films to meet the demands of an avid audience, so the companies struggled to release a certain film in advance of others. Achieving this commitment consolidated its prestige. The lack of an acceptable cinema, or privileging the opening of a competitor's film, caused premieres to be postponed. We also must point out the limitations imposed by local jurisdictions that regulated the premieres of foreign titles. Spanish-language Hollywood films accustomed the Latin American public to see and hear themselves in their own language. They were the prelude to domestic film industries that burst onto the Latin American market in the mid-1930s, although Hollywood did not initially realize that such a threat was in the wings.

The Rise and Fall of Spanish Versions (1929-1931), According to *Cinelandia* Magazine

Esteve Riambau

The introduction of sound, which quickly developed as a result of the unexpected success of *The Jazz Singer* (1927, Alan Crosland), created a need for alternatives to tackle the issue of language barriers. In conjunction with dubbing and subtitling, used alternatively to the present day, the practice of filming multiple versions of the same story was also employed in the early years of talkies, using actors proficient in as many language combinations as required for the markets they were aiming to conquer. It was, in short, a new application of a practice that was as old as cinema itself: the recording of several versions of the same film, as had previously been done extensively throughout the silent film era, with simultaneous filming by several cameras or even to suit different censorship parameters.

Although the practice of producing multiple versions to account for language differences was to continue sporadically for a few more years, Hollywood hosted the shooting of some seventy U.S.-produced Spanish-language feature films in the period between 1929 and 1932. The first of these films, *Sombras de gloria* (1930, Andrew L. Stone and Fernando Tamayo), a version of *Blaze O' Glory* (1929, George Crone and Renaud Hoffman), was based on a story by Thomas Alexander Boyd that starred José Bohr and María Rico as Spanish-speaking alternatives to the English-speaking Eddie Dowling and Betty Compson. This practice, developed by most of the major Hollywood studios—with the exception of RKO and United Artists—attracted actors, screenwriters and even directors, representing numerous Latin nationalities to the "Mecca of Cinema," and even prompted English-speaking comedians, such as Buster Keaton, and Stan Laurel and Oliver Hardy, to speak in Spanish in the corresponding Latin American export versions of their film projects.

Despite version production being integrated into the industrial standards of Hollywood, its limitations soon manifested themselves. In theory, the process involved the adaptation of a plot and dialogue originally written in English to Spanish, recycling the sets and hiring directors, scriptwriters and actors capable of substituting for the original cast and crew members. In reality, the duplicate Spanish versions were B-movie productions, promoted as if they were the A-productions from which they originated, but with budgets four times smaller than the originals. Latino actors often lacked the necessary theatrical experience to rise to the dramaturgical and interpretative demands of the talkies and, for the most part, were unknown to audiences in their respective countries of origin. Last, but not least, under the Spanish label Hollywood also assembled actors within a single cast that represented a variety of different Hispanic nationalities, complete with their entire range of accents, sparking in the process criticism from all quarters. In the Spanish version of *Drácula* (1931, George Melford), Andalusian actor Carlos Villarías replaced Bela Lugosi to head up a Hispanic cast which also included Lupita Tovar from Mexico, Barry Norton from Argentina, and Madrid-born Pablo Álvarez Rubio. Although the talkies had obliged movie studios to look for alternatives to English, the curse of Babel still persisted under the apparent common denominator of Spanish.

The limited number of surviving multi-language films makes the study of this phenomenon problematic and suggests subtle differences. The Spanish version of *Dracula*, for example, displays a more interesting *mise-en-scène* than that of the original, as well as being subject to less censorship. Historical studies such as those of Juan B. Heinink and Robert G. Dickson, and Lisa Jarvinen[1], allow the general conclusion that "in late 1930 and early 1931, when producers began to receive reports of their films' fortunes, only a few films had become major hits and many had received withering criticism in the Spanish-language press."[2]

One of the magazines that followed the fortunes of Spanish-language versions most closely was *Cinelandia*. Published in Los Angeles by the Spanish-American Publishing Co., it was a Spanish-language journal, essentially aimed at a female audience, while promoting American cinema within Spanish-speaking markets. Launched as *Cinelandia y Films* in 1927, its title was changed simply to *Cinelandia*[3] in September 1930, the name by which it would be known until its closure in 1936. During the later period, the magazine was headed up by journalist Juan J. Moreno, author of the "Cinelándicas," monthly editorials that closely followed the development of Spanish-language film versions from the end of 1929 to the end of 1934; they now serve as primary sources for the study of their rise and fall, based on the position the magazine assumed in January 1930, when it pointed out to the relevant production companies that "our position in the industry allows us to serve as interpreters for the wishes of the fans in Spanish-speaking countries and our knowledge of these countries offers benefits that you can well imagine and that we are happy to provide."

As early as December 1929, the director of the publication echoed the expectations created in the Spanish-speaking market by writing: "One of the desires that we are all eager to see become a reality in the very near future is the large-scale production of talking films in our language!" A month later, he reiterated the imminent arrival of "a new era of major significance and interest for film enthusiasts in Spanish-speaking countries. Naturally, we are talking about Spanish talkies, featuring actors who represent our own race and made in Hollywood: the most important filmmaking center in the world." The association between the powerful American industry and *Hispanidad* patriotism set the bar very high in terms of expectations, which it soon became apparent, reality would fail to meet.

1 Juan B. Heinink and Robert G. Dickson, *Cita en Hollywood. Las películas norteamericanas habladas en español* (Mensajero, Bilbao, 1990); Lisa Jarvinen, *The Rise of Spanish-Language Filmmaking. Out from Hollywood's Shadow, 1929-1939* (New Brunswick, N.J.: Rutgers University Press, 2012).

2 Jarvinen, 54.

3 An almost complete collection of *Cinelandia* is held at the Filmoteca de Catalunya and was used as reference material for this paper.

Following a report, also in January 1930, that "five major and other less important studios have announced a program of talking pictures featuring Hispanic artists, some of whom are our national idols," the first disappointment arrived with *Sombras habaneras* (1929, Cliff Wheeler): "An absurd plot, poorly directed, with even worse acting and featuring Spanish dialogue that sounds like a literal translation of the English," according to a news piece published in the same issue. Barely a month later, Juan J. Moreno himself reported the "setback suffered by the first synchronized film—Universal's *Broadway* (1929, Paul Fejos)—that was received in Buenos Aires and Mexico with spirited expressions of disapproval." The enthusiasm remained intact, however, thanks to announcements of future projects from a number of studios, so the editorial signed off with a traditional Spanish saying: "Let's see what kind of stew comes out of this pot!"

As the numbers of projects increased, Moreno tempered his negative criticism in March 1930 of the previously mentioned *Sombras de gloria*: "... the film in question does not live up to expectations, given the material elements at its disposal, (...) the result is worth watching and listening to and, as a first attempt, we need to overlook many things that would, under different circumstances, be unforgivable." This forced indulgence is offered, however, along with an observation that reveals the depth of the problem: "As long as the current shortage of first-rate artistic and literary elements in Hollywood continues, all efforts to produce top-quality talkies will be to no avail. Reviewing the list of top Hispanic stars that have become established and have flourished on the American big screen, there is not one who has had any experience in spoken theatre." Hope then became focused on the imminent arrival of the Catalan leading man, Ernesto Vilches, "who promises to form the vanguard of an army that will soon come from all Spanish-speaking countries in a determined effort to besiege and occupy this citadel of dollars and fame."

In the next issue—April 1930—expectations were further heightened with the rumour that "one of our own idols, Ramón Novarro, will soon be appearing in a Spanish-language talkie under the auspices of the highly renowned company, Metro-Goldwyn-Mayer." During the silent movie era, this Mexican heartthrob had rivalled Rudolph Valentino as a Latin lover, thanks to his leading roles in *Scaramouche* (1923, Rex Ingram) and *Ben-Hur* (1925, Fred Niblo). The impact of this high-profile collaboration far surpassed that of other strictly local actors so that even Moreno felt "obliged to add the caveat that the news is somewhat premature and that there is currently no indication that such a thing will happen in the near future, or, indeed, ever." That, however, was not enough to deter him from promoting the potential of Spanish-language versions as the best antidote to the infiltration of English in Spanish-speaking countries, since "there will soon be enough Spanish talkies for Hispanic audiences not to be required to listen to a language that, for the majority, is as intelligible as Chinese."

The misgivings were confirmed in the following issue, which reported that Novarro had withdrawn from the *La Casa de la Troya* project, because "he quite understandably has qualms about striking out on a new, unexplored path that could lead him into a quagmire, rather than to the glory he deserves."[4] Buster Keaton, having fallen on hard times, didn't however hesitate to agree to appear in *Estrellados* (1930, *Free and Easy*), "speaking in broken Spanish" under the direction of Salvador de Alberich. The news also reported that *Men of the North* (1930, Hal Roach) would be shot in five languages, including in Spanish as *Monsieur Le Fox* (1930) with Hal Roach and Roberto E. Guzmán at the helm. Having openly condemned the poor quality of initial attempts, *Cinelandia* now also ran the risk of strangling the goose that laid the golden egg: "The gold rush sweeps up numerous individuals of our racial heritage who, with the new innovation of the talkies, see a mountain of gold prompting them to line their pockets with gay abandon. (...) Films without art or *raison d'être* are produced as quickly as possible to be 'the first,' and the result is disastrous for our *raza*'s pagan audience."

The premiere of *El cuerpo del delito* (1930, Cyril Gardner, A. Washington Pezet), reviewed in June, seemed to dispel any previous bad omens. Moreno praised the quality of the sound recording of this Paramount production and allowed himself "to announce with great pleasure, that the production of Spanish-language talking pictures with Hispanic artists has begun in every way and with such a resounding success that it surpasses my highest expectations." Two months later, the announcement of new titles further boosted this feeling of optimism, headlined by stars, capable of expressing themselves in Spanish, notable among which were *Amor audaz* (1930, Louis J. Gasnier) with Adolphe Menjou, *El hombre malo* (1930, William McGann) with Antonio Moreno, *Monsieur Le Fox* with Gilbert Roland, *Cascarrabias* (1930, Cyril Gardner) with Ernesto Vilches, and *Olimpia* (1930, Chester M. Franklin) with José Crespo. In November, further new titles were reported: *Sevilla de mis amores* (1930, Ramón Novarro) with Ramón Novarro finally in a leading role, *Wu Li Chang* (1930, Nick Grinde) with Ernesto Vilches, *El presidio* (1930, Ward Wing) and *El dios del mar* (1930, Edward D. Venturini), prompting the proclamation that

> photophonic production in Spanish is progressing by leaps and bounds and I firmly believe that the day in which the production of Spanish-speaking films reaches the degree of artistic perfection that we all wish for is not far off. (...) The production companies have at last realized the importance of making every effort to produce talkies in Spanish and it is natural that we should rejoice in seeing that the position assumed by *Cinelandia* is on the verge of being amply justified.

This euphoria resulting from the films' crucial technical improvement was, however, ephemeral. Just a month later, at the same time that Paramount moved its European market version production to its studios in Joinville near Paris, another powerful production company decided to shut down its foreign language film operations: "The Pathé company alleges that the foreign audience—in this case the Hispanic audience—wants to continue watching their established idols and cannot get excited about the prospect of supplanting those idolized shadows of the screen with people of their own blood. (...) Maybe the Pathé Company is right," says Juan J. Moreno in December 1930. Although an

---

4 Novarro starred in the English-language original, *In Gay Madrid* (1930, Robert Z. Leonard), but a Spanish-language version was never released.

exception, the Company's decision was the result of a strategy that consisted of "producing talking pictures with a maximum amount of action and a minimum amount of dialogue; films that can be shown in foreign lands, without any strange accent assaulting the senses of the viewer or hampering their understanding of the drama unfolding before their eyes. Could this be the year that solves the difficulties that are now beleaguering talkie production in our language?"

Another alternative was put forward in an article published in January 1931 in which the Chilean director Carlos F. Borcosque supported the selection of Spanish or Latin American-themed sources that were more accommodating for Latin actors. Moreno in the editorial of the same issue contradicts him, however, referring to a number of examples of silent films and the recent successes of Frenchman Maurice Chevalier, who acted in English. "Speaking plainly, the current situation in Hollywood is that there is barely a single Latin artist, aside from those who are already established, who can play their role in a convincing and rational way. Whether playing Americans, as in the case of *Olimpia*, or Chinese, as in *Wu Li Chang*, or Hispanics, as in *El hombre malo*, their mediocre work comes down to a lack of talent in playing the roles with which they have been entrusted."

These failures required those responsible to be called out, in order to compensate the public for their disappointment:

> Many of our readers want to know what is wrong with the production of Spanish talkies. They are attracted to the theatres by glowing promises of Spanish pictures on par with the American output, and leave the show embittered and disillusioned. (...) They reason that the American producers with their unlimited resources and vast experience should be able to give them a product worthy of their acquired taste for the best of acting and direction. (...) Briefly the trouble begins right at the top: The producer.[5]

Moreno calls for Spanish-speaking directors, scriptwriters with cinematic experience and Latin-American sympathies, and concludes with great pessimism: "An apathy towards Spanish talkies can be observed in many areas that augurs financial disaster for this incipient industry. (...) The fact that they themselves question whether they have done what they should to produce a first-class article that will bring them the artistic and financial success they desire. (...) We will then have a product that is not an insult to our intelligence."

The collapse in the production of Spanish versions is explicitly addressed in March 1931:

> After a hectic period of Spanish picture production, we find most of the Hollywood studios marking time in this branch of the industry (...) with the producers anxiously scanning income reports from the various theatre fronts along the line." To avoid catastrophe, "we would have considered it wiser to

5 As of this issue, Juan J. Moreno's editorial was simultaneously published in both Spanish and English. Although the translation is not always orthodox, nor even literal, the English version of the text as it was published in the magazine is included here.

Cover of *Cinelandia*, February 1930, featuring Lupe Vélez.

> continue to supply the Spanish markets with quality American talkies with a minimum of English dialogue that could be easily gapped by the insertion of subtitles or some other method. In the meantime, a Spanish organization could have been formed at each studio by slowly and carefully coaching the various elements involved, in the principles of motion picture making.[6]

M-G-M's decision to halt production of Spanish-language films, including those that, by April 1931, were already being shot, seems to confirm the gloomy predictions previously suggested by *Cinelandia*: "We certainly sensed that a certain something was in the air that promised well needed changes in this incipient branch of the industry." Moreno, still optimistic, conjectured

> that the Metro-Goldwyn-Mayer Studios have found a way to successfully present their original pictures made in English with the original characters talking in our language. It also means that the Spanish fans have made their wishes felt through the ultimate and definitive medium of the well-known box-office receipts. As they have often expressed in their letters to *Cinelandia* they want to continue seeing their screen favorites and are not yet ready for substitutes that have been forced on them from Hollywood.

According to the magazine, the solution lay in dubbing. In other words:

> The pictures would revert to the old standard of action technique leaving the word and sound to supplement the telling of the story rather than to form the basis for it. With pictures of this kind it will be extremely easy to make the characters express themselves in any language, or they can in many places, be shown in English without loss of interest on the part of the foreign spectator.[7]

Contrary to the official decision regarding Metro's secession of version filmmaking, the May editorial reported that one film, *El proceso de Mary Dugan/The Trial of Mary Dugan* (1931, Marcel De Sano), had in fact been completed, "directed by a man who does not know Spanish. With two Spanish-speaking directors available, the reason for this selection remains unexplained and little understood." This, however, was an exception to the rule, since "after *Mary Dugan* there will be a period of inactivity." Fox also came in for criticism, because the studio "has produced no better Spanish films than its competitors, has recently imported a number of actors from the Spanish stage. This news has been received by everyone in the industry with raised eyebrows and a feeling that something is missing somewhere. It gives new evidence of the inefficiency and confusion attending the making of Spanish talkies so far."

6 In English in the original.
7 In English in the original.

Lastly, Paramount received a mention for its commitment to continue Spanish-language production, "but actually they are merely marking time, waiting for the final returns that will tell the tale as nothing else will. The final balancing of the books will show them the fatal effects, rather than reveal the causes of failure. This must be found out and corrected by people of good judgment and knowledge of conditions." The key, in short, lies in the technical quality of the films and, faced with a Spanish-speaking audience, seduced by *The Love Parade* (1929, Ernst Lubitsch) and *All Quiet on the Western Front* (1930, Lewis Milestone), "these people know how good talkies can be, and are loudest in their denunciation of the Spanish productions they have seen."[8]

With the problems identified, "the Spanish talkie situation seems to be as muddled as it was a month ago. (...) Confusion everywhere adds to producer's well-founded fears and wisely they reef sails until the squall blows over,"[9] the June 1931 editorial stated. Exceptionally, the director Carlos Borcosque waded into the controversy with an article published in the November issue that posed the idea that the lack of Spanish-language films produced an increased demand, since an actor speaking the local language is preferable to the incomprehensible dialogue of a star in the original version. Despite these expectations, and a few sporadic final gasps, the editorial published in January 1932 seemingly heralded the death of Spanish-language film production: "The Hollywood studios, with the exception of Universal and a privately-owned company, are no longer making Spanish talkies. (...) The great phalanx of Hispanic actors and actresses who for many months swarmed over Hollywood, have returned to their homelands." The notice was not completely true, though, since Fox continued producing Spanish-language originals until at least 1934. Finally, by way of a swan song, an overview of the seventy productions filmed between the end of 1929 and the middle of 1931 was published in March 1932, with just half a dozen titles that "constituted significant and definitive successes in each and every one of the language's countries."

Juan J. Moreno remained in his position at the helm of *Cinelandia* until 1934. The magazine continued publishing until 1936—the start of the Spanish Civil War—maintaining its identity as a publication catering for a predominantly female audience and, although it stopped reporting on Spanish versions, the impressions expounded in the "Cinelándicas" editorials produced by its director serve as extraordinarily useful sources through which we are able to follow the development of this phenomenon.

---

8 In English in the original.
9 In English in the original.

Buried in the Vaults: The Restoration of Hollywood's Spanish-language films

Roberto Green Quintana

A film buried in a vault is not unlike a hidden treasure. It might be in a safe place (by no means a trivial fact considering the dire consequences of poor storage), but it fails to fulfill its *raison d'être*. Since it cannot be enjoyed or admired, it cannot bring any pleasure or have an impact on people's lives, and, because it remains unseen, its value cannot be assessed. In fact, we can argue that availability plays a key role in the creation of film histories and the establishment of film canons. Films like *Gone with the Wind* (1939, Victor Fleming), *The Wizard of Oz* (1939, Victor Fleming) or *Casablanca* (1942, Michael Curtiz) would have hardly achieved the legendary status they enjoy today had they not been regularly re-released and enjoyed by new generations. And would Frank Capra's *It's a Wonderful Life* (1946)—a box-office flop when first released—be the perennial Christmas classic it is nowadays, were it not aired on television every year? Probably not, as evidenced by the fact that another Christmas classic, *Miracle on 34th Street* (1947, George Seaton), is practically unknown in several European countries where it is seldom shown on television and has not always been available on home video.

Therefore, if we accept that availability is the first step to visibility, it is not difficult to understand why Spanish-language films that Hollywood produced during the transition to sound have fallen into oblivion. Either hidden in vaults or lost, many of these movies haven't been seen since they were first released or reprised in the 1930s; thus, until fairly recently, they had attracted the attention of only a few film historians, while being relegated to a mere footnote in film history books.

However, between 1929 and 1939, Hollywood studios and different independent production companies made more than 170 films in Spanish.[1] Many of these titles were Spanish-language versions of English-language originals, one of the first solutions that studios

1 See Lisa Jarvinen, *The Rise of Spanish-Language Filmmaking: Out from Hollywood's Shadow, 1929-1939* (New Brunswick, N.J.: Rutgers University Press, 2012), 8.

conceived to cope with the problem that the advent of sound posed to non-English-speaking audiences before the techniques of subtitling and dubbing had been perfected.[2] Other titles, however, were original productions aimed at the Spanish-speaking market.[3]

The fact that so few of these films have survived is not that surprising. Before the advent of television, studios saw little value in their old titles, so most prints were destroyed after a film's theatrical run, though a few were usually saved, and preprint material was generally shelved and sometimes used for clips.[4] However, until the implementation of 35mm cellulose triacetate safety film base in 1948, film stock was made of highly flammable cellulose nitrate. As a result, film fires were not uncommon. One of the most notorious examples is the 1937 fire of a storage facility in Little Ferry, New Jersey, which resulted in the loss of many silent and early sound negatives from the Fox Film Corporation. Due to storage costs and the increasing insurance premiums for keeping nitrate on the backlots, most studios began disposing of their original nitrate materials after 1950. In the best cases, films were transferred onto safety stock and/or deposited in film archives; in the worst cases, they were just destroyed.[5] But even when studios kept original nitrate film elements, over time, many deteriorated beyond repair, and were lost forever.

The Spanish-language features were even less fortunate than other early sound films. "It is more difficult to find extra prints of them because they were never re-released," says Josef Lindner, Preservation Officer for the Academy Film Archive.

"There was probably no TV sale; there were probably no 16mm prints made because there was no market for them; they weren't super successful, so they weren't kept for remake purposes. When studios duplicated some of their films, these would have been at the bottom of their list of priorities."[6] The same is true for the German and French films that Hollywood made during the transition to sound. As Scott MacQueen, Head of Preservation at UCLA Film & Television Archive, observes:

> M-G-M's German-language version of *Anna Christie* survives because (a) M-G-M copied everything they still held, and (b) Garbo starred in it. But they don't have the French version of *The Unholy Night* (*Le spectre vert*, 1929), and Warner Bros. does not have the German *Moby Dick* (*Dämon des Meeres*, 1931) directed by Michael Curtiz. Only the Vitaphone sound discs survive at UCLA.[7]

---

2 For more information about some of the solutions that studios came up with for foreign markets, read "Modes of Translating Hollywood Films, 1930-1935" in Jarvinen, 102-118.

3 Lisa Jarvinen argues that the reason why American Spanish-language films were produced as late as 1939, when dubbing and subtitling were already standard, is because Hollywood wished to maintain its position of power in Spanish-speaking countries. See Jarvinen, 3.

4 See Annette Melville and Scott Simmon, *Film Preservation 1993: A Study of the Current State of American Film Preservation, Vol. 1* (Washington, D.C.: Library of Congress, 1993), https://www.loc.gov/programs/national-film-preservation-board/preservation-research/film-preservation-study/current-state-of-american-film-preservation-study/ .

5 Metro-Goldwyn-Mayer, for example, started a duplication program in the 1960s. Every surviving film from the studio and its affiliated companies was copied on safety stock, and many nitrate originals were donated to George Eastman House. Besides, since the 1930s M-G-M had given prints or negatives for some of its features to American archives. Universal, on the other hand, destroyed most of its silent film negatives in 1948. See David Pierce, *The Survival of American Silent Feature Films: 1912–1929* (Washington, D.C.: Library of Congress, 2013), 1, 6-7, 31; Michael Binder, *A Light Affliction: A History of Film Preservation and Restoration* (Lulu, 2014), 56, 104-5.

6 Josef Lindner to author, December 21, 2017.

7 Scott MacQueen to author, December 20, 2017.

While the neglect suffered by these titles back in the day when movies were just regarded as commodities might be understandable, the obscurity of the ones that still exist is, at the very least, puzzling. Why have studios and archives paid so little attention to the few surviving Spanish-language films? There are probably several reasons for this.

For instance, studios, always concerned with profits, have usually prioritized the restoration of familiar titles, even though, as Anthony Slide wrote in 1992, "for every 'glamorous' restoration project such as *A Star Is Born* or *Lawrence of Arabia*, there are literally hundreds of 'little films,' forgotten B-pictures, Westerns and serials in desperate need of preservation."[8] An added problem in the case of the Spanish-language films is that, besides being virtually unknown, their reputation is not exactly stellar. Until recently, Spanish-language versions of English-language originals were usually dismissed as cheap, fast-made copies, while original productions were regarded as phony, Hollywoodized products. Even Jesús García de Dueñas, author of one of the few books devoted to these films (*¡Nos vamos a Hollywood!*), supported this idea. "It is difficult to make a critical analysis of the Spanish movies filmed in Hollywood during the '30s," he wrote. "They are what they are, or, better said, what they wanted to be: a senseless and mistaken colonialist ploy."[9] On top of this, most of the thespians who starred in these productions have fallen into oblivion. Names like Juan Torena, Rosita Díaz Gimeno, Raúl Roulien or even Conchita Montenegro, mean little or nothing to modern audiences from the United States or Spanish-speaking countries. And the same can be said about those who directed them in these American ventures.

Taking this into account, it is not difficult to see why the studios might have had misgivings about the profitability of these Spanish-language films, even today when online distribution and retail allows them to obtain benefits from titles in their deep catalog. Although companies like Warner Bros., Universal, 20th Century-Fox and Sony-Columbia have released some of their rarer films on Made-On-Demand DVDs or online streaming services, almost all the surviving American Spanish-language films remain locked in the vaults. The fact that some of them require costly restorations, due to the poor condition of the surviving film elements, as well as the extra expense of creating subtitles for English-speaking audiences, might have had something to do with this.

Josef Lindner, however, believes that the main reason why studios and archives have not paid much attention to these films is because they are still completely unknown. "People are not even researching them yet. That's part of the problem," he says.

---

8 Anthony Slide, *Nitrate Won't Wait: A History of Film Preservation in the United States* (Jefferson, N.C.: McFarland & Company, 1992), 6.

9 "Resulta difícil hacer un comentario crítico de las películas españolas rodadas en Hollywood en los años 30. Son lo que son o, mejor dicho, lo que pretendieron ser: una insensata y equivocada argucia de penetración colonialista." Original quote from Jesús García de Dueñas, *¡Nos vamos a Hollywood!* (Madrid: Nickel Odeon, 1993), xviii.

> We don't have a good grasp on what Fox has, we don't have a good grasp on what the other studios have. I think there's a lot more work that needs to be done about the research of these films, about finding elements, and just awareness of what they are. But, because they're unknown, no one is even asking for them."[10]

Jan-Christopher Horak, Director of the UCLA Film & Television Archive, shares this opinion. "There was no real history of these Spanish-language films and nobody was asking for them. In the Archive our priorities are (a) materials that are decomposing and (b) requests from outside, and in all these years we obviously did not get many requests," he points out, adding that "when you have such a large archive, it takes time to get around to things."[11] Scott MacQueen also comments that the obscurity of these Spanish-language films can pose a problem when it comes to finding funds to restore them. "Most archive work is grant-funded, and donors and agencies are often unaware of these films, which exist on the margins of the studio system," he observes.[12]

Not surprisingly, one of the first Spanish-language films that was rescued from the shadows of oblivion and the threat of decay featured one of the most popular characters of all time: Dracula. In 1930, Universal produced a film adaptation of Bram Stoker's classic novel, starring Bela Lugosi as the mysterious count and the ill-fated Helen Chandler as his love interest. Tod Browning, a master of the medium, was in charge of direction. Simultaneously, the studio made a Spanish-language version, filmed at night on the same sets that Browning and his crew were using during the day. The Spanish-born actor Carlos Villarías and the Mexican beauty Lupita Tovar stepped into the main roles, while George Melford took over the directorial reins.[13] After a preview on the Universal lot in January 1931, the Spanish-language *Drácula* opened to good reviews in Mexico City on April 4, and, a month later, on May 8, at the California Theatre in Los Angeles.[14] But while Browning's version has become a classic, Melford's film fell into oblivion, even though, according to Dracula expert David J. Skal, it was shown theatrically in Spanish-speaking countries until the 1950s.[15]

When in the late 1970s, Universal found the negative in a New Jersey storage facility, it was too late: certain parts had deteriorated beyond recovery due to nitrate decomposition. With the help of the Library of Congress, some of the lost fragments were located, but the entire third reel was missing.[16] Unfortunately, this reel featured some key moments, like Dracula's sea voyage to England or the theater scene in which the vampire meets the character played by Lupita Tovar. All the same, archival prints were struck, and an incomplete copy was shown in a Universal retrospective at the Museum of Modern Art in 1977.[17]

---

10 Josef Lindner to author, December 21, 2017.

11 Jan-Christopher Horak to author, January 8, 2018.

12 Scott MacQueen to author, December 20, 2017.

13 For more information about the filming of the Spanish-language *Drácula*, see "La Sangre Es la Vida," the sixth chapter in David J. Skal's *Hollywood Gothic: The Tangled Web of Dracula from Novel to Stage to Screen* (New York: Faber and Faber, 2004).

14 See David J. Skal, *Hollywood Gothic: The Tangled Web of Dracula from Novel to Stage to Screen* (New York: Faber and Faber, 2004), 225-6.

15 See Skal, 229.

16 Ibid; Reynaldo González, "Drácula resucitó en la Habana" (Program notes, Aula de Cultura ARABA, 1991); Robert Rosen to Teresa Toledo, January 7, 1990.

17 See Skal, 218-9; 229.

Lobby Card for Spanish *Drácula* (1931, George Melford).

But there was a rumor that a complete print survived at the Cuban Film Archive (Cinemateca de Cuba) in Havana, something that the institution apparently confirmed to the International Federation of Film Archives (FIAF).[18] The Cinemateca had held a nitrate print of the film in the past, which they had copied to safety stock in the 1960s, when, for safety reasons, they had started disposing of their nitrate assets.[19] In 1989, David J. Skal was able to travel to Havana to study in detail this complete copy. After the publicity that the original edition of his book *Hollywood Gothic* generated, Universal decided to restore the film. However, due to the United States embargo against Cuba, Universal could not deal directly with the Cinemateca, so the UCLA Film & Television Archive had to act as an intermediary.[20] Being both an educational institution and a member of FIAF, this archive had more leeway to negotiate. On April 12, 1991, the Cinemateca sent the film to UCLA and, the following year, in November 1992, a restored version was finally screened at the Director's Guild Theatre in Los Angeles.[21]

To this day, Melford's *Drácula* is one of the few Hollywood Spanish-language films available on home video, even though it is presented as a bonus feature on the Universal DVD and Blu-ray editions of Tod Browning's version. Another rare exception is the 2006 DVD release of *Eran trece* (1931, David Howard), the Spanish-language version of a lost Charlie Chan film, *Charlie Chan Carries On* (1931). Twentieth Century Fox included it as a DVD bonus feature on *Charlie Chan in Shanghai* (1935, James Tinling). The answer to why these films have fared better than other titles is probably found in the popularity of the two main characters they feature.

Not by chance, the other Hollywood films in Spanish that have been available on home video are from Laurel and Hardy. Between 1929 and 1931, the popular comic duo made multilingual versions of eleven of their shorts, which allowed foreign audiences to hear them speak in Spanish, German, French and even Italian. Eight of these versions were in Spanish, and, apparently, they were very popular.[22] In 1980, Hal Roach recalled: "Those foreign pictures were extremely successful. The prices we got in South American countries and Spain were fantastic."[23] The original film elements for the Laurel and Hardy Spanish-language films were rediscovered in 1986, and are now housed at the UCLA Film & Television Archive.[24] "It's interesting that so many of the Spanish titles exist, but none of the German or French or Italian iterations," Scott MacQueen observes. "We don't know why Roach or his staff elected to retain the Latin versions and not the others. Based on the plentiful reissue posters and advertising material that circulate, I suspect that Spanish titles were still in wide distribution in South America into the 1950s, so the negatives still had commercial value to the owner."[25]

---

18 See Alfredo Muñoz Unsaín, "Drácula en Cuba," *AFP* (Havana), April 22, 1991.
19 See Silvia Isabel Gámez, "Comparte cine la crisis de Cuba," *Reforma* (Mexico City), June 11, 1994.
20 See Skal, 229.
21 See Teresa Toledo to Robert Rosen, April 15, 1991; Skal, 229.
22 The Laurel and Hardy Spanish-language films are: *Ladrones* (1930, version of *Night Owls*); *La vida nocturna* (1930, version of *Blotto*); *Tiembla y titubea* (1930, version of *Below Zero*); *Radiomanía* (1930, version of *Hog Wild*); *Noche de duendes* (1930, version of *The Laurel-Hardy Murder Case* and *Berth Marks*); *Politiquerías* (1931, version of *Chickens Come Home*); *Los calaveras* (1931, version of *Be Big* and *Laughing Gravy*); *De bote en bote* (1931, version of *Pardon Us*).
23 Randy Skretvedt, "Catching Up with Laurel & Hardy in Spanish," www.cinema.ucla.edu/support/laurel-hardy-spanish .
24 Ibid.
25 Scott MacQueen to author, December 20, 2017.

Unlike the domestic version materials, which were overused to make new prints and are now worn out, the Spanish-language elements were in pristine condition when found.[26] As part of a major preservation effort to restore all the surviving negatives of Laurel and Hardy titles, the UCLA Film & Television Archive had already restored *De bote en bote* (1931, James W. Horne), *La vida nocturna* (1930, James Parrott), *Politiquerías* (1931, James W. Horne) and *Tiembla y titubea* (1930, James Parrott) by 2017. These films are interesting, especially because they sometimes feature new sequences that were not in domestic versions. According to Randy Skretvedt, "longer pictures meant higher rental fees, and the team's popularity was such in Spanish-speaking countries that their short films were often billed over the feature attraction. As a result, some of the two- and three-reel domestic films were lengthened to four or five reels."[27]

The UCLA Film & Television Archive has also restored other Spanish-language titles, including several of the Fox films that were deposited in the Archive in the early 1970s. Two Fox movies were restored thanks to a generous $45,000 donation made in 1998 by film historian Bob Dickson, who eight years earlier had published *Cita en Hollywood*, along with Juan B. Heinink, a groundbreaking book about Spanish-language features made in Hollywood during the 1930s that has since inspired other researchers. His first choice was the romantic drama *Nada más que una mujer* (1934, Harry Lachman), a Spanish version of *Pursued* (1934, Louis King) that features Juan Torena, Luana Alcañiz and Berta Singerman, in a rare film appearance. Dickson had been captivated by Singerman's unique performance and Rudolph Maté's cinematography, and wanted new audiences to enjoy the movie. *No dejes la puerta abierta* (1933, Lewis Seiler), a Spanish version of the comedy *Pleasure Cruise* (1933, Frank Tuttle), starring Raúl Roulien, Rosita Moreno and Mona Maris, was the second restoration he funded.[28]

However, it was thanks to the Getty-led project *Pacific Standard Time: LA/LA*, which aimed to explore the connections between Latin American art and the City of Los Angeles, that in 2014 the UCLA Film & Television Archive embarked on a major preservation project in which several Spanish-language films, including some American productions from the '30s, were restored. "Under the leadership of Jan-Christopher Horak, we were asked to identify holdings in our collections and several sister archives," Scott MacQueen recalls. "The first criterion was for the selected titles to have played the Spanish-language theaters in Los Angeles on their initial release, so that these were titles seen by Latinos in Los Angeles back in the day. Titles were then floated based on importance, availability, and the time and money available to prepare them."[29]

Among the restored titles are two Fox vehicles with the prominent opera star José Mojica: *La cruz y la espada* (1934, Frank R. Strayer) and *El rey de los gitanos* (1933, Frank R. Strayer). Mojica was the most popular Spanish-language star of the early 1930s, with the exception of Carlos Gardel, and *La cruz y la espada* was his favorite film.[30] The Acad-

---

26 Randy Skretvedt, n.p.
27 Ibid.
28 Bob Dickson to author, April 5, 2017.
29 Scott MacQueen to author, December 20, 2017.
30 Jarvinen, 121.

emy Film Archive had considered restoring it a decade earlier, but there were some film elements missing.[31] UCLA was finally able to do a definitive 35mm film restoration using three original nitrate sources. This was possible thanks to the generous support of 20th Century-Fox which, apart from granting UCLA permission and access to other elements in the studio's collections held at the Academy Film Archive and MoMA, underwrote the entire cost of the restoration.[32]

More problematic was the preservation of *El rey de los gitanos*. The only surviving copy of this title was a badly warped 16mm print with vinegar syndrome decay, held by a South American collector. This print was scanned and a 35mm duplicate negative was made. However, audiences will at present only be able to enjoy it digitally. "The results were unsatisfactory due to the extreme shrinkage and buckling of the deteriorating 16mm print, and it was futile to make 35mm prints," says Scott MacQueen. "The preservation result is not an accomplishment we are proud of for visual or sonic beauty, but it is all that could be achieved in the last hour of the celluloid's life. The film now survives even though in a heavily mutilated form."[33]

Other titles that UCLA wanted to restore were less fortunate. *Hollywood, ciudad de ensueño* (1931, George Crone), with José Bohr and Lia Torá, and *Granaderos del amor* (1934, John Reinhardt), starring Raúl Roulien and Conchita Montenegro, are among the films that have been shelved, due to the poor condition of the surviving elements.[34]

Luckily, this was not the case of *La vida bohemia* (1938, Josef Berne) and *Verbena trágica* (1939, Charles Lamont), the only two titles made by the independent production company Cantabria Films. The first is an adaptation of Henri Murger's popular novel, *Scènes de la vie de bohème*, featuring Gilbert Roland and Rosita Díaz Gimeno as the unfortunate lovers. The legendary John Alton, in charge of the cinematography, once said: "If I were to give myself an award for the most artistic black-and-white photography, this would be it."[35] New audiences will finally be able to enjoy it thanks to a new 35mm restoration made from the original camera negative (on loan from the Library of Congress) and a nitrate print that was used to cover small losses and damage in the negative.[36]

As for *Verbena trágica*, UCLA created a DCP for exhibition purposes in 2017, but, unfortunately, there was no funding available to make film prints or preservation elements. "We are still hoping that will happen, and it remains high on our radar for film preservation; it's an important film," says MacQueen.[37] As a matter of fact, this drama, set in a Hispanic neighborhood in New York, was inducted into the National Film Registry in 1996. Directed by Charles Lamont—responsible for some of Shirley Temple's early shorts —*Verbena trágica* features Fernando Soler as a boxer who returns home after spending

31 Josef Lindner to author, December 21, 2017.
32 Scott MacQueen to author, December 20, 2017.
33 Ibid.
34 Ibid.
35 Todd McCarthy, "Through a Lens Darkly: The Life and Films of John Alton," in John Alton, *Painting with Light* (Los Angeles: University of California Press, 2013), xxv.
36 Scott MacQueen to author, December 20, 2017.
37 Ibid.

some months in jail, only to discover that his wife has fallen in love with one of his best friends. The rest of the cast includes Luana Alcañiz, Juan Torena, Romualdo Tirado and Pilar Arcos, who provides some of the film's funniest moments.

Although best remembered for her singing career, Arcos acted in a handful of American Spanish-language films, including the independent production for Monogram Pictures *Castillos en el aire* (1938), directed by the prolific screenwriter and filmmaker Jaime Salvador. Only a 16mm print of this light romantic comedy, held at Filmoteca de la UNAM, is known to have survived. After UNAM digitized it, the UCLA Film & Television Archive did some digital cleanup and made a DCP for theatrical exhibition. The outcome was not completely satisfactory, due to the quality of the surviving copy, but at least allows us to rediscover this curious title, which, when released, the *New York Times* described as "the first of what the Monogram concern hopes will be a series of Hollywood-made Spanish language films able to compete with Mexican and Argentine producers for the favor of motion picture patrons in Hispano-America."[38]

The UCLA Film & Television Archive also restored one of the most famous Mexican films of the classical period, *Enamorada* (1946, Emilio Fernández), starring María Félix and Pedro Armendáriz. Borrowing the original nitrate camera negative from Televisa in Mexico City, UCLA created a new preservation master, utilizing a 4K scan of UNAM's original nitrate print to fill in imperfections, then digitized the material for further cleanup, before it premiered at the Cannes Film Festival in 2018. The Archive has also received funding to preserve another early Mexican classic, *El fantasma del convento* (1934, Fernando de Fuentes), which will premiere in 2019.

UCLA's three-year preservation effort of Spanish-language titles culminated with the 2017 film series *Recuerdos de un cine en español: Latin American Cinema in Los Angeles*, where over thirty-five Spanish-language films were screened, including several American productions from the 1930s. Aside from the UCLA restorations mentioned above, the series featured titles like *¡Asegure a su mujer!* (1935, Lewis Seiler), a delightful comedy that the Academy Film Archive preserved in 2007, in order to screen it at the Los Angeles Latino International Film Festival.

After going through its collections, the Academy found four original Spanish-language productions: two José Mojica vehicles, *Un capitán de cosacos* (1934, John Reinhardt) and *La cruz y la espada*; one of Fox's last films in Spanish, *Los hijos mandan* (1939, Gabriel Soria); and the amusing *¡Asegure a su mujer!* Because funds to preserve only one title were available, a decision had to be made. The elements for both *La cruz y la espada* and *Los hijos mandan* were incomplete, so the options soon narrowed down to two. *¡Asegure a su mujer!* was finally chosen for several reasons. In the first place, its elements were the easiest to preserve, as a complete nitrate dupe negative had survived. Also, the film presented numerous artistic qualities. Its screenplay, co-written by the renowned Spanish writer Enrique Jardiel Poncela, offers a very original premise: after getting into trouble, a womanizer creates an insurance policy against marital infidelity,

38 H.T.S., "At the Teatro Hispano," *New York Times*, May 21, 1938.

which will eventually complicate things for him. If we add a cast full of some of the most important thespians making Spanish-language films, it is easy to see why the Academy finally selected this title. Josef Lindner also points out that when he chose *¡Asegure a su mujer!* over *Un capitán de cosacos*, he thought that it would probably be a better film to promote the forgotten Spanish-language productions that Hollywood once made. He was not mistaken. Ten years later, when the movie was shown again at the 2017 FIAF Congress, several archives expressed their interest in screening it in the future. Unfortunately, to this date, no digital transfer has been made and, therefore, only those who are able to attend a screening of the Academy's 35mm print will be able to enjoy it.[39]

Other American Spanish-language films soon to be available for reevaluation feature Carlos Gardel. Before his early death in a plane accident at the age of forty-four, the legendary Argentinian singer starred in several Paramount features that, aside from contributing to the popularity of sound films in Argentina, were very successful in many countries.[40] Actually, Gardel's films were so popular that, when he renegotiated his contract with Paramount in 1934, he was able to obtain an unusual degree of autonomy: his films were be produced by his own company, Exito Productions, although Paramount would go on distributing them.[41]

It is unclear what happened to the original film elements after the artist's death, but, for many years, these titles have only been available in DVD editions that used poor transfers from worn-out prints. Because of Gardel's popularity and iconic status, there was an urgent need to restore them back to their former glory. Several international institutions had shown an interest in undertaking this enterprise, but Marcela Cassinelli, President of Fundación Cinemateca Argentina (FCA), was adamant: the films had to be restored in Argentina; the country owed it to Gardel. Her late husband, the writer and filmmaker Guillermo Fernández Jurado, who had presided over FCA almost until his death in 2013, had acquired copies of most of the singer's films. However, due to the limited financial resources of the institution, it was impossible to restore them until Santander Bank provided funding in 2016, thanks to the support of the Buenos Aires City program, Mecenazgo.[42]

The titles initially restored were *Así cantaba Carlos Gardel* (1935, Eduardo Morera) and *El día que me quieras* (1935, John Reinhardt). The first title is a compilation of ten shorts that the singer made in Argentina in 1930, considered to be the first Argentinian sound-on-film productions. *El día que me quieras*, on the other hand, is an American production. It was Gardel's last film and his personal favorite. FCA had an acetate dupe negative, which was scanned at 4K resolution at Cinecolor Argentina. The soundtrack presented problems, so it was restored from a print owned by collector Walter Santoro,

---

39 Josef Lindner to author, December 21, 2017.

40 The Carlos Gardel films were: *Las luces de Buenos Aires* (1931), *Espérame* (1933), *Melodía de arrabal* (1933), *Cuesta abajo* (1934), *El tango en Broadway* (1934), *Tango Bar* (1935) and *El día que me quieras* (1935). Gardel also appeared in *The Big Broadcast of 1936* (1935), although his scene was only included in the version made for the Latin American market.

41 For more information about Gardel's American films, see Jorge Finkielman, "Carlos Gardel as a Film Star and His Tragic Death", in *The Film Industry in Argentina: An Illustrated Cultural History* (Jefferson, N.C.: McFarland & Company, 2004), 184-97.

42 Marcela Cassinelli to author, December 7, 2017.

who generously gave access to it. Because there are no longer labs that work with celluloid in Argentina, it was not possible to manufacture new safety elements, only DCPs for theatrical exhibition.[43] Still, Gardel fans will finally be able to see and listen to their idol without worrying about the quality issues that marred this film's theatrical and home video presentations in the past.

Once other Gardel titles are restored, they will be shown at different festivals and venues where, hopefully, new generations will discover them. However, there is still much that needs to be done to further raise awareness of the existence of Hollywood's 1930s Spanish-language films. Some titles are still hidden in the vaults of archives and studios, and unless some of the recent restorations make it to home video, they will remain obscure curiosities, only occasionally enjoyed (if ever) by audiences who have a film archive or a repertory cinema nearby. Nevertheless, the efforts made during the past years are already a giant step in the right direction. The time has come to restore a page that's long been missing from the books of American film history.

43 Ibid.

II
Production

Cita en Hollywood

Juan B. Heinink and Robert G. Dickson

With the advent of talking pictures, but before the development of successful dubbing and subtitling techniques, the major Hollywood studios and several independents produced versions of some of their films in foreign languages, including Spanish, French, and German, because they were fearful of the loss of international markets for their American films. Film production in the United States was dominated by five large companies: Metro-Goldwyn-Mayer, Paramount, Fox Film Corporation, United Artists and Warner Bros. The first four, well-established companies, had subsidiaries and agents all over the world, while Warner Bros. had recently become a major by being the first aboard the sound bandwagon after merging with First National. Harry Cohn's Columbia and Carl Laemmle's Universal were considered mini-majors. These companies produced 60% of all released films and possessed their own film factories, located in Hollywood and surrounding areas of Los Angeles. Some, like Paramount or Warner Bros., also owned studios in New York. A group of Poverty Row producers survived without their own studios in the shadow of Hollywood's majors, such as Metropolitan, Tiffany, Educational, Darmour, Tec-Art, Chesterfield, World Wide, Tiffany, Sono-Art and Mascot. A peculiar case, worth noting, was Hal Roach's studio. Based in Culver City, near the gigantic M-G-M, with which Roach had a distribution agreement, Hal Roach Studios had developed a formula for successfully producing comedy shorts. Roach, like the majors, would attempt Spanish-language film production after the coming of sound.

Some production companies organized contests outside the U.S. to find new faces. María Alba and Antonio Cumellas came to Hollywood as winners of a beauty contest that took place in Barcelona, promoted by Fox. María Alba did produce good results, but Cumellas failed. However, many other Spanish-speakers had previously arrived in Hollywood: Ramón Novarro, Antonio Moreno, Dolores del Río, and Gilbert Roland, followed by Lupe Vélez, Raquel Torres, Barry Norton, Mona Maris, Andrés de Segurola, Paul Ellis, Mona Rico, Soledad Jiménez, Lia Torá, Donald Reed, José Crespo and Lupita Tovar. In some cases, these actors had already started bringing to life Hispanic characters in sound films. Some production companies also had departments responsible for writing both the publicity materials, titles and intertiles in Spanish for films exported to Spain and Latin America. From this existing infrastructure, the studios considered producing directly in Spanish, but they waited for other companies to take the first step.

Spanish-language film production by the studio majors attracted Spanish-speaking writers, actors and directors to Hollywood, who—far from their familiar linguistic and cultural backgrounds—discovered that the promised land was not what it appeared to be. There was opportunity for writers from Spain to write Spanish dialogue, including Francisco Moré de la Torre at Fox, Salvador de Alberich at M-G-M, Carner Ribalta at Paramount, and Baltasar Fernández Cué at Universal. Instead of a life of luxury, they wandered from studio to studio in search of work. Carmen Guerrero, Alfonso Pedroza and Nancy Torres arrived from Mexico; María Calvo, Luis Llaneza, Carlos Villarías, and Rosita Granada from Spain; Vicente Padula from Argentina, and Ralph Navarro from the Philippines. Actors of Hispanic origin, like George Lewis, had to relearn a language they had forgotten. After a number of roles in shorts, Mexican baritone Rodolfo Hoyos couldn't find work at any of the studios, while his wife, not an artist, was offered a contract. Also part of the unseen face of Hollywood were rehearsals, photo and screen tests, and unexpectedly low salaries, as well as plenty of other hidden miseries. A good remedy to forget these sorrows was to wear the most elegant dress in the closet and get an invitation to attend the gala premiere of the latest Spanish-language film, produced by a Hollywood studio. Moreover, it was necessary to be seen in the lobby of the Teatro México, the Million Dollar or the California, to snatch information about future projects, and to be noticed, in case a producer needed to discover a new face. Around midnight, members of the Hispanic community in California and their friends would attend the premiere party with news reporters, critics, and studio executives. While the hopefuls would roam around networking, trying to be photographed, a worried smile would cross the faces of the film's producers and members of the cast. It was common for the sound reproduction systems to malfunction and no one could guarantee that it would not occur again. In any case, the technical mishap could very well become a good pretext to justify the failure of the film itself.

It is usually said, and perhaps it is true, that the first words in Spanish in a movie filmed in Hollywood were the ones pronounced by Soledad Jiménez, born in Spain, who was cast as a Mexican in the western *In Old Arizona* (1929, Irving Cummings). A silent version of the film premiered in Spain, but there are no records to prove it. It is not, however, a matter of great importance, because various productions were filmed along the border with Mexico, meaning any one of them could have produced a film with phrases or words in Spanish.

While the Hispanic world waited for Hollywood to present something more substantial than brief Spanish scenes in shorts, which gave local ambiance to typical songs, news from New York became a headline: Empire Productions Inc., a new company of independent producers, associated with the Latin American Underwriter Syndicate, announced the production of a group of twelve two-reel films, solely spoken and sung in Spanish. This would be the first sustained distribution of independent Spanish-language shorts. Presided over by Maurice A. Chase and Edmund Lawrence, a former associate producer at Paramount, Empire hired Arcady Boytler as their principal director, as well as Spanish baritones Fortunio Bonanova and Juan Pulido, among a roster of actors. *Sombras vengadoras* (Shadows of Revenge) opened the series, followed by Lawrence's *Flor de pasión* (Flower of Passion), and comedies, such as *Los Bombones del Abor* (Abor's Chocolates), musicals, such as *Granada*, concert and dance acts, and vaudeville numbers. Filmed through the latter half of 1929 at the Metropolitan Studios in Fort Lee, New Jersey, the films left few traces, making exact identification an impossible mission. After announcing an ambitious plan to produce forty-two new titles in 1930, Empire suddenly moved to Mexico.

Headed by impresario Juan J. Pablo, better known as the magician Li Ho Chang, Hispano America Movitonal Films, based in New York, launched a group of shorts that combined comedies and musical pieces, featuring performances by Mexican baritone Rodolfo Hoyos, Puerto Rican Orquesta Sanabria, and Madrid-born actress Carmen Rodríguez. A compilation, *Revista Hispano-Americana* (1930), was released to little acclaim in New York in January 1930. Carmen would return to Spain in 1935, after a lengthy career in Hollywood, and remained active until the late 1950s.

Hollywood reacted against the East Coast threat by releasing a number of short film comedies or musicals that had been in the works. It also introduced an invention that would generate much talk: dubbing. While a subsidiary of Universal Pictures, directed by the Chilean journalist Lucio Villegas, was quietly achieving success with the presentation of singer/dancer José Bohr in the short *Una noche en Hollywood* (A Night in Hollywood), Universal experienced a notable failure with the synchronized Spanish version of the musical *Broadway* (1929, Paul Fejos). A few months later, in a poll taken in Cuba, the dubbed version of *Broadway* received twelve favorable votes cast out of 3,098, ending up in last place among Spanish-language films released. Other markets chose to ignore this version, projecting the original sound version and rejecting this first dubbing experiment.

Enter René Cardona, a twenty-three-year-old Cuban who had acted as a young leading man next to Raquel Meller in the 1926 short *La mujer del torero* (The Bullfighter's Wife). The adventurer had the audacity to produce the first American feature film, spoken in Spanish. Using minimal capital, he founded the Cuban International Company, shooting *Sombras habaneras* (Shadows of Havana) in Hollywood's Tec-Art studios in September, 1929. The director was Cliff Wheeler, an Austrian aristocrat and military man, who would later return to film work under his real name, Alexis Thurn-Taxis. Unfortunately, the hopeful Cardona, who cast himself in a starring role, was the victim of an exaggerated streak of bad luck. It started with losing a good deal of the exposed negative, due to a fire at Consolidated Laboratories, and culminated with the cancellation of a crowded gala premiere in Los Angeles, due to a malfunction of the sound equipment. The businessman Rodolfo Montes offered to pay for the bills if the company changed its name to Hispania Talking Film Corp., which Cardona accepted. However, because the star of the film, Jacqueline Logan, did not speak a word of Spanish and her voice was dubbed by a Cuban, the critics denied Cardona the honor of having produced the first Spanish-language feature film. It was said that *Sombras habaneras* had an absurd subject, was badly directed, and even worse acted, with Spanish dialogue that sounded like a literal translation from English. Perhaps too much was expected, but to witness the screen debut of the Filipino Juan Torena, whose only artistic merit was to have played for a Barcelona soccer team, and to see Paul Ellis, an Argentine, sporting a French accent of his own invention, or the dancer Joyzelle exclaiming "ke-rram-ba!" elicited laughter to no end.

Sombras habaneras paved the way for *Sombras de gloria* (1930, Andrew L. Stone), which took home all the honors in 1930, thanks to great publicity, not only casting a shadow on its predecessor, but also shamelessly borrowing half its title. *Sombras de gloria* was the first picture filmed in Hollywood in two versions. The entrepreneurs O.E. Goebel, who made a fortune producing religious films, and George W. Weeks, an expert in film distribution, had founded a small company, Sono-Art, whose survival depended on a careful strategy of expansion. They looked for material that the market was not supplying. After trying a few shorts, starring Luana Alcañiz, they reached the conclusion that there was a business opportunity in making simultaneous versions of the same story, one in English for the domestic market, and another for export to the Spanish-language market. *Sombras de gloria* used the sets and technicians of the original *Blaze O' Glory* (1929, George J. Crone, Renaud Hoffman), during the day, with Spanish-speaking actors repeating the scenes at night. Logically, the English version set the mark, but it sometimes occurred that variations introduced by the nocturnal group worked better, so the English-language cast had to reshoot the scene. *Sombras de gloria* achieved a significant success wherever it was shown, making José Bohr, the film's protagonist, a very popular figure.

The majority of these films have been lost forever, the California Theatre long demolished for a parking lot, but the footprints left by those glorious premieres remain alive in press clippings. At the premiere of *Sombras de gloria*, film critic Lucio Villegas commented that José Bohr seemed to be singing when he spoke, and when he sang, he seemed to be reciting. After polling the public in attendance, R.M. Saavedra wrote that it was improper to showcase *Un fotógrafo distraído* (1930, Xavier Cugat) in first-class theatres because, simply put, the acting was indecent. Although he wanted to provide constructive criticism, Gabriel Navarro wrote with sadness after watching *La rosa de fuego* (1930, W. L. Griffith):

> And the public, our good public, saw it without the least sign of protest, without losing composure, not in one single instant, with that almost oriental fatalism of our race, ... Why is the film called *La rosa de fuego*? Where is the story supposed to take place? In what time period? The exterior scenes are out-of-synch, and on the sets, the slightest noise resonated like a cannon. Renée Torres forgets one of her lines and starts all over from her previous paragraph, as if it was a theatrical rehearsal.

Simultaneously filming two versions was a method that would have been forgotten, if it had not been for the mythical, bilingual, *Dracula* (1931, Tod Browning). Because Hispanics acted during the night shift, one might ask whether the moonlight could have produced the extraordinary effect of the film? In reality, simultaneous versions were seldom filmed. The method of repeating takes, using the same setup, but in different languages, started after the first bilingual comedies by Hal Roach. When only a small number of actors were substituted, problems were minimal, but with bigger casts, these productions became unwieldy.

Reviewing Hal Roach's multilingual comedies provides unsuspected surprises. Stan Laurel and Oliver Hardy, the most famous comic duo in the history of cinema, lived happily and quietly in Hal Roach's small studio, dedicating themselves to the noble profession of punches, falls, chases, pie fights and flirts. In contrast to other comedians of the silent era, the coming of sound worked in their favor and their popularity was on the rise. As they told it, one day in fall 1929, Hal Roach announced they would have to make their shorts in English, French, German, Italian and Spanish. Roach thought that a few hours of language tutoring and a supervisor on set would be enough. Roach appointed Robert O'Connor as their coach. The son of an Irish father and a Spanish mother, born and raised in Mexico, he had spent five years working on the studio's comedies. A few days later, Stan and Ollie started shooting *Night Owls*, or *Ladrones*. The studio hit upon a formula to avoid destroying sets and props by eliminating dialogue in action scenes, allowing them to reproduce the scene in the lab as many times as necessary. The dialogue in the different languages was written on blackboards and panels, outside of the camera's field of view, allowing the comedians to read words with greater accuracy, even though they had not the slightest idea of what they were saying. But Laurel and Hardy were brilliant and knew how to transform that ignorance into a comic ingredient that could not be surpassed nor substituted. Years later, once dubbing was normalized, it would be very difficult to find voices that could imitate them.

At the Hal Roach Studios, Laurel and Hardy and Charley Chase continued producing Spanish-language versions, lasting between 15 and 70 minutes. The majority of actors were of Mexican origin, under the direction of James Parrot, Chase's brother, or the efficient James W. Horne, one of the fathers of film serials. *Ladrones* (1930, James Parrott), the first comedy in the series, produced by Hal Roach in Spanish, was never an exact copy of the original, but rather included additional footage of the actors inventing variations on gags, along with other new and funny jokes that prolonged the film, doubling its original length. The same held true for other Laurel and Hardy shorts in Spanish. *La vida nocturna*, the Spanish-language version of *Blotto* (1930, James Parrott), was extended to forty minutes. With a script by Leo McCarey, and photographed by George Stevens, it was Laurel and Hardy's most recent commercial success, in which the duo wreck a night club, while a furious Linda Loredo chases them with bullets. In *Tiembla y titubea* (1930, James Parrott), Laurel and Hardy—*Los Sangrigordos*, as they are known in Puerto Rico—are street musicians, determined to play "In The Good Old Summertime" over and over, half buried in snow in the middle of winter, a gag that becomes surrealistic when they repeat the show in a residence for the deaf, and are thrown out for being obnoxious. *Radiomanía* (1930, James Parrott) is continuous slapstick mayhem from the moment Hardy decides to install a radio antenna on his roof with the help of Laurel. Little by little, Spanish-speaking actors Enrique Acosta, Linda Loredo, Luis Llaneza and Alfonso Pedroza became familiar to audiences.

Charley Chase was a first-class comedian, funny and original, and also a skillful director. Despite his premature death, he left behind an extensive *oeuvre*, spanning twenty-five years of uninterrupted activity, fifteen of these at Hal Roach Studios. Awkward, skinny and with a little mustache, looking like a second-rate playboy, his character was always involved with problems of love. He became very popular in some Spanish-speaking countries, and not quite in others. Along with Laurel and Hardy, Chase made eight Spanish-language films. Charley Chase takes advantage of an invitation to the golf club of Linda Loredo's father in *El jugador de golf* (1930, Edgar Kennedy). In *Locuras de amor* (1930, James W. Horne), Charley Chase's second short in Spanish, Carlos mistakes an escaped lunatic for his girlfriend's father; in *¡Huye, faldas!* (1930, James W. Horne), he shows an extreme case of shyness towards women.

Roach comedian Harry Langdon was a guinea pig in the hands of a wise lunatic in *La estación de gasolina* (1930, Warren Doane). Langdon wasn't lucky in the Spanish-speaking market, nor in his own country; his kind of comedy, based on pantomime, was not successful, and in spite of his great friendship with Hal Roach, his contract was not renewed. The gap was filled by a new series, *The Little Rascals*, from an idea by George Stevens; it was a reboot of the *Our Gang* series, whose actors had left their childhood years ago. Regarding *La Pandilla*, the Spanish version of *The Little Rascals*, it seems Roach had problems and preferred to use dubbing. The kid actors fumbled their way through other Spanish-language shorts, under the supervision of Laura Peralta, in *Los pequeños papás* (1930, Robert F. McGowan) and *Los fantasmas* (1930, James W. Horne).

Away from his studio for a couple of weeks, Hal Roach went on vacation to neighboring M-G-M, not exactly to rest but to direct a very demanding adventure: *Men of the North* (1931, Hal Roach), multiplied by five languages. The epic story of miners in the Canadian gold mines, involving avalanches and mounted police chases, was not a complicated affair for an expert like Roach. The problems started with casting: Gilbert Roland would play in the English and Spanish versions, *Monsieur Le Fox* (1930), Barbara Leonard in all except the Spanish one, Lillian Savin in all, minus the English version, Arnold Korff in the French and German films, also called *Monsieur Le Fox* (1930), George Davis in the English, French and Spanish, Frank Lackteen in the English and Spanish versions. Simultaneous production was so complex that during the filming the actors and the director didn't know what they had completed nor what they had left to do. *Luigi La Volpe* (1931) for the Italians, and the other versions featured the jolly fake bandit accused of stealing gold, played by four faces: André Luguet, John Reinhardt, Franco Corsaro and Gilbert Roland. Roland, whose real name was Luis Alonso, made use of the language he learned as a child, south of the Rio Grande, reading from a script written by the actor/writer Roberto E. Guzmán. After the complicated shoot, the five versions were edited and the films were released with considerable delay. The experience gathered from making these simultaneous versions called for a radical change in the production: the original version had to be filmed and edited, before producing the foreign versions. This way, the original version could serve as a guide in making other versions—even more, if the film was released first and its appeal tested—streamlining the technical process and bringing down the costs.

Another pioneer was Xavier Cugat, the Rumba King, who became well-known for his appearances in M-G-M musicals during the 1940s, and also for live performances with his orchestra. What many don't know is that he produced at least two Spanish-language original films in 1929. Born in Spain in 1900, he moved to Havana with his family at age three. In 1928, he performed with his own orchestra at the Cocoanut Grove in Hollywood's Ambassador Hotel. For a musician to be involved in sound cinema was a must, and without realizing it, Cugat found himself immersed in a ruinous affair that he would have liked to forget, namely a two-reel short, *Un fotógrafo distraído* (1930, Xavier Cugat), starring Romualdo Tirado. It was an appetizer for the program's main dish, a sort of Hispanic-themed musical triptych, reminiscent of government-produced tourism brochures, called *Charros, gauchos y manolas* (1930). As writer/director, Cugat resorted to an old stage cliché, in which a struggling painter attempts to win a contest by illustrating folkloric scenes from different countries. The result was a survey of Hispanic cultures that jumped from Mexican *charros* to the Argentine pampas of the *gauchos*, and ended up with Spanish bullfighters, *señoritas* and other outrageous clichés. The castanets sketch, played by José Peña ("Pepet"), María Alba and Martín Garralaga is the highlight of a film that would pass through Barcelona's theatres almost unnoticed.

Beginning in 1930, the production of Spanish-speaking films in Hollywood increased significantly. Projects started the previous year were released, including the first films with synchronized sound. Pathé released *Su íntimo secreto* (*Her Private Affair*) and *La gran parada* (*The Grand Parade*), both with Emile de Récat directing the dubbing, while Universal produced the failed *La dama de Shanghai* (*Shanghai Lady,* 1929, John S. Robertson), and RKO announced *Rio Rita* (1929, Luther Reed), with the dubbed voices of Ramón Pereda, Romualdo Tirado and Martín Garralaga.

The March 30, 1930 issue of *Mensajero Paramount*, a monthly magazine for internal circulation, published by the company's foreign department, presented an overview of Spanish-language material, produced by the studio and supplied to film exhibitors. It made note of musical shorts with popular songs, performed by José Bohr, Rodolfo Hoyos, Alfredo Cuadra or Tito Schipa, some being produced by other companies (for example, Sono-Art, initially distributed by Paramount). The journal documented growing studio interest in the Hispanic market. Mentioned were: *La serenata* and *Flor del mal*, both starring dancer Luana Alcañiz, *Mosaicos líricos* with Fortunio Bonanova and Dolores Cassinelli, and *Palabras y obras*. The last named, *¡Que viene papá!*, a comedy short directed by an American at New York's Paramount Studios, was a potpourri set in Spain with music by Rondalla Usandizaga, starring Peruvian Alberto de Lima and Mexican Margarita Duval; Hispanic brotherhood at its best.

Sono-Art, a small company, kept expanding, first by associating with World Wide and later with James Cruze's independent production outfit. It produced a vehicle to showcase José Bohr and his songs: *Así es la vida* (1930, George J. Crone). It tells the story of a tramp who becomes the chauffeur of a grand lady, and falls in love with her daughter, but their social differences make the relationship impossible, until it's discovered that the young man is in reality a detective, hired to protect the family's jewels, thus making the happy ending possible. The same plot would be repeated multiple times in later Spanish-language films, but not by Sono-Art, because this was their last Spanish-language production. By 1931, the company was renamed Sono Art–World Wide Pictures, Ltd., finally merging with Fox Film Corporation.

Another intrepid actor, Benjamin Ingénito, better known as Paul Ellis, who sometimes appeared as Manuel Granado, probably thought the atmosphere of his native Argentina had not been represented authentically. He therefore wrote the screenplay *Alma de gaucho* (1930, Henry Otto), similar to *Así es la vida*, but without a jewel robbery: An elegant *gaucho* (Paul Ellis, of course) falls crazily in love with a rich and flirtatious girl (Mona Rico), while he looks for a golf ball she's lost; the girl makes fun of him behind his back, until she finds herself profoundly in love and makes matters right. Independently produced by Chris Phillis, *Alma de gaucho* does not appear to have premiered in Argentina. Paul Ellis did not repeat the experience, but continued working as an actor.

Under the management of Geoffrey Shurlock, a serious student of Spanish languages and literature, Paramount stepped away from the musical genre, and entered fully into the whodunit genre with *El cuerpo del delito* (1930, Cyril Gardner, A. Washington Pezet), based on a Philo Vance novel written by S.S. Van Dine. Paramount finished the English version, before making the sets available for the Hispanic team. Adapted by Spanish novelist Josep Carner Ribalta, the film relates a criminal investigation, involving a stock-broker. In light of the 1929 Wall Street Crash, Paramount hurried to premiere the film at Madrid's Callao Theatre in May 1930, to exploit the topic's tremendous relevancy. It featured a larger than average number of Spanish actors, including Antonio Moreno, a Madrid native who had been a silent cinema superstar, playing the role of the killer, and Ramón Pereda as Philo Vance. They headed an excellent Spanish cast: María Alba, Andrés de Segurola, Carlos Villarías, and María Calvo. Also cast were the Argentines Barry Norton and Vicente Padula. The program was complemented by *La Paloma* (1930), a Dave Fleischer cartoon with the well-known Spanish song by Yradier, interpreted by Juan Olivier and La Rondalla Usandizaga.

Universal, founded and presided over by German-Jewish magnate Carl Laemmle, needed a new image to counter charges of nepotism and elevate its prestige. Yet, against all business logic, it promoted Carl Laemmle Jr., his twenty-one-year-old son to head of production. A notable preference for everything related to the family's German origins shaped the production slate. With *All Quiet on The Western Front* (1930, Lewis Milestone), the young Laemmle hit the bull's eye. Paul Kohner, a former journalist, was put in charge of supervising foreign productions, including those produced in Spanish. With dubbing still on hold until further notice, Universal resumed production, announcing two shorts in Spanish: *Sólo un sueño* and *Caprichos de Hollywood,* starring Lupita Tovar and Andrés de Segurola. The publicity department released a revealing statement about the company's foray into foreign-language productions, announcing that filming had begun on twelve two-reel films with foreign casts, to be spoken in French, Italian, Spanish and Mexican [sic].

In the meantime, Metro-Goldwyn-Mayer announced its upcoming attraction, *Sevilla de mis amores*, the Spanish-language version of *Call of the Flesh* (1930, Charles Brabin), to star and be directed by Ramón Novarro, while Buster Keaton was secretly filming his first comedy directly in Spanish: *Estrellados* (1930, Salvador de Alberich, Edward Sedgwick), the Spanish-language version of *Free and Easy* (1930, Edward Sedgwick), an intriguing picture by a creative comedian of the silent era who had reinvented himself. In the film, Miss Rioseco (Raquel Torres), a small-town girl, wants to be a star. With an adaptation and dialogue supervised by Salvador de Alberich, Metro took advantage of the story premise to produce an almost documentary look at its studio, promoting—not without a flair for publicity—stars like William Haines and Lionel Barrymore, leaving no doubt that the picture was made in Hollywood.

American cinema owes its endurance to the work of a generation of tough, multi-faceted and intuitive pioneers, whose passion for adventure pushed them to experiment with risky ideas in a matter-of-fact way. James Cruze, a theatre actor, became a prestigious filmmaker by directing Wallace Reid and "Fatty" Arbuckle in many shorts, and *The Covered Wagon* (1923). He tried his fortune as independent producer with the coming of sound. He green-lighted the Spanish-language version of his production *The Big*

Fox Film Corp. Spanish-language department, ca. 1932. Front row, from left: Gregorio Martínez Sierra, John Stone, Catalina Bárcena, Sol M. Wurtzel, Mrs. Lou Moore, and Miguel de Zárraga. Middle row, from left: Sam Wurtzel, José López Rubio, Raúl Roulien, Lillian Wurtzel, José Mojica, Hilda (Mrs. John) Stone, Gene Forde, Duncan Cramer, and Royer. Third row, from left: Louis King, Luis Saslavsky, Mrs. Sol Wurtzel, Sam Kaylin, Max Golden, John Reinhardt, unidentified man, and Louis Moore. Courtesy of Academy of Motion Picture Arts and Sciences.

Fight (1930, Walter Lang), written by Andrés de Segurola. While Walter Lang directed the original, Ralph Ince, one of the actors and an expert filmmaker, took notes to direct the Hispanic cast. Despite his contract with Sono-Art, Cruze signed a distribution agreement with Paramount to ensure proper distribution. The film premiered as *La fuerza del querer* (1930), a curious title—the power of love—to sell a drama about the underworld, with gangsters, boxing fights, and an attempted bribe. María Alba, the Uruguayan boxer Carlos Barbé as "El Tigre," Tito Davison, in his first important role, and Andrés de Segurola, headed the cast of this modest but dignified production, filmed at Educational Studios.

Without evaluating the performances in *El cuerpo del delito*—Paramount's first important foray in Spanish—the executives of the company, presided by Adolph Zukor and Jesse Lasky, approved the utilization of a newly built studio complex for foreign versions in Joinville, in the outskirts of Paris. The creation of a production center for films spoken in different languages had been the idea of Robert T. Kane, a well-established Paramount executive based in Paris, who had the full support of the company. During pre-production of the comedy *Un trou dans le mur* (1930, René Barberis), produced by Kane and distributed by Paramount, Kane was promoted to general director of Joinville Studios. Soon after, Pedro Muñoz Seca wrote an adaptation of this French-language film with the action transferred to Madrid, and other important character changes. Benito Perojo, the most international of Spanish filmmakers at the time, was assigned to direct *Un hombre de suerte* (1930). In spite of the play's French origin, it was the only Paramount film—and one of the few Spanish-language versions overall—where the characters, situation and dialogue appear to be genuinely Spanish.

The opening of the Joinville Studios coincided with the filming in Hollywood of *Amor audaz*, the Spanish-language version of *Slightly Scarlet* (Louis J. Gasnier, Edwin H. Knopf) that made use of props and costumes planned for other English-language productions. After a successful test in New York, Rosita Moreno—a Mexican dancer and daughter of Spanish actors—and Adolphe Menjou were cast in this film about jewel thieves, which paradoxically takes place between Paris and Nice. The French (*L'énigmatique Monsieur Parkes*) and Spanish versions of *Slightly Scarlet* were filmed during the last two weeks of April 1930, two months after the premiere of the original version. Paramount thereafter gave strict orders to produce foreign-language versions in Joinville after English versions had been completed.

Very quickly, the studio also produced *Paramount on Parade* (1930, 11 directors), a musical revue with stars and contract players, followed by a dozen foreign versions. Taking their cue from M-G-M's *The Hollywood Revue of 1929* (1929, Charles Reisner, Christy Cabanne) and Warner Bros.' *The Show of Shows* (1930, John G. Adolfi), Paramount staged some twenty musical numbers and comedy sketches, some in black and white, others in Technicolor. In contrast to other studio revues, *Paramount on Parade* was adapted for foreign-language audiences by keeping some original sequences, while substituting others with numbers filmed exclusively for each country, with different actors and presenters. Director Charles de Rochefort, based in Joinville, was in charge of the versions destined for European markets, with the exception of the Spanish-speaking countries. That version was supervised by Geoffrey Shurlock, with Edward D. Venturini, as Eduardo

Venturini, directing additional segments, because *Galas de la Paramount*—as the Spanish version was called—included alternative scenes, depending on whether the film was released in Mexico, Cuba, Argentina or Spain.

Rosita Moreno, Ramón Pereda and Barry Norton were the presenters in the Spanish-language versions, which comprised Maurice Chevalier's numbers, including Lubitsch's sketch, *Origin of the Apache*. Juan Pulido sang flamenco for Spain, but *Carmen*'s "Habanera" for Cuba and Venezuela, and Mexican popular songs for that country. Spanish actor Ernesto Vilches was featured as the magician Wu Li Chang, the womanizer Don Juan, and other characters in his repertoire. Encarnación López, "La Argentinita," sang and danced to maestro Luis Yance's guitar; Rosita Moreno danced *fado* and appeared with Nino Martini with Venetian gondolas in the background. But there is no record of a performance by Jeanette MacDonald, nor the fragment prepared by George Bancroft and Hal Skelly, speaking Spanish.

In the shadow of *Galas de la Paramount*, Universal produced a musical revue with less dazzling stars but more coherence. Filmed in two-color Technicolor, John Murray Anderson's *King of Jazz* (1930) was one of the best musicals of the time. Spanish-speaking hosts were inserted by Kurt Neumann, a director from Germany, who filmed additional takes with Lupita Tovar and Martín Garralaga as masters of ceremony. There are also a couple of musical segments with Jeanette Loff singing "La Paloma", and John Boles in a sketch set in Mexico. Paul Whiteman and his orchestra provided the music. These variety films, clearly intended to publicize studio stars, reached screens at a rate of one per year per studio. Produced with a short shelf life of twelve months maximum, they were soon replaced with next year's new faces and latest fashionable songs. The formula was repeated until Busby Berkeley refurbished the genre, contributing ideas that would shape Hollywood's film musical style.

The Wall Street crisis drastically cut attempts by the ambitious William Fox to take near-monopolistic control of the film industry. As he did not have enough financial liquidity to pay for the loans with which he had acquired an important packet of M-G-M stock, Fox relinquished his movie empire in 1930. However, at the end of 1929, Fox hired the Mexican tenor José Mojica from the Chicago Opera. His English-language debut film was *One Mad Kiss* (1930, Marcel Silver, James Tinling), featuring Mojica as a Hispanic Robin Hood who defended farmers from the abuses of the town boss. Directed by Marcel Silver, with Antonio Moreno as an advisor, the final result did not convince the studios, leaving the launching of the film in limbo. Months later, the chief of the foreign film department, John Stone, assigned filmmaker James Tinling to re-shoot *One Mad Kiss*, and to film additional material for a version specifically edited for the Spanish-speaking market. When *El precio de un beso* (1930, James Tinling, Marcel Silver) was ready to be premiered, no one suspected that José Mojica would become so popular, nor that Fox would continue to produce films in Spanish regularly over the next five years.

Between May 1930 and April 1931, the studios produced more Spanish-language films than at any other time until 1939. Foreign-language versions were produced both in Hollywood and its European subsidiaries, but at a diminishing rate, due to their lack of profitability. Dubbing, the technique of replacing actors' voices with anonymous voiceovers, ultimately prevailed. Aesthetically dreadful but commercially viable, dubbing eliminated the need to re-film in different languages. But for the moment, the Hollywood machine was operational, producing at maximum capacity.

Warner Bros. had been a key player in sound's arrival. A pioneer of synchronized sound, the studio had signed a contract in 1926 with Western Electric to produce shorts with music and sound effects. These Vitaphone shorts employed a sound-on-disc technology, that was successfully used in the part-talkie, *The Jazz Singer* (1927, Alan Crosland), which revolutionized the film business.

Berlin-born Henry Blanke had arrived in Hollywood with Ernst Lubitsch in 1922, and in 1930 was head of foreign-language productions at Warners. Blanke favored making German and French versions of English-language originals, importing directors from those countries, including the renowned William Dieterle. Only four Spanish-language versions were shot in 1930, all directed by William McGann, a veteran cameraman but novice director. Warners' lack of good international networks lead to poor distribution; these versions were also not on a par with their German and French counterparts. According to several sources, Baltasar Fernández Cué wrote half a dozen short stories for Warner Bros., but it's not known whether they were filmed. Fernández Cué also wrote *El hombre malo* (1930, Roberto E. Guzmán, William McGann), the adventures of Mexican bandit Pancho López, without any Mexican actors in lead roles. The "bad man" is played by Antonio Moreno; he robs a bank and kills the town boss, who threatens his protégé, so the latter can live happily ever after on his ranch, now debt- and villain-free. The French version, *Lopez, le bandit* (1930, John Daumery), was filmed on the same sets with Geymond Vital as Pancho López.

These first Spanish-language versions gave rise to a heated controversy in the Spanish-speaking world about the cacophony of accents in these pictures, called "la guerra de los acentos," the war of accents. It should be noted that Americans were always careful about the linguistic details that could affect the credibility of film stories. Just as the great Garbo played a foreigner in her first sound film role, *Anna Christie* (1930, Clarence Brown), in order to justify her Swedish-accented English, Vivien Leigh had to provide a Southern accent in *Gone with the Wind* (1939, Victor Fleming). These demands concerned the English-speaking world. No one was a stickler for accents or dialects in a film about the French Revolution as long as it was understandable in English.

The Spanish situation was more complex. For a Spanish-speaker, it would be ridiculous to hear Pancho Villa speak with an Andalusian accent, or listen to a flamenco singer attempting tango inflections. But American producers couldn't distinguish regional Spanish variations, leading to linguistic disasters when the films played in Spanish-language markets. Spanish-language newspapers, specialized magazines and critics were relentless in pointing out the inconsistencies in accents and idioms. There was always a paragraph on the topic, defending particular points of view, further complicating the matter for Hollywood executives. The solution was to promote a neutral "Hispano" Spanish for stories taking place in non-specific locales. Mexicans, however, threatened to boycott productions coming from Hollywood, if they weren't spoken in Mexican-inflected Spanish. Some companies tried to please everyone by providing a wide variety of accents, but it was an unsuccessful strategy, since the actors themselves could not understand each other. To make matters worse, the Spanish Latin American Film Bureau Inc., an entity sponsored by Sono-Art, fought tooth and nail for the idea of a Spanish Esperanto, an international unified "Hispano" Spanish. The idea was laughed off as ridiculous. The war of the accents ended up exhausting the contenders without solving the issue. What was liked in some locations was not accepted elsewhere. Ironically, only films garnering unanimous rejection achieved a desired consensus between Spanish-speaking peoples. There were, however, a few films that were highly praised.

Many times, those English-speakers hired to direct the Spanish versions had no understanding of the language and were unable to comprehend nuances. As a direct consequence of the controversy over accents, the role of the dialogue director became increasingly more important, since he was present during the shoot to supervise the actors' diction and make sure the dialogue made sense. Although their role was considered of secondary importance, dialogue supervisors were in many instances the real directors, with a decisive capacity to approve takes, control the development of sequences, and contribute to the directing process.

Ernesto Vilches, the "Man of a Thousand Faces," a Hispanic Lon Chaney, arrived in Hollywood, hired by Paramount, after a Latin America theatrical tour. He was renowned for the speed with which he could step into a role, e.g., when he played a female role in the Spanish Golden Age classic *Juan Tenorio*, substituting for the actress. A larger than life figure, Vilches believed he had been anointed by God to be a successful actor! During his stay in Hollywood, he was the community's highest-paid Spanish-speaking actor; he also spelled trouble for colleagues and studio executives, blaming everybody for his failures and being unable to accept criticism. *Cascarrabias* (1930, Cyril Gardner), a film that was a good fit for the actor, was considered very funny by the reviewers of the *New York Times* and *Variety*, but Vilches was so upset with Paramount, because he could not shape the performance the way he wanted, that he ended up leaving the studio.

The filming of *Cascarrabias* intensified the linguistic battle between Spaniards and Mexicans. When an actor pronounced phrases in a Mexican-inflected Spanish, Vilches responded by cussing in Castilian, thus making the take unusable. Carner Ribalta, in charge of Spanish-language adaptations for Paramount, saw his efforts continually sabotaged by the actor. Spanish is a language allowing for little abstraction, and translations from English prolonged the scenes, affecting the rhythm and flow of the action, ruining much of the English original's qualities. Since Spanish-language productions in the Joinville Studios supplied the Hispanic market with plenty of films, executives took it easy, successfully slowing down filming in Hollywood.

By mid-1930, Paramount, Warner Bros., Fox, Metro-Goldwyn-Mayer, Universal and Hal Roach Studios began shooting Hispanic productions more or less regularly. When the enthusiasm started to wane, a little before 1931's radical cut, Columbia arrived, contributing several films. During those months of euphoric full employment, much was accomplished, even great achievements. Some were taken by surprise, like Luis Buñuel, who was paid a salary for doing nothing.

The story of the first months of Spanish-language filmmaking in the U.S. is the prologue to activity that would continue without much variation during the 1930s. The leading actors of the story changed with the passage of time, but this did not prevent similar patterns and problems from repeating themselves. Writers such as Edgar Neville, Miguel de Zárraga, Antonio de Lara, Paul Pérez, Eduardo Ugarte, José López Rubio and René Borgia worked in the Hollywood studios, adapting Spanish pictures that had already been filmed in English. Others had the same task in Joinville and London, e.g., María Luz Morales, Camilo Aldao, Ceferino Palencia, Luis Fernández Ardavín, Honorio Maura, José Luis Salado, Claudio de la Torre and Carlos de Batlle. Hundreds of Spanish-speaking actors paraded in front of the cameras, but almost always under the direction of filmmakers who in the majority of cases did not understand the dialogue. By fall 1931, the press considered Spanish-language film production in Hollywood and Europe to have ceased.

However, six months later, Fox called José Lopez Rubio again; for three more seasons he worked on film versions of theatrical plays by Gregorio Martínez Sierra, and other Spanish or South American authors. He also adapted musical comedies for José Mojica, as well as dialogue from various operettas, highlighting his fine sense of humor and sharp irony. Moreover, López Rubio overcame a paucity of resources with great imagination by taking advantage of sets designed for higher-budget films. In the end, he almost managed to completely control the production of *Rosa de Francia* (1935, Gordon Wiles), a scathing review of sacred cows in Spain's history. Likewise at Fox, Miguel de Zárraga had the opportunity to work on *La cruz y la espada* (1934, Frank Strayer), with a script especially written for the film. Enrique Jardiel Poncela also hit the bull's eye with the adaptation of his play, *Angelina o el honor de un brigadier* (1935, Louis King, Miguel de Zárraga), which became a memorable picture.

In all, Fox was the most prolific among Hollywood studios in terms of Spanish-language production—a total of thirty-nine features and six shorts. Of those, twenty-one were versions and twenty-four were originals.

Except for a few sporadic releases by Universal, Columbia and Warner Bros., the only Spanish-language productions produced regularly after 1931 were the films of Mojica at Fox and Carlos Gardel at Paramount. The latter, however, did not know how to exploit the popularity of the Argentine singer, until his death in an airplane accident in 1935 elevated him to myth.

An exotic group of independent producers attempted in vain to continue the work abandoned by the big studios: Fanchon Royer in 1933, Moe Sackin in 1934-35, and George A. Hirliman in 1935-36, but their films ended up being screened in second-run theatres, as fillers on the bottom of double bills, or they were simply not distributed at all. It is usually said that with the outbreak of the Spanish Civil War in July 1936, the American film industry definitively ended the production of films destined for Spanish-speaking markets. However, that was not the case.

Spanish-language film production was about to resume. In mid-1937, the actress and ballet dancer Rosita Moreno brought to the screen a project she had written, and her husband Mel Shauer produced. In spite of a close relationship with Paramount, Shauer organized his own independent company, Victoria Films Inc. He moved into the Grand National studios, which were about to make a hit by signing James Cagney. Director John Reinhardt, a Spanish-language film expert, shared screenwriting duties and directed *Tengo fe en tí*, a melodrama about a dance professor (Frank Puglia) who is disappointed when a promising student whom he secretly loves decides to abandon ballet; years later, he falls in love with her daughter. Fascinated by Hollywood, the young woman decides to become a dancer, falling in love with a film director (José Crespo), who becomes the victim of the jealous old man. Rosita Moreno, playing dual roles as she had in Gardel's *El día que me quieras* (1935, John Reinhardt), shows her skills as a dancer, and also as a songwriter with Shauer and her father, actor Paco Moreno. Unfortunately, Rosita became ill in mid-production, halting it. Shauer and Victoria Films abandoned the project, taking a $60,000 loss. RKO apparently bought the rushes in 1939, shooting more footage with doubles in a failed rescue attempt. It was released in 1940, unnoticed. Alternating between radio shows and Lux soap advertisements, Rosita Moreno had been featured in Argentine productions, such as *El canillita y la dama* (1938, César Amadori), and also in Hollywood pictures through the 1940s, but her career was in decline.

In contrast, José Crespo's was taking off. After starring in *Tengo fe en ti,* he joined the biggest Hispanic Hollywood production, *La vida bohemia* (1938, Josef Berne). A Spanish-American multimillionaire, film aficionado, son of the illustrious Gregorio del Amo, Jaime del Amo founded Cantabria Films to produce films in Hollywood, destined for the Spanish-language film market. He hired Rosita Díaz, who had recently arrived from war-torn Spain, to star in his first venture. Shortly before that, her agent announced that she had been shot by a Francoist firing squad. He denied the story shortly thereafter, but the publicity trick succeeded because Rosita's arrival did not go unnoticed. Initially, Jaime del Amo announced the filming of *El camino de Hollywood*, starring Antonio Moreno and Andrés de Segurola, but later switched to *La vida bohemia*, a version of the French classic *Scènes de la vie de bohème*, filmed as *La Bohème* in 1926 by King Vidor. It was adapted by José López Rubio, in what was to be his last Hollywood job. With a cast of important actors that included Miguel Ligero, who came from Cuba to participate, Gilbert Roland, Rosita Díaz and José Crespo, *La vida bohemia* was shot by the Hungarian-born cinematographer John Alton, who had also worked in France and Argentina.

Hollywood was ready for a new wave of projects for the Spanish-language market. Having premiered a semi-Hispanic film, produced by Dorothy Davenport and released in Spain in 1946 as *El nuevo Zorro* (*Rose of the Rio Grande*, 1938, William Nigh), Monogram Pictures sponsored a project proposed by Venezuelan musician Eduardo Le Baron, in close collaboration with writer/director Jaime Salvador. The team released *Castillos en el aire* in May 1938. It did not have the impact Monogram expected. Their follow-up film, *La última melodía*, also directed by Jaime Salvador, was released by Películas Cubanas, as a Cuban film. *Castillos en el aire* was a romantic comedy about a humble typist, who wins a contest to visit Hollywood. During the trip, she falls in love with an office worker, who impersonates a Russian prince to impress the typist, who in turn poses as an aristocrat. Comedian José ("Pepet") Peña gave one of his best performances as the sidekick.

In New York, distributors Rafael Ramos Cobián and Julio Bruno, owners of a chain of theatres in Puerto Rico and the Dominican Republic, formed Cobián Productions Inc., to make films with the popular Mexican singer Tito Guízar, who was classically trained in opera, and had performed in Chicago and New York. He had later become a popular music singer, making a hit in Mexico with *Allá en el Rancho Grande* (1936, Fernando de Fuentes). Fox and Paramount saw in Guízar the ideal substitute for José Mojica, who had retired, and Carlos Gardel, who had died in June 1935. Cobián had Tito Guízar under an exclusive contract, and after negotiating with both companies, Cobián signed a deal with Paramount for distribution. He bought an original script by José Antonio Miranda and hired Miguel de Zárraga, Sr. and Jr., to work on the adaptation and dialogue. Blanca de Castejón, who was also Puerto Rican, was cast as the protagonist of *Mis dos amores* (1938, Nick Grinde). The film is considered the best of the five Spanish-language features Tito Guízar made in Hollywood.

A story by playwright and screenwriter Jean Bart had circulated for some time under its original English name. It served as the basis for *Verbena trágica*, the second and last production of del Amo's Cantabria Films. With Miguel de Zárraga writing dialogue, the film veered from the classicism of *La vida bohemia* towards the melodrama conventions of Mexico and Argentina's cinema. Set in New York's Spanish Harlem, it told the story of a boxer, jailed for a minor offense, who comes home and hears rumors of his wife's infidelity. Tragedy unfolds once he confirms the rumors are true. Mexican actor Fernando Soler was cast with Luana Alcañiz and Juan Torena, who had just starred in Ramón Peón's *Sucedió en La Habana* (1938), one Cuba's first sound features. *Verbena trágica* was directed by Charles Lamont, a prolific director of comedy shorts, but unfamiliar with the style the film required. *Verbena trágica* ended up at the bottom of a double feature, precipitating Jaime del Amo's end as a film producer.

The multi-faceted William Rowland, an actor-producer-director of musical comedies and vaudeville, was also interested in the Hispanic market, and proposed a production plan to RKO. In New York's Astoria Studios, William Rowland produced *Di que me quieres* (1939, Robert R. Snody), his first film for RKO. Behind Robert Snody, a lackluster director on the roster of Astoria Studios, were William Rowland with his musical expertise, and a plot that was a pretext to justify a series of cabaret numbers, performed by Argentine singer Azucena Maizani, the key publicity draw of the picture. After being relegated to supporting roles, George Lewis played the lead in *Di que me quieres*, a composer of popular songs who immigrates to New York and opens a luxurious cabaret, with help from an admirer. Paul Ellis is the antagonist, bent on ruining him, while Martín Garralaga plays a kindhearted gambler. Francisco J. Ariza, a critic for the Spanish-language magazine *Cine-Mundial*, wrote the dialogue. After the film was finished, Rowland directed the other titles stipulated by RKO in Mexico. Although the budgets were smaller, the results were better, resulting in the award-winning pictures *Perfidia* (1939) and *Odio* (1940, alternate title *Harvest of Hate*).

In November 1938, Tito Guízar and Ramos Cobián parted ways. Cobián produced one of the most lavish Spanish-language films made in Hollywood, *Los hijos mandan* (1939), directed by Gabriel Soria and starring Blanca Castejón, Fernando Soler and Arturo de Córdova. Excessively melodramatic, *Los hijos mandan* was based on the play by Spanish playwright José Lopéz Pinillos, *El Caudal de los hijos*, a staple of the María Guerrero Company, touring the Hispanic world. Blanca de Castejón adapted it to the screen, and also played the lead. The misfortunes of a peasant from rural Valencia who sacrifices the love of her life to take care of the Duke of Montesino's son, failed to attract the audience who had flocked to the stage play. This was Ramos Cobián's last film production venture.

Tito Guízar stayed at Paramount, working on a tight schedule of one film per month, which required half a dozen new songs for each. He starred in four films, directed by Peruvian-born director Richard Harlan. After visiting Spain in 1933, where he directed *La viuda quería emociones* (1935, co-directed by Francisco Elías) and *Odio* (Hate, 1935), Harlan returned to Hollywood, where he had directed three of Fox's Spanish-language films.

El trovador de la radio (1938), a melodrama about a popular tenor who loses his voice through the machinations of his doctor and his secretary, marked Harlan's return to directing. *Papá soltero* (1939) tells the misadventures of a young heir traveling to Los Angeles to take charge of his family fortune; forced to care for an orphan girl once in Los Angeles, he can find neither his fortune nor his protégé's family. *El otro soy yo* (1939) is about two brothers, both played by Guízar, one of whom has to impersonate the other secretly. Filmed entirely on location, *Cuando canta la ley* (1939, alternate title, *El rancho del pinar*) sought to capitalize on Guízar's *charro* image. All four films were produced by Darío Faralla, an Italian businessman, featuring almost identical casts, including Paul Ellis, Pilar Arcos, Martín Garralaga, Robina Duarte, Amanda Varela and Tana. Richard Harlan and Tito Guízar teamed up again in Argentina, where they filmed *De México llegó el amor* (1940). The director met old acquaintances in Buenos Aires, such as John Reinhardt, Carlos Borcosque, Tito Davison, Manuel Romero and Adelqui Millar. Harlan directed three more films in Buenos Aires before returning to Hollywood as an assistant director.

Independent producer Jack Skirball decided to make a Spanish-language version of *Miracle on Main Street* (1939, Steve Sekely), *El milagro de la Calle Mayor* (1939, Steve Sekely), filming simultaneously in English and Spanish, with different casts. It was an intriguing decision, in light of past experiences regarding the profitability of this strategy. Set in a Mexican neighborhood in Los Angeles, the film's miracle consists of a woman, attempting to escape the police, finding a newborn baby hidden in a Nativity set. José Crespo, who had been living in Mexico, was cast in the Spanish version, written by Enrique Uthoff; he reputedly learned his lines during the trip from the airport to the studio. Steve Sekely, who had recently emigrated from Hungary, landed his first assignment, directing both films simultaneously. The niece of Xavier Cugat, Margo (born Maria Margarita Estella Castilla), the female lead of *Crime Without Passion* (1934, Ben Hecht, Charles MacArthur), was cast as the young woman in both versions, which were made by Arcadia Pictures for Grand National, a company on the verge of bankruptcy; the Spanish version was released by 20th Century-Fox in December 1940, several months before *Miracle on Main Street*, a Columbia Pictures release.

Producer Maurice Cohen signed a distribution deal with United Artists for the release of his Atalaya Films production, *La Inmaculada* (1939, dir. Louis J. Gasnier), another Mexican-style melodrama set in Mexico but filmed in Hollywood. A rich womanizer (Fortunio Bonanova) falls in love with a small-town girl (Andrea Palma), and after living together as husband and wife, he ends up paralytic and ruined, while she falls in love with another man. She remains loyal to him, but he commits suicide; tragically, the other man has married someone else. Based on a novel by Catalina D'Erzell, the story foreshadowed the fate of Louis J. Gasnier himself, the director of the popular serial *The Perils of Pauline* (1913), who had been unemployed since 1942, and was found dead at age eighty-one on a Hollywood Boulevard bench in 1963, with no family and penniless.

With the onset of World War II, the era of the Spanish-language productions came to an end. What remained of the Spanish-speaking film community dispersed, with most of them returning to their countries of origin. The Spaniards, whether for political motives, or to avoid harsh conditions in post-war Spain, stayed in Spanish-speaking America, for more or less longer periods. José Crespo, Rosita Díaz, Luana Alcañiz, Ramón Pereda, Carlos Villarías, among others, moved to Mexico. Gregorio Martínez Sierra and Ernesto Vilches went to Argentina. Fortunio Bonanova, Luis Alberni, Antonio Moreno and Martín Garralaga stayed in Hollywood, acting for many years in mostly Hispanic supporting roles, but in English. Conchita Montenegro spent some time in Brazil, where she made a film with her then-husband, Raúl Roulien, and later joined the Spanish film industry; she also made films in Italy, where, like Juan de Landa, she was very popular, since M-G-M had distributed Spanish-language film versions, instead of the originals, dubbed into Italian. José López Rubio returned to Spain via Mexico at the end of World War II, and was elected to the Royal Spanish Academy of Language.

EPILOGUE

Since the publication of *Cita en Hollywood* in 1990, several of the films discussed in the book have been recovered and subtitled in English. They include titles from Hal Roach and Fox; Universal's *Drácula;* the four films of Carlos Gardel's Exito Productions; and titles from independent producers, such as Ramón Novarro, Jaime del Amo and Eduardo Le Baron.

Translated by Fabricio Espasande and adapted by Robert G. Dickson, María Elena de las Carreras and Jan-Christopher Horak.

Carlos Borcosque: Learning the Ropes in Hollywood (1927-1938)

María Elena de las Carreras

In September 1927, Carlos Francisco Borcosque, born in Valparaíso, Chile, in 1894, arrived in Los Angeles from Santiago, with his wife Lucía Lizana and their baby daughter María Elena. He had secured an appointment as Vice Consul from the Chilean government to study the U.S. film industry's handling of the coming of sound. He was also interested in exploring how to bring a more accurate portrait of Latin America, its people and cultures to the Hollywood screen. He must have thought, too, about finding an opportunity to work in "la Meca del Cine," the Mecca of Cinema, in the phrase of the times.

The *Los Angeles Times* noted that:

> believing that film stories based on historical and fictional South American data would prove popular in the Latin American countries, Carlos Francisco Borcosque, Santiago, Chile, has arrived in Los Angeles and proposes spending a year in close contact with the film industry. At the present time, according to Señor Borcosque, there are a number of films produced dealing with the topics that are uppermost in his mind, but, in a large number of instances, they lack conformity to detail that makes them appear ridiculous to the initiated in South America. The visitor presents credentials from William Miller Collier, Ambassador of the United States to Chile. He has obtained an apartment at 3218 Sunset Boulevard.[1]

A few days later, *Film Daily* wrote in the same vein: "Carlos Francisco Borcosque of Santiago, Chile, is here to promote the making of pictures based on historical and fictional South American data that will prove popular in Latin American countries."[2] Borcosque was well prepared professionally to observe up close the workings of Hollywood in the midst of massive technological changes, and to eventually participate in studio projects. He had lived in Buenos Aires from 1906 to 1921, where he had been a journalist, writing for various magazines, such as *El Hogar*, *Caras y Caretas* and *Plus Ultra*. An aviation enthusiast and licensed pilot, he had also been involved with the pioneers of Argentine aviation.

---

1 *Los Angeles Times*, September 27, 1927.
2 *Film Daily*, October 10, 1927.

He had moved back to Santiago in 1922, where thanks to his father's financial help he had set up Estudios Cinematográficos Borcosque, a production company and lab. He had directed several silent movies: *Hombres de esta tierra* (1923); *Traición* (1923); the cartoon *Vida y milagros de Don Fausto* (1924), adapted from the comic strip of the newspaper *El Mercurio*; *Martín Rivas* (1925); *Diablo fuerte* (1925); and the short *El huérfano* (1926). He had also directed actualities and human-interest stories.

Friendly, gregarious and a great conversationalist who spoke fluent English and French, Borcosque seems to have had no problems in quickly becoming an established journalist in Los Angeles, as *Variety* wrote in July 11, 1928:

> Carlos F. Borcosque, who is a member of the Hollywood Association of Foreign Correspondents, has been granted studio privileges by the credentials committee of the WAMPAS [Western Association of Motion Picture Advertisers]. Borcosque has resigned his position as Vice Consul of Chile and is devoting his entire time to journalism. He represents three papers in Chile, one in Madrid, and also a Spanish magazine for Latin American consumption in Hollywood.

The Borcosques' second daughter, Lucía, was born in Los Angeles, as announced by the Spanish-language film magazine *Cine-Mundial*, in April 1928. The Chilean's first studio assignment was as technical advisor on the M-G-M film, *The Bridge of San Luis Rey* (1929, Charles Brabin), the production of Thornton Wilder's Pulitzer-winning novel. A year later, he worked in the same capacity on *In Gay Madrid* (1930, Robert Z. Leonard), an adaptation of the beloved novel of student life, *La casa de la Troya*, written by Alejandro Pérez Lugín, starring Ramón Novarro.[3]

> As a reporter of the Hollywood scene, Borcosque professed strong opinions about the possibilities open to Spanish-language talent. He told the *Hollywood Filmograph*: Amongst many players now in Hollywood suitable for making talkie pictures in Spanish, are Dolores del Río, Ramón Novarro, Antonio Moreno, Gilbert Roland, Lupe Vélez, and Barry Norton—all of whom speak a pure Spanish. Other players who speak Spanish with very little accent are: Raquel Torres, Don Alvarado, Lili Damita, Mona Rico, George Lewis, Donald Reed, and Lia Torá. (...) It seems that there is real opportunity here for some enterprising producer.[4]

Among the topics he covered in particular in 1930 and 1931 were the unique features of the Spanish-language film, making it transatlantic and multicultural. Often cited is his article, "La nueva Babel," in *Cinelandia* (September 1930), about the difficulties of making Hispanic pictures—a controversy addressed by other authors in the present volume.

3 "*The Bridge of San Luis Rey* is Garden Film", *The Davenport Democrat and Leader* (Davenport, Iowa), April 28, 1929; "Novarro comes to the Rialto Sunday in *Gay Madrid*," *Hamilton Evening Journal* (Hamilton, Ohio), 18 October 1930.

4 *Hollywood Filmograph*, June 8, 1929.

Borcosque observed that the root of the problem was a lack of a "common Spanish, shared by Spain and the many nations of Hispanic America. (...) A producer had noted that the studios had to come to some kind of agreement as to how Spanish should be spoken."

In 1930, Borcosque was involved in another journalistic endeavor, sensing that there was a readership in Chile and neighboring Argentina for a film magazine that would combine reports on the film business with Hollywood gossip. With friends in Chile, he founded *Ecran*, a monthly magazine whose first issue featured a drawing of Greta Garbo on the cover. Borcosque co-edited *Ecran* until 1934, and continued thereafter filing articles about the industry and the stars.[5]

BORCOSQUE'S FOURTEEN HOLLYWOOD CREDITS [6]

Borcosque's connections and experience made him an asset when the Hollywood studios began to produce films in Spanish. The Chilean was the proverbial case of being in the right place at the right time. Based in Los Angeles, Borcosque was first in line when M-G-M opened its Spanish Department in 1930. Headed by Frank Davis, it produced thirteen pictures until it was closed in early 1931.[7] Borcosque worked on seven of these titles, in increasingly more important capacities. He collaborated with the top Spanish talent hired by the studio, such as directors Miguel de Zárraga, Salvador de Alberich; writers Eduardo Ugarte, Edgar Neville and José López Rubio; actors José Crespo, Ernesto Vilches, Conchita Montenegro, María Alba, Juan de Landa, María Fernanda Ladrón de Guevara, and Rafael Rivelles.

The seven film credits are: assistant director of *Olimpia* (1930, Chester M. Franklin), the Spanish version of *His Glorious Night* (1929, Lionel Barrymore); dialogue director of *Wu Li Chang* (1930), Spanish version of *Mr. Wu* (1927, William Nigh); *Sevilla de mis amores* (1930, Ramon Novarro); assistant director and dialogue director of the Spanish version of *Call of the Flesh* (1930, Charles Brabin); dialogue director of *Su última noche* (1931, Chester M. Franklin), Spanish version of *The Gay Deceiver* (1927, John M. Stahl); dialogue director, *En cada puerto un amor* (1931, Marcel Silver), the Spanish version of *Way for a Sailor* (1930, Sam Wood); and directing credits for *La mujer X* (1931), the Spanish version of *Madame X* (1929, Lionel Barrymore) and *Cheri-Bibi* (1931), Spanish version of *The Phantom of Paris* (1931, John S. Robertson).

Borcosque's directing efforts in *La mujer X* were praised in favorable reviews, such as the one in the *Los Angeles Times* (April 13, 1931) by Salvador Baguez: "Signalized by the exquisite and sensitive emotional acting of Señora María Ladrón de Guevara and by the

5 http://www.memoriachilena.cl/602/w3-article-588.html#imagenes.

6 Borcosque has a total of fourteen credits in films made in Los Angeles between 1930 and 1946: Seven for M-G-M (Spanish-language versions); three for Fanchon Royer Pictures (one in Spanish, two in English); one for Universal Pictures; one for Metropolitan Pictures. He worked as a technical advisor for two M-G-M films, but no IMDb or AFI catalog credits could be found.

7 Juan B. Heinink and Robert G. Dickson list the following thirteen films produced by M-G-M: *Estrellados* (1930, Edward Sedgwick), *Monsieur Le Fox* (1930, Hal Roach), *Olimpia* (1930, Chester M. Franklin), *De frente, marchen!* (1930, Edward Sedgwick), *Wu Li Chang* (1930, Nick Grinde), *El Presidio* (1930, Ward Wing), *Su última noche* (1930, Chester M. Franklin), *En cada puerto un amor* (1931, Marcel Silver), *La fruta amarga* (1931, Arthur Gregor), *La mujer X* (1931, Carlos F. Borcosque), *Cheri-Bibi* (1931, Carlos F. Borcosque), *El proceso de Mary Dugan* (1931, Marcel De Sano). See Juan B. Heinink and Robert G. Dickson, *Cita en Hollywood. Antología de las películas norteamericanas habladas en español* (Bilbao, España: Mensajero, 1990).

splendid direction of Carlos F. Borcosque, *La Mujer X*, Spanish film, opened Friday evening with a gala premiere at the California Theater." *La mujer X* was singled out in the same review as an example of a first-rate Spanish language film with box-office appeal:

> Now that the problem of making Spanish talkies seems to again confront producers, and major companies have almost completely abandoned foreign-picture production, along comes a picture whose box-office qualities should attract once again the attention of executives. It is the only Spanish-speaking picture made so far, which possesses sufficient Latin-American and Spanish flavor to make it appealing to audiences of those countries.

The studio's marketing effort was evident in the Spanish-language advertisement for the two films Borcosque directed. The campaign also included *Su última noche*, where he had been the dialogue director; and *La fruta amarga* (1931, Arthur Gregor), with José López Rubio as the Spanish dialogue director, the Spanish version of *Min and Bill* (1930, George W. Hill). Ironically, this last hurrah for the studio's Spanish versions was the flag-waving one-page ad that appeared in May 1931 in *Cine-Mundial* (p.352). M-G-M, the studio of Leo the Lion, presented itself as "acclaimed by Hispanic nations—"los pueblos de abolengo hispano"—as the most important producer of films spoken entirely in Spanish." There is a drawing of the trademark king of the jungle, thanking the Spanish-speaking audiences and the film businessmen who have written him about how much they like this type of film.[8]

It is interesting to notice that, working as an assistant director and dialogue director in *Sevilla de mis amores*, Borcosque developed a warm professional relationship with Ramón Novarro, the M-G-M star who directed the film. On several occasions, the Hollywood press would report on projects Borcosque, Novarro and his brother Carlos Novarro were developing. During an interview with the author, his son Carlos Borcosque Jr. mentioned that his father represented Ramón Novarro, an assertion that can be understood in the light of some never-realized projects.

During those two years at M-G-M, Borcosque also developed personal and professional relationships with other prominent members of the Hispanic colony, such as Antonio Moreno, the Spanish-born star of the silent era, and the Mexican Dolores del Río, whose exotic persona was made even more so by her Spanish accent with the coming of sound. Among his group of friends were the Chileans Tito Davison and José Bohr, who parlayed their Hollywood experience into long careers in Mexico and Argentina. Together with Borcosque, Bohr and Davison warrant a closer look, as emblematic Hollywood-trained film professionals who brought knowledge and experience to the Latin American film industries in which they later worked.

As a Spanish-language director, Borcosque was often associated in the press with the group of Spaniards who had arrived under contract with the studios in Hollywood in 1930. The *New York Times* mentions Borcosque, albeit as a Spaniard, in an article about the in-

---

8 *Cine-Mundial*, May 1931, 352.

creased presence of foreign talent in Los Angeles: "Arrival in America of European screen players to appear in foreign language versions of dialogue pictures may be said to have begun in earnest. (...) Miguel de Zárraga, founder of the Spanish theatre in New York and author of 'Morals of the Immoral' and other Spanish plays; (...) and Carlos Borcosque, Spanish writer and producer of the Spanish film *Martin Rivas*, are others on the creative staff of the studio's foreign plays department." [9]

In an article published in *Cine-Mundial* (March 1931), "Los directores hispanos," Carlos Borcosque is mentioned as the first Hispanic director hired by M-G-M to make a Spanish version. Also listed are Richard Harlan, from Peru; Jorge Delano, from Chile; the Spaniards Benito Perojo, Luis Buñuel, Edgar Neville and Salvador Alberich; and Ramón Novarro, already an established Hollywood figure. The article wonders what all of them could do if they are put in charge of original Spanish versions. "Are they better than the Americans? Frankly speaking, no. Until now, ours have followed what the Americans have done, which is after all, relatively easy. What we have not seen is what they will be able to do when they direct original versions, that is, without imitating what the U.S. directors are doing?"[10]

It was a prescient question then, and today, when studios, production companies and audiences are given a chance to see what Alejandro González Iñárritu, Guillermo del Toro or Alfonso Cuarón are doing with films where they have creative control as writers, directors and producers. The May 1931 issue of *Cine-Mundial* notes again that "the only Hispanic directors in the Hollywood studios are: Richard Harlan, from Peru; Carlos Borcosque, Chile; Benito Perojo, Spain; and Jorge Delano, Chile". [11] The cases of Richard Harlan, the son of an American diplomat in Peru, and Jorge Delano, a distant relative of Franklin Roosevelt, also merit further study.

After M-G-M closed its Spanish Department in May 1931, Borcosque tried to put together some independent projects. They were reported in the press, such as the article in the October 1931 issue of *Cine-Mundial*: "Carlos Borcosque announces he is going to produce Hispanic films on his own, and is requesting works that are a fit for our audiences."[12] *Variety* informed readers about a Spanish-language film to be produced by Ramón Novarro: "[the actor] is reported financially interested in a company being formed to make Spanish pictures. Carlos Borcosque, former Metro foreign-version director, is promoting the venture with Carlos Novarro, brother of the actor, also interested. Production will be made in Hollywood."[13]

In a matter of months, however, Borcosque found himself in the directing chair again, this time for independent producer Fanchon Royer.[14] An Iowa native in Hollywood since the early 1920s, Royer was not the only producer of small-budget films to step into the vacuum left by the trickling down of these productions by the big studios. But her com-

9 *New York Times*, June 29, 1930.
10 *Cine-Mundial*, March 1931, 197-198.
11 *Cine-Mundial*, May 1931, 403.
12 *Cine-Mundial*, May 1931, 821.
13 *Variety*, December 22, 1931, 11.
14 For a profile of Fanchon Royer, see Michael R. Pitts, *Poverty Row Studios, 1929-1940. An Illustrated History of 53 Independent Film Companies, with a Filmography for Each* (Jefferson, N.C.: McFarland & Company, 1997).

Carlos Borcosque (center) with Spanish actress, María Fernanda Ladrón de Guevara, and cast on set of *La mujer X*, 1931). Courtesy of Academy of Motion Picture Arts & Sciences.

pany made a significant contribution in this area. B.R. Crisler, of the *New York Times*, noted in 1938 that "around 1930 she cornered all the Spaniards in Hollywood just before a big Spanish vogue broke out and cleaned up on them like Rockefeller did in oil."[15] Previously, the same publication had observed that in the production field Rose Judell Reisman and Fanchon Royer "have been active in the independent market, making films at rather unpretentious cost."[16] It should be noted, however, that Fanchon Royer took advantage of this pool of Spanish-language actors and directors *concurrently* with the big studios, but not before them.

Borcosque was the associate director of Royer's English-language production *Trapped in Tia Juana* (1932), and the writer of the dialogue in Spanish.[17] He made two other films for this Poverty Row studio: *Dos noches* (1933), the Spanish version of *Revenge at Monte Carlo* (1933, B. Reeves Eason), for which he was the director, and *Fighting Lady* (1935), Borcosque's only English-language directing effort in Hollywood.

Dos noches brought together two Spaniards with whom Borcosque was very familiar: José Crespo (*Olimpia, Wu Li Chang, En cada puerto un amor,* and *La mujer X*) and Conchita Montenegro (*Sevilla de mis amores, Su última noche,* and *En cada puerto un amor*). The Spanish version was originally titled *La República no peligra,* and began filming in January 1933, three days after the studio had finished *Revenge at Monte Carlo,* as the *Hollywood Filmograph* noted on February 4, 1933.

In April 1933, *Cine-Mundial* published a profile of producer Fanchon Royer, signed by Don Q. It discussed the bilingual production plans of her company. She had joined forces with Mayfair Pictures, and made seven films in seven months. Don Q. noted that Royer's intention was to alternate English and Spanish-language films. The writer deplored the withdrawal of the big studios from the Spanish-speaking market. Their strategy was to use subtitles or to dub the English dialogue, except for Fox, whom Don Q. praised for providing original Spanish versions with José Mojica, Catalina Bárcena and Raúl Roulien. Fanchon Royer stepped into this context, her Spanish version of *Revenge at Monte Carlo* tapping into a remarkable pool of talented people in front of and behind the camera. The author singled out Borcosque, praising the streamlined budget of *Dos noches,* and the efficiency in making a film for a fifth of the studio cost. Don Q. was optimistic that the success of these films in the Hispanic market would encourage the studios to become their distributors.

In the following issue, May 1933, *Cine-Mundial* reviewed *Dos noches,* noting that it was filmed in five days, "a great triumph and a great lesson." The reviewer added that "the greatest praise should go to Carlos Borcosque who has directed the film with extraordinary skill."[18] The *New York Times* also reviewed *Dos noches,* when it opened at the Teatro Variedades on July 28, 1933: "The outstanding feature (...) is the absence of any

15 "People in the films," *New York Times*, May 15, 1938.
16 "Activities on the West Coast," *New York Times*, June 17, 1934.
17 This western, set in 1930, tells the story of twins separated by an Indian kidnapper. Both were played by Duncan Renaldo, as a soldier from West Point serving on the Mexican border, and a *bandido*, who gains the love of the young Anglo woman about to marry the other twin. It's an intriguing twist on the trope of the Hispanic woman falling for the British or Anglo hero.
18 *Cine-Mundial*, May 1933.

real hero or heroine in what the program labels 'an emotional love picture.'" [19] A short article in the *Los Angeles Times* informed readers a month later about the production schedule of Fanchon Royer Productions, at its Glendale Boulevard studios: "José Crespo will star in his second English film, *Diamonds Preferred*, by Leonard Levinson, with Carlos Borcosque probably directing, and a Spanish version planned. *For Value Received*, played by an all-star cast, will be another offering. Edward Earle in charge of dialogue in both cases. *Outside the World* is still another picture, a flying opus in the Andes, for which exteriors are already being made."[20]

Cine-Mundial reported in September 1933 about the plans of the outfit, noting again that it was run by the only female producer in Hollywood. She had begun a series of fifteen films in English, with six planned in Spanish, in an alternate shooting schedule. The huge success of *Dos noches*, released throughout Latin America, had prompted her to increase her Spanish-language slate, featuring José Crespo, who would be working in English and Spanish.[21] The column also announced that Carlos Borcosque was writing the screenplay of a very interesting film about aviation, taking place in Chile and over the Andes. "The assistant director will be Tito Davison [Borcosque's compatriot and friend], who is forsaking an acting career for the megaphone."[22]

I have found no records that those six Spanish-language projects ever went into production. José Crespo made a handful of Spanish-language films for Fox and independent companies in Hollywood after 1933, before moving to Mexico in 1940. None of these titles were for Fanchon Royer. The producer did not make films in Spanish again. Borcosque's only directing credit in English, *Fighting Lady*, for Fanchon Royer Pictures, Inc., is neither an aviation film, nor in Spanish.

In the midst of this flurry of activity, the Borcosques welcomed, on October 9, 1933, a third child, as announced by *Variety*: "Mr. and Mrs. Carlos Borcosque, [a] daughter, in Santa Monica. Father is a film director and Hollywood correspondent for a number of South American papers." [23]

In the same month, Fanchon Royer announced the start of her next film, *For Value Received*, based on a play by Robert Ober, and directed by Carlos Borcosque as his first assignment in English, starring Peggy Shannon.[24] The film was completed by early November, and was now titled *Fighting Lady*.[25] This was to be Borcosque's third and last film for Fanchon Royer Productions. It was released in 1935, with a copyright date of February 1, 1934. I have not been able to account for this gap between production and release dates.

---

19 *New York Times*, July 29, 1933.

20 *Los Angeles Times*, August 26, 1933. None of these films were apparently completed, except eventually the Andes project, which apparently moved to Universal. Both Leonard Levinson and Edward Earle were associated with Fanchon Royer Pictures at this time, but none of their credits match any of these project titles.

21 The only Fanchon Royer production José Crespo is credited with in this period is *Hollywood Mystery* (1934, B. Reeves Eason), which was apparently only shot in English.

22 *Cine-Mundial*, September 1933, 539.

23 *Variety*, October 17, 1933, 59.

24 *Variety*, October 24, 1933, 2.

25 *Film Daily*, November 8, 1933, 2.

I have found no records so far of Borcosque's filmmaking activity throughout 1934. When I asked his son, he simply said that maybe he had not worked that year. I am still researching this period, so far without success.

In 1935, Borcosque was back in business, having completed an assignment for Universal Pictures, as the assistant director of *Alas sobre el Chaco* (1935, Christy Cabanne), with Spanish dialogue written by René Borgia. The original English version, *Storm over the Andes,* was also directed by Christy Cabanne. *Cine-Mundial* reported that in *Alas sobre el Chaco*, Carlos Borcosque directed Lupita Tovar, recently married to Universal executive Paul Kohner. Her co-stars were José Crespo and Antonio Moreno. The magazine complimented the Spanish version for paying careful attention to details of setting and character.[26]

TANGEE'S HOLLYWOOD REPORTER: RADIO SHOW IN SPANISH - 1936-1938

The year 1935, however, marked the beginning of Borcosque's last stage in Los Angeles. He continued writing about the Hollywood scene for *Ecran* in Chile and *Sintonía* in Argentina—the magazines for which he was officially listed as their Hollywood correspondent. However, a new possibility opened up: the creation of a radio show that would tap into materials he produced for the print press. The first notice I found came from *Film Daily,* in a short piece describing the trip of Jaime Yankelevitch, the owner of several radio stations in Argentina:

> (...) Yankelevitch has signed Lupe Vélez to make several personal appearances in Buenos Aires and to also do radio work. She will begin her engagement August 15. Conchita Montenegro and Raúl Roulien have been signed as a team, while Rosita Moreno has also been put under contract. They will go to South America early in 1936. Yankelevitch, who has been in Hollywood, is now en route to London to buy television equipment. He has signed Carlos Borcosque to give weekly talks in Spanish on Hollywood sidelights. These will be electrical transcriptions and will be airmailed to Buenos Aires.[27]

By September 1935, *Broadcasting* informed readers that "Carlos F. Borcosque, 2419 Charitan St., Los Angeles, foreign language director for film companies, in August completed arrangements to send to Radio Belgrano, Buenos Aires, a weekly transcribed program of Hollywood film gossip. Talks will be airmailed to be on the air six weeks after recording."[28] However, it was only in 1936 that the radio show was on the air. It was sponsored by the cosmetics company Tangee. I have found no further mention of Jaime Yankelevitch, a topic that warrants further study. The earliest description so far about the Tangee show comes from *Broadcasting* magazine, in its issue of July 15, 1936: "Carlos Borcosque, Hollywood Spanish-language reporter, will soon add broadcasting to his

26 *Cine-Mundial,* September 1935, 605.
27 *Film Daily,* June 25, 1935, 8.
28 *Broadcasting,* September 1, 1935, 32.

activities. For many years Borcosque has acted as Hollywood reporter for leading newspapers of Latin America. He recently signed a contract with Broadcasting Abroad, Ltd., a New York transcription company, which states that a sponsor has been secured for the first series of 26 programs which will be shortly released throughout Latin America."[29]

A subsequent issue, dated September 1, 1936, gave technical and legal information about the show, under the title "Tangee Placing Discs Over 21 Latin Stations." It noted that the show premiered on August 12, and consisted of a 26-week series of 15-minute transcriptions on twenty-one Latin American stations:

> The program is modeled after Tangee's domestic success with Jimmy Fidler, *Hollywood Reporter*, and is titled *Tangee's Hollywood Reporter*. It features Carlos Borcosque, popular Spanish-speaking Buenos Aires movie columnist whose writings are syndicated in more than 60 Latin American newspapers. The Tangee export account is handled by the Export Adv. Agency, New York City. Stations were selected by Broadcasting Abroad Ltd., New York City. Stations securing the placements are in Argentina, Chile, Cuba, Colombia, Dominican Republic, Ecuador, Mexico, Panama, Peru, Puerto Rico, and Venezuela. Other Latin American stations will be added to the list shortly. Newspaper tie-ins publicizing the program are being used extensively.[30]

Cine-Mundial promptly informed its readers, too, about the radio show. In September 1936, it noted it would be heard between 8 and 10 pm, according to each country. It would include news from the studios and actors, and a segment by a fashion designer describing the gowns wore by the stars. *Cine-Mundial* recommended the show as something new and very entertaining.[31]

The radio show was recorded weekly in Hollywood in electrical transcriptions, which were then mailed to radio stations throughout Latin America, airing a week later, still keeping its freshness.[32] I have listened to several of these shows and they all follow the same format: the Tangee announcer introduces Borcosque; he offers tidbits about actors and actresses, interspersed with the announcer publicizing Tangee cosmetics; and an unnamed female fashion reporter describes gowns worn by the stars. One of the segments is an "open letter" Borcosque reads about a specific topic, whether it is advice to Lily Pons to sing opera staples to delight her audience, or a request to actor Warner Baxter to stop playing "bandidos." The fifteen minutes end full circle, with the announcer promoting the virtues of the lipstick, and inviting listeners to the next show.

Unfortunately, none of these shows are dated. The collection is listed as "circa 1937." It is not difficult, however, to date the shows individually, most of them at least by month, doing minimal detective work: for example, the funeral of M-G-M's top producer Irving

---

29 *Broadcasting*, July 15, 1936, 44.
30 Broadcasting, September 1, 1936, 26.
31 *Cine-Mundial*, September 1936, 541.
32 One of Borcosque's daughters donated a collection of 38 discs of *Tangee's Hollywood Reporter* to the Margaret Herrick Library, Academy of Motion Picture Arts and Sciences. Their Music and Recorded Sound Collection holds 50 programs that are available to researchers on compact discs, made from these original electric transcriptions.

Thalberg in September 1936, or the shooting of Cukor's *Camille* with Greta Garbo, a few months before its release in January 1937. Dating a show where Borcosque described how the belongings of John Gilbert were auctioned may take some digging; but figuring out when Borcosque spotted Charlie Chaplin and Paulette Goddard at the Brown Derby in Hollywood is anyone's guess. *Cine-Mundial* promoted these radio shows in various columns over several months, and also featured paid advertisement, with Borcosque's name as a brand, as can be noted by the articles in the January and May 1937 issues.[33]

1936 is the year of Borcosque's last Hollywood credit: he was the supervisor and dialogue director for *El carnaval del diablo*, the Spanish version of *The Devil on Horseback* (1936, Crane Wilbur), for Metropolitan Pictures, distributed by M-G-M. Except for reports about a project here and there, it seems that by 1936, the filmmaking side of Borcosque's Hollywood activity was drying up. *Cine-Mundial* informed readers about a project entitled "Fuera del mundo," starring Dolores del Río, who is often featured in Borcosque's articles and radio show. It would have been the first Spanish-language film of the star in Hollywood before she returned to Mexico in 1943.

However, as a foreign correspondent and radio show commentator, Borcosque had a full plate. There are many references to his journalistic activities and social life in 1937 and until mid-1938, the year he left Los Angeles for Buenos Aires. The *Motion Picture Daily* reported in November 1936 that the newly formed Foreign Press Society had elected Joseph Polonsky as its president and Borcosque as vice-president.[34] This organization of international journalists, in which Borcosque was actively involved, was the precursor of the Hollywood Foreign Press Association, founded in 1943 as the Hollywood Foreign Correspondents Association.

BORCOSQUE AND THE HOLLYWOOD STYLE TRANSPLANTED TO ARGENTINA (1938-1966)

In 1938, the Mentasti family, owners of Argentina Sono Film, one of the most important film studios in Buenos Aires, founded in 1933, offered Borcosque an excellent contract. "Luis César Amadori [ASF's top director, and a high school friend of Borcosque's] came to Hollywood to get him," Carlos Borcosque, Jr., told me, adding that his father also had offers from Mexico, but chose to return to Buenos Aires, a familiar base. Argentina Sono Film was importing to Buenos Aires a seasoned professional with the skills and experience necessary to bring the studio to the next level by implementing the techniques and practices of the American studio system, and working with speed and efficiency. The Borcosque family arrived in Buenos Aires on May 31, 1938, on board the *Northern Prince*. They settled in San Isidro, a suburb north of Buenos Aires, where they immediately became active in the social side of the film business. Borcosque's second daughter, Lucía, married actor Carlos Cores, who was cast by her father in ... *Y mañana serán hombres* (1939).

33 *Cine-Mundial*, January 1937, 57, and May 1937, 252.
34 *Motion Picture Daily*, November 26, 1936.

Borcosque brought with him an American assistant, his friend from California, Jack Hall. Hall had worked in the *Tangee's Hollywood Reporter* show, capitalizing on his work as an announcer and news commentator with FSFO, a radio station in San Francisco. *Variety* listed both of them as foreign correspondents for *Sintonía* magazine in Buenos Aires.[35] According to Borcosque's son, Jack Hall was his father's right-hand in Buenos Aires, until the American went to the Argentine province of Mendoza to set up Film Andes, the only production company in an Argentine province with its own studio. Hall eventually returned to the U.S. with his wife and children. Jack Hall co-wrote with Borcosque ... *Y mañana serán hombres* (1939), *Nosotros, los muchachos* (1940), *Una vez en la vida* (1942), *Un nuevo amanecer* (1942), *La juventud manda* (1943), and *Valle Negro* (1943).

Borcosque's lucrative contract with Argentina Sono stipulated that he would direct six films in two years. During the seventeen-day boat trip from Los Angeles to Buenos Aires, he was busy writing the script for his first picture, *Alas de mi patria*, about the history of aviation since 1908, a precursor of the semi-documentary genre.[36] Jack Hall is listed in the opening credits as "colaboración en la dirección."

Borcosque's contributions to the Argentine film industry were important and long-lasting: he streamlined the filmmaking process, beginning with the use of daily call sheets to organize shooting schedules. He favored fluid camera movements for continuity, used tracking shots extensively, and tightened editing. The director made twenty-nine films in Argentina between 1939 and 1966; his last picture was released a year after his death. One can watch them today and discern an American style in the visuals and storytelling. Perhaps, we can apply to Borcosque what the Spanish writer Max Aub said of his friend Buñuel: "He learned to *make* cinema in Hollywood. To put it together and take it apart. I'm speaking, naturally, of the profession. His cinema is very 'Spanish' at heart, but (...) his way of arranging things (...) is North American." [37] Or, as phrased affectionately by his son, at the end of our interview: "Papá siempre hablaba de Hollywood."

35 *Variety*, October 7, 1936.

36 Claudio España, *Argentina Sono Film. Medio siglo de cine* (Buenos Aires, Editorial Abril, 1984), 60, 173; Personal communications with Carlos Borcosque Jr., January 13, 2017 and April 3, 2017.

37 Román Gubern and Paul Hammond, *Luis Buñuel: The Red Years, 1929-1939* (Madison, WI: University of Wisconsin Press, 2012), 70.

Ramón Peón: A Cuban in the Babel of Languages

Luciano Castillo

In the midst of the tense environment provoked by the arrival of sound, the Cuban filmmaker Ramón Peón (1897-1971) arrived in a Hollywood filled with "stars" who had been done in by their tinny voices, and directors fired for their inability to adapt to the sudden changes brought about by the new technology. After the Havana premiere of his twelfth feature film, *La Virgen de la Caridad* (1930), a film that has become a classic of the silent Latin American cinema, Peón left for Los Angeles, due to political and economic instability on the Caribbean island. With the help of Peruvian-born filmmaker Richard Harlan, he was hired as an assistant director by Fox Film Corporation, which in 1935 would become 20th Century-Fox. Peón had made several short films for Harlan, who established a film company in Havana in 1926 with the somewhat pretentious name, Pan American Pictures Corporation. The idea was to produce two-reel shorts with Cuban actors and technicians through a New York company, Canfield & Clarke, intended for the voracious North American market. It was an unsuccessful attempt to make quality short films in imitation of those of the Golden Age of silent comedy.

Peón's name appears on the studio's payroll with five other Cubans, which included more than a hundred people from Spanish-speaking countries. They were part of the Hollywood studios' efforts to capture Spanish-speaking film markets with productions made directly in Spanish. "Hollywood must make films spoken in five languages—English, Spanish, French, German and Italian—if it wants to keep for its films its great foreign markets," declared Mr. N.D. Golden, head of the Film Division at the U.S. Department of Commerce.[1] In October 1929, it was announced that preparations were being made by the main studios to film "Spanish talkies."

A month earlier, another recently arrived Cuban, René Cardona (1905-1988), who was just twenty-three at the time, took a risk when he financed and starred in the very first Spanish-language feature film, *Sombras habaneras* (1929, Cliff Wheeler). It was filmed in Hollywood at the Tec-Art Studios, one of the low-budget rental studios that survived in the shadow of the majors. Founded by Cardona on a shoestring budget, the company's original name was Cuban International Film Productions, but was later changed to

1 Quoted in John King, "Cinema," in Leslie Bethell, ed., *A Cultural History of Latin America: Literature, Music and the Visual Arts* (Cambridge: Cambridge University Press, 1998), 463.

Hispania Talking Film. The plot involved a man who resorts to forgery in order to cover his gambling debts, while being threatened by a greedy gambler who pines for his sister. Wheeler's poor direction, the weak, soap-opera plot, and lousy performances rapidly ended Cardona's dreams.

Released in some countries as *Bajo el cielo de La Habana,* its failure allowed *Sombras de gloria* (1930), the first Hollywood film made under the multiple-language version system, to receive more publicity. Directed by Andrew L. Stone and Fernando C. Tamayo, *Sombras de gloria* is the Spanish-language version of *Blaze O' Glory* (1929, George Crone), filmed on the same sets as the English-language original. Much like Ramón Peón, Cardona would later go on to become a prolific director in Mexico during the later 1930s. He would return only once to Cuba, to film the co-production *Una gallega en La Habana* (1954, René Cardona).

The majority of Latin Americans and Spaniards who arrived in Los Angeles to work in Spanish-language productions were often poorly paid and their talents underutilized. They often went from one studio to another seeking work worthy of the prestige and experience that they had acquired in their native countries. There was practically no communication with the Anglo filmmakers they assisted, many of whom were totally unfamiliar with Spanish. Around sixty movies were filmed in Spanish in California facilities between the end of 1929 and mid-1931. Most came from Fox, which financed seventeen films, followed by Metro with thirteen titles, and Paramount, which produced seven Spanish-language films. The participants of this "American adventure" agreed that the language used was Spanish in name only.[2] In addition, a hodgepodge of Spanish and Mexican costumes was very common. The participation of Latin Americans during the production process however mitigated to a certain extent the grotesque depiction of foreigners in Hollywood films.

One strategy used by the Hal Roach studio to solve the problem of language was to have comedians under contract to deliver their lines in Spanish, utilizing their inability to do so as just another part of the fun. When Peón arrived in Hollywood, the comic duo Stan Laurel and Oliver Hardy were struggling to say their lines "in Spanish," while creating mayhem in *Ladrones* (1930, James Parrott), *Tiembla o titubea* (1930, James Parrott), *La vida nocturna* (1930, James Parrott) and *Noche de duendes* (1930, James Parrott); the kids in Our Gang were making mischief in *Los pequeños papás* (1930, Robert F. McGowan) and *Los cazadores de osos* (1930, Robert F. McGowan); Harry Langdon's face emphasized his astonishment and powerlessness in the face of the unintelligible lines which he had to repeat in *¡Pobre infeliz!* (1930) and *La estación de gasolina* (1930). Meanwhile, Charley Chase went through the same ordeal in *El jugador de golf* (1930, Edgar Kennedy) and *¡Huye, faldas!* (1930). Buster Keaton, the eternal and impassive "Great Stone Face," starred in *Estrellados* (1930, Edward Sedgwick) and *¡De frente, marchen!* (1930, Edward Sedgwick).

2 Álvaro Armero, *Una aventura americana: españoles en Hollywood* (Madrid: Compañía Literaria, 1995).

It is difficult to give an exact timeline of how long Ramón Peón stayed in Hollywood during this period when he learned everything about sound films, working on multiple-language versions as an assistant director and actor. He could not have chosen a better moment to join the crowd of Latin Americans in the Babel of languages. He received screen credit for two films that, due to their artistic merits and box-office grosses, stand out among the Spanish-language productions: *Del mismo barro* (*Common Clay,* 1930) and *La gran jornada* (*The Big Trail,* 1931), both directed by David Howard for Fox. But he also worked on others as assistant director. According to some biographies included in pressbooks for his films, Peón remained in Los Angeles for a year and a half. However, in some interviews he claimed that he stayed just over a year and in others that he stayed two, which seems truly impossible. I consider it more probable that his time on American soil did not even last twelve months. By November 2, 1931, Ramón Peón was at Nacional Productora Studios in Mexico.

Before arriving in Mexico, Peón went through an exhausting period. Perhaps the intensity with which he lived and the variety of activities he carried out led him to believe that this stage of his life was longer than it seemed. Richard Harlan got him a job as assistant director to David Howard (1896-1941), a former King Vidor assistant, on the crew of *El precio de un beso* (1930), a wildly successful vehicle for former opera singer José Mojica. Due to some problems with his work—his films likely went over-budget –Fox had punished Howard by relegating him to directing foreign versions. According to one of his actresses, Ana María Custodio (1903-1976), however, the commercial triumph of *Eran trece* (*Charlie Chan Carries On*, 1931) redeemed him. Between June and July 1930, Howard filmed *Del mismo barro* for Fox, a Spanish-language version of Cleves Kinkead's 1915 play *Common Clay*. On October 3, not even a month after the successful release of *Del mismo barro* in September, *El último de los Vargas* premiered at New York's San José Theatre. Filmed by Howard between July and August with Peón as his assistant, it was the Spanish-language version of *The Last of the Duanes* (1930, Alfred L. Werker), with dialogue written by the Spaniard Francisco Moré de la Torre, who adapted the screenplays of the first Fox Spanish productions.

Juan de Landa and Carlos Villarías, who played supporting roles in *El último de los Vargas*, also appeared in the short film *El valiente* (1930), a drama that Richard Harlan filmed in August. It was then extended to a feature thanks to additional takes shot in September. Infected with the prevailing production fever, Ramón Peón worked alongside Eli Dunn as an assistant director on this Spanish adaptation of the screenplay by Tom Barry and John Hunter Booth, based on the 1924 play by Holworthy Hall and Robert Middlemass. The original English-language version, *The Valiant* (1929), was directed by William K. Howard and starred Paul Muni in the role of the soldier who, at the end of World War I, returns to the States and kills a friend who once betrayed him. Using a false identity, he turns himself over to the police and is sentenced to death.

Metro-Goldwyn-Mayer hired Edgar Neville (1899-1967) to write and work as a dialogue director for the Spanish version *El presidio* (1930). This film offers a testament to the extreme lengths to which studios would go to reproduce in Spanish-language versions every detail of the American originals, produced with North American actors and directors. Neville describes how, in order to accurately remake George Hill's original *The Big House*, he forced actors, especially Juan de Landa, to copy all the gestures and movements of the actor who played Butch, Wallace Beery. For the sake of achieving this mimesis, a Moviola was installed on set so that before filming each scene, the actor could watch and study Beery's performance in order to copy it. It was not unusual for the directors of Spanish-language versions to have a Moviola within reach to recreate the shots and framings of the original.

Some elements varied, such as the names and nationalities of the cast and crew, or melodramatic components that spiced up the plot, but all the studios followed the same recipe. These films were not truly different language versions, but rather word-for-word translations of plots, which were often remade shot-for-shot. Still, it is difficult to make any critical assessment, as it is difficult to locate prints of these films, which have been scattered, lost, eroded by time, subject to indifference, or destroyed by nitrate decomposition.

THE BATTLE OF THE "Z"

At a time when bitter moments were not uncommon among those involved in the "canned theatre" (as Spanish-language versions were often referred to), a "war of the accents" broke out. Any American producer could identify and notice the differences between the English of natives of Oklahoma, Georgia or New York, but, due to their lack of knowledge of Spanish, they did not care about the origins of the speaker. For them, Castilian, Mexican and Cuban Spanish were all the same. Latin Americans proclaimed themselves the masters of the authentic Spanish-language, and attacked Spaniards, doing whatever they could to get their contracts cancelled. While there was a plan to arrive at a neutral Spanish, the Mexicans, defending their idioms during another scuffle in this linguistic battle, threatened to boycott any production made in Hollywood that did not use their accent. As a truce, the ridiculous idea of promoting a sort of Esperanto or unified international Spanish was considered. The declaration of the "battle of the 'Z'"—so called because of the dramatically different way in which Spaniards and Latin Americans pronounced this particular letter—was to become a dispute for the history books, without an apparent victory for any of the sides involved.

Ramón Peón was determined to be on the front lines of these skirmishes and looked for work with any film crew he could. For him, the important thing was that movies won the battle, and that they remained unbeaten after each battle, as sound technology progressively improved. Thanks to his chameleonic versatility, Peón went from drama to comedy when he worked as assistant director on Sidney Lanfield's *El barbero de Napoleón* (1930).[3] It was a remake of John Ford's comedy *Napoleon's Barber* (1928), starring Otto Matieson. The original plot by Arthur Caesar relates how a small-town barber's obsession with seeing Napoleon dead changes into fervent admiration when the emperor uses his professional services. Manuel Paris wrote the Spanish dialogue and starred as the protagonist. This modest movie is noteworthy for being the first talkie directed by Ford, who went on to film numerous classics like *Stagecoach* (1939) and *The Searchers* (1956).

3 The Fox film premiered at the California Theatre in Los Angeles in January 1931.

Ramón Peón directing *La Virgen de la Caridad* (1930).

Peón's frantic working rhythm, making him a ubiquitous presence at the studios during this period, earned him a job as David Howard's assistant for *A media noche*. This dramatic crime film, an adaptation of Ethel Clinton's *Evidence Only* by Francisco Moré de la Torre, features Lia Torá as the woman who is staying under a false name at the hotel where Juan Torena, wounded and running away from the police, bursts in. Peón also accepted the opportunity of assisting Howard in this film, which opened on December 1930, and also worked on *La gran jornada* between November and December. *The Big Trail* (1930), a large-scale Western, was directed by Raoul Walsh, who, throughout his career contributed numerous significant titles to the genre, and was also responsible with co-directors for the Italian (1930, *Il grande sentiero*) and German (1931, *Die grosse Fahrt*) versions, featuring John Wayne, Franco Corsaro and Theo Shall respectively. Hal G. Evarts' original screenplay, adapted by Paul Pérez and with Spanish dialogue by Francisco Moré de la Torre, tells the story of a young adventurer determined to avenge the death of the old man who raised him as a son. In order to do so, he leads a caravan of determined settlers who are on their way west to unexplored regions, as he believes that the murderers are traveling in it.

While working as Howard and Lanfield's assistant at Fox, Ramón Peón, eager to learn as much as possible and to delve into the secrets of sound films, signed an acting contract with Columbia Pictures. On December 1930, he managed to split his time between the filming of Fox's *La gran jornada* and as an actor in a Columbia picture, playing Runch in Phil Rosen's *El código penal*, a diluted Spanish-language version of Howard Hawks' jail melodrama *The Criminal Code* (1930), based on a Broadway flop by Martin Flavin. It tells the story of a young man sentenced to ten years for the murder of a dancer's "protector," who goes through numerous vicissitudes while waiting for his pardon. Hawks' film features Walter Huston, Phillips Holmes and Constance Cummings in the main roles. In this original version, one of Hawks' finest early films, Clark Marshall played Runch.

Lupita Tovar, the Mexican actress who starred in Hollywood movies like *La voluntad del muerto* (1930, George Melford) and *El tenorio del harem* (1931, Kurt Neumann), was chosen to star as Mina in the Spanish-language version of *Dracula*, which, actually, copied the original "shot by shot and line by line." Director George Melford (1877-1961), who launched Valentino's career with *The Sheik*, shot the movie between October and November 1930 at Universal studios. This Spanish *Dracula*, based on a play adaptation of Bram Stoker's novel, was filmed at night, using the same sets that were being used for Tod Browning's classic during the day. Carlos Villarías played the Transylvanian vampire, arousing more pity than fear; and Barry Norton, who worked with Peón in *El código penal*, played the victim's fiancé. However, Tovar's dresses were more suggestive than the ones used in the American version. Actually, some film historians believe that this version is, in many ways, superior to the one starring Bela Lugosi, especially in its more mysterious atmosphere.

Back again at Fox Films in January 1931, Peón accepted Richard Harlan's offer to play one of the characters in *Del infierno al cielo*. The rest of the cast included Juan Torena, María Alba, Ralph Navarro and Carlos Villarías. For the Spanish version, Paul Pérez adapted Edwin Burke's screenplay, based on *The Man Who Came Back* (1931). The American version had been directed by Raoul Walsh and featured Janet Gaynor, Charles Farrell, and Kenneth MacKenna. *Del infierno al cielo*, also distributed under the title *Camino del infierno*, opened at the San José theatre in New York, on February 27, 1931, then played the Los Angeles California Theatre in April 1931. Juan Torena—the lead actor, and a thespian who, thanks to his prestige and discipline, was among the top tier of imported actors—would later star in Ramón Peón's *Sucedió en La Habana* (1938), the first movie he made when he returned to Cuba; it was a great success among the audiences of the island and elsewhere in Latin America, due to plentiful amounts of comedy and Cuban music. Ramón Pereda (1897-1986), one of the actors in another American Spanish-language production, Cyril Gardner and A. Washington Pezet's *El cuerpo del delito* (1930), would later become associated with Peón in Mexico, beginning a fruitful collaboration that resulted in more than ten films.

Lewis Seiler, also known as Lew Seiler, was under contract to Fox where he filmed four movies between February and December 1931: *El impostor, Hay que casar al príncipe, La ley del harem* and *Mi último amor*; Ramón Peón assisted in the last title. *Mi último amor* opened at the California Theatre in Los Angeles on November 28, 1931. By then, however, Ramón Peón was already in Mexico.

In spite of Peón's frenetic work habits, he had to do whatever it took to make a living. Peón, who had directed one of the great silent films made in Latin America, *La Virgen de la Caridad,* had no choice but to resort to his remarkable ability to cry at will. At Venice Beach, Peón appeared in the illusionist show "John the Baptist's Head," a work he had performed during his younger years in Havana and other Cuban cities. He caught the attention of Robert L. Ripley (1893-1949). Since 1918, Ripley had been writing a newspaper feature called "Believe It or Not," which, due to the unusual facts and abilities it compiled, appeared in the newspapers of more than thirty countries and was translated into seventeen languages. When Ripley discovered Peón, who was tied to an enormous wooden cross on the beach, surrounded by a dumbfounded audience as he cried profusely, he was so stunned that he devoted an article to him. Raymond, "the man who cries," as Ripley called him, cried convincingly in order to earn a living in that "city of foreigners." The Cuban had no other alternative to earn some money, when most of the major studios suddenly stopped making Spanish-language films and he lost his job. In the fall of 1931, production of Spanish-language films was abruptly halted; the same thing happened with European market versions, produced at Joinville Studios in France.

Various facts and circumstances influenced the sudden decision to stop filming foreign-language productions and to permanently close down the departments in charge of this "minor genre." In a June 1932 article published in *Cinelandia*, a magazine that championed Spanish-language productions, one author observed that: "Hollywood producers have no intention of reviving that part of the industry, as they don't believe it is vital for the rest of it."[4] She affirmed that "the major film studios in the Mecca of Cinema," always on guard against new competitors, producers "are not interested at all in

4 Martha Durán B., "El prestigio de la cinta en español," *Cinelandia* No. 6, June 1932, 34.

pleasing Latin American markets, as films in English take all of their time, and besides, are profitable enough to allow them the luxury of not worrying about any other financial headaches in terms of the commercial side of the industry."[5]

The careless selection of plots, actors and directors, as well as the hastiness and low budgets with which these "translations and betrayals of, in some cases, less than popular films with a notorious lack of quality" were filmed, resulted in "mediocre versions that, gradually, failed to interest the public," as Spanish historian Ángel Zúñiga once observed. He added: "The great Spanish-speaking family, not being able to make its own movies, had to endure the increasing avalanche of mediocre films that, whether on purpose or not, managed to completely discredit Spanish-language productions and, little by little, consolidate the dominance of foreign films."[6]

When asked about the failure of this venture, Julio Peña (1912-1972), who played a significant role in it, concluded that the "Spanish" films made in Hollywood were never really Spanish films. He stated: "They looked Spanish, but they were Yankee in spirit."[7] Another actor, José Nieto (1903-1982), known as "the Spanish George O'Brien," believed that the reason for this failure was the chaotic organization of production that completely failed to account for the tastes of their targeted audience. "All Spanish-language versions were adaptations of bad American films, because, in our countries, good American movies were easily marketable in their original language. Besides, in the movies we made in Hollywood, they used all the leftovers from the American productions: directors, cinematographers, etc."[8]

Spanish-speaking technicians and artists, displaced by the California studios, were forced into exile. American productions could not absorb that many people. Some of them went to Europe (Rosita Moreno, Roberto Rey, Pablo Álvarez Rubio, Catalina Bárcena), others returned to their native countries (like the Mexicans Miguel Contreras Torres and Gabriel Soria, among others). Some went to Latin America (like Carlos F. Borcosque, who went to Argentina); and there were also those who committed suicide, like the Spanish actor Alfonso Quintana.

Although Ramón Peón was determined to film in his native country, returning to Cuba was out of the question, due to increasing conflicts during the dictatorship of Gerardo Machado, as well as the total absence of any cinematic activity: no films had been produced on the island in 1931. Things looked more promising in Mexico, the next stop on his cinematic journey. Peón's period of apprenticeship in Hollywood (1930-1931) came to an end. About that "land of abundance," that city of glory and misery, naive and childish, according to those who worked there during that hectic period, playwright Gregorio Martínez Sierra observed: "The intense industrialization of cinema (after all, Hollywood is just a huge factory) has killed any artistic curiosity famous actors might have had."[9]

---

5 *Ibid,* 44.
6 Ángel Zúñiga, *Una historia del cine.* Vol. 1 (Barcelona, Ediciones Destino, S. L., 1948), 390.
7 Florentino Hernández Girbal, *Los que pasaron por Hollywood* (Madrid, Editorial Verdoux, S.L., 1992), 112.
8 Ibid, 89.
9 Ibid, 72.

A few months later, Ramón Peón and Lupita Tovar were in Mexico, ready to work respectively as actress and assistant director on *Santa*, directed by the actor Antonio Moreno. It was the second Mexican sound film ever made, and the first one to use live sound. Peón would become a sound film pioneer in his adopted country, Mexico. Cinematographer Néstor Almendros, who defined him as "the Cuban Griffith" after watching *La Virgen de la Caridad*, observed that this prolific filmmaker, who worked in almost every genre, showed his versatility and his narrative talent, even though he made cheap, simple, and effective movies. He would always brag about having learned in Los Angeles everything about the use of sound. Peón's Mexican filmography, which spans twenty-three years, includes forty-eight feature films. He returned to Cuba twice, and made six films there. His romantic determination and his quixotic tenacity in fostering a film industry in his homeland is unforgettable. But that's another story.

Gabriel García Moreno: Inventor in Hollywood, Innovator in Mexico

María Esperanza Vázquez Bernal and Xóchitl Fernández

Gabriel García Moreno was multitalented. In the course of his career, he ventured into screenplay writing, film producing, directing, editing, and even had a stint as an exhibitor. He was also a noted film technician and prolific inventor, who co-founded one of the largest film studios in Mexico. Born in Tacubaya, Mexico, in 1897, into a family of public servants and military officers (some of them distinguished), who had excellent connections to powerful politicians, landowners, and entrepreneurs, Gabriel's family was nevertheless of modest means. His father died when Gabriel was still a boy, and his older brother, Vicente, became a father-figure to him. Gabriel became interested in cinema as a teenager. He gained experience as a cinematographer, but then proceeded with a career in banking. Before long, García Moreno reached a managerial position that took him to Sonora and El Paso, Texas. In Sonora, he met Hortensia Valencia, whom in time he married.

In spite of being on a promising professional path, he was not happy. Cinema was in his blood and he ultimately decided to follow this calling. So, he resigned from the bank and sold his shares. With the money he bought a Universal camera and embarked on a new profession. In 1924, he and his wife moved to Mexico City. There he leased a movie theatre and also made his first feature film, *El buitre* (1925), an adventure film featuring a band of hooded scoundrels, possibly inspired by Francis Ford's serials, which were very popular in Mexico. García Moreno toured with his movie, as an itinerant exhibitor. Aware of the difficulty of maintaining a constant speed while shooting or screening films, he looked for a way to solve this problem.

He made countless trials at Jesús Abitia's Mexico Film Studios. Evidence of such tests is still extant, thanks to García Moreno's friend, Carlos Villatoro, who preserved some of the footage. The results were unexpected: the filmmaker discovered that a shutterless camera was the answer to film movies at a constant speed. However, the lack of financial support and the unavailability of the high-precision parts he needed for building a prototype halted the project for a few years.

In 1926, Gabriel and Hortensia moved to Orizaba, Veracruz. They rented a large property, called "El Molino de la Marquesa," which offered splendid locations for García Moreno's film projects. He moved to Orizaba with the certainty of finding the support he needed for establishing a film production company. And so he did, with the backing of some rich local businessmen. They founded the Centro Cultural Cinematográfico. The partners intended to build a film studio and lab in the Molino de la Marquesa's grounds and issued bonds for such purpose. The company first produced some fiction films, as well as documentary short subjects. Then, they made *Misterio,* a feature film, in 1926, with García Moreno behind the megaphone. Only a seven-minute fragment of *Misterio* is extant, thanks (again) to Carlos Villatoro, the movie's leading man.

El tren fantasma was their second movie, also made in 1926. It is an eight-part serial; an entertaining adventure featuring modern box cab electric locomotives that had just begun running between Orizaba and Mexico City. García Moreno showed his filmmaking skills, shooting sequences, like fights on moving trains, chases, and an accident avoided in the nick of time. Filming started in September and the movie was finished in December. Juan Vasallo was the leading man in this as well as in all García Moreno's feature films. The Centro Cultural Cinematográfico organized an intensive publicity campaign for the movie.

El puño de hierro followed in 1927; García Moreno made it in about five weeks. The story is about a serious problem that plagued Veracruz and other Mexican regions at the time, namely, the addiction of increasing numbers of people smoking opium. The film features striking sequences, e.g., documentary footage showing the effects of the drug on addicts and on their children. The fictional scenes, portraying addicts at an opium den, are gruesome. His wife Hortensia played the leading female part and Octavio, his brother-in-law, also participated. Carlos Vasallo, a well-known still photographer and cinematographer from Orizaba, was in charge of the camera. Original negatives of *El tren fantasma* and *El puño de hierro* were kept by the family of William Mayer, one of the Centro Cultural Cinematográfico's partners. The Filmoteca de la UNAM rescued them, thanks to Dr. Aurelio de los Reyes, noted historian of the Mexican silent film era. Later, the institution had both films restored. Esperanza Vázquez, co-author of this paper, was in charge of editorial restoration. It is worth pointing out that two of García Moreno's films were distributed and exhibited in the United States: *El buitre* and *El tren fantasma.*

The Centro Cultural Cinematográfico ceased to operate in 1927, in spite of having a pair of projects in the making; it closed without explanation. It was a serious setback for García Moreno, but he refused to give up his goals. His brother Vicente came to the rescue and helped Gabriel and Hortensia move to Tijuana. As the chief engineer of the Barbachano's Light and Telephone Company, Vicente was a prominent man there. He was also the Grand Master of the Scottish Rite Lodge in the North Baja California Territory. Soon, Gabriel was running a movie theatre in Tijuana. He did not intend to stay there long; it was only a transitional step to resume his project of developing a continuous-speed camera and projector. He knew such an endeavor was only possible in Hollywood, where he hoped to find both the financial and the technological support needed for its completion.

Staying in Tijuana meant an opportunity to earn some money for his next move, and also to establish the necessary business contacts. Apart from counting on his brother Vicente's relations, Gabriel also had some friends in the Hollywood film industry. By that time, at least a dozen Mexican technicians had positions at studios either in Culver City or in Hollywood. These relations were instrumental in García Moreno's plans. Once he felt well equipped to take his next step, García Moreno moved in December 1928 to California with his wife. They stayed first in San Ysidro, near the border. In those days, his camera was still designed to run at sixteen frames per second, which was later adjusted to twenty-four. The continuous-speed projector's design was ready, too. One of the projector's advantages was that it needed only two sprockets and two idlers to work, instead of the eight or more used by standard equipment. Purportedly, a firm of lawyers was already working on the patent applications.

After a few months, García Moreno and his wife moved to Los Angeles. As most of the Mexican technicians and higher-ranked actors did, the couple chose to live in Hollywood. It was socially and professionally convenient. Being well-educated and bilingual, they were not subject to the discrimination experienced by most of their fellow Mexican-Americans. Mexican film technicians in Hollywood were employed in fields like animation, stop-motion, set design, miniatures and backgrounds, cinematography (even color) and laboratories. Thanks to one of them, García Moreno found a position at the Hal Roach Studios' miniature and background department.

Later, García Moreno was admitted as one of the inventors to Howard Hughes's technology incubator, called the Hughes Development Company. Caltech engineer Howard Lewis was its manager. Lewis and his team recruited more than twenty-five engineers to develop diverse projects, and Gabriel (among other Mexicans) was one of them. The incubator was located at 700 Romaine Street, Hollywood, site of the magnate's legendary business empire. García Moreno started to build the first prototype of his continuous-speed camera there. Projects at the incubator included some related to color cinematography (Hughes had bought Multicolor, Ltd., a few years earlier), slow-motion film, and 3-D, and he became interested in those areas, too.

During his time at the incubator, García Moreno unknowingly made his first contribution to the formation of a Mexican film industry, when he helped Joselito and Roberto Rodríguez join Hughes's team of inventors, coaching them, while the brothers developed their optical sound system. This system eventually allowed Mexico to make the transition to sound film without the need of leasing costly foreign equipment. Only three countries were able to do that: the United States, Germany and Mexico. Unfortunately, García Moreno was unable to finish his prototype for the continuous-speed camera at the Hughes incubator, when the tycoon abruptly had it closed in 1931.

Times were tough in Hollywood, as well as all over the country. Film production dropped severely, with film studios and all business related to distribution and exhibition suffering from the effects of the Great Depression. The financial crisis fueled strong xenophobic sentiments and Hollywood was no exception. If some outbreaks had been visible since 1926, among cinematographers, for instance, the Depression made the situation far worse. Contrary to popular mythology, the National Origins Act of 1924 limited

Gabriel García Moreno and his wife Hortensia, in Hollywood, n.d.

overall immigration into the United States to 150,000 per year, but did not specifically restrict Latin Americans. Nevertheless, after 1929, many actors and technicians were deported or voluntarily left the country, because they lacked proper documentation or had not formally applied for U.S. citizenship; overall, 138,000 Mexicans were "repatriated" in 1931 alone. For many Mexicans, it was the end of their Hollywood dreams, but not for García Moreno. He was a legal resident, had excellent relations, and bore total confidence in the viability of his inventions.

In 1931, García Moreno founded a new company in partnership with the influential editor, Snyder, and a financial adviser, William Fairbanks. Curiously enough, the purpose of the company was quite similar to that of Howard Hughes's incubator. The development of the continuous-speed camera was only one of a myriad of projects the company was interested in endorsing in fields like aviation, automobile production, publicity and editorial. The partners soon found financial support for building ten prototypes of a shutterless camera. Seven of them were made, and test results were promising. Among other things, it was proven that the camera could shoot in slow motion at a very high speed without getting damaged, a usual occurrence with cameras in the market.

The so-called Moreno-Snyder camera used an optical intermittent system consisting of eight Plano concave lenses which supplement the camera's regular lens and moved with the film to correct its continuous motion. The effect was a steady, motionless image on each frame. The system allowed an exposure time of 24 fps, twice the time a regular camera did, so only 50% of the usual lighting was needed. This camera could run at 125 ft. per minute, and had a maximum aperture of 360 degrees. It featured a great depth of field. It was equipped with an exposure meter, which allowed the operator to quickly measure light intensity for each take. The camera operated noiselessly. Tests made at a lab proved the camera was suitable for slow-motion shooting for scientific purposes.

García Moreno and his partners launched an intensive publicity campaign promoting the camera and the reviews were encouraging. In 1931, the company exhibited a prototype at the non-trade apparatus exhibit at the spring meeting of the Society of Motion Picture Engineers (SMPE) in Hollywood, where it got a good deal of attention. The company applied for patents for the camera and five devices related to it. It seemed the corporation was bound for success, until its financier was accused of having invested embezzled funds in the company. As a consequence, all of Moreno-Snyder's assets, including the prototypes of the camera and other devices, were seized. It marked the end of an ambitious project. All the patents they had applied for were granted; alas, it occurred years after the company was forced to close.

This did not discourage García Moreno. He was a resourceful man, always full of new ideas. He abandoned the idea of the camera. However, one of the prototypes for the continuous-speed projector appeared in Mexico some time later and trade agent Tomás Maya made some effort to promote sales, to no avail. García Moreno independently patented a device and went to work again in the field of miniatures and backgrounds, this time for RKO-Pathé. He was there during the making of *King Kong* in 1932. According to a Los Angeles newspaper, he contributed some innovations in miniatures for the movie, but his work went uncredited, as often happened to film technicians.

In October 1933, García Moreno was ready to undertake a new project: a color film process he called Opti-Color. The Craigs, a rich, high-society New York gentleman and his mother, became interested in this venture as his capitalist partners. The Crosene Company introduced the four-color, additive, bipack process in 1935, continuing to operate until the early 1940s, after García Moreno had already returned to Mexico. Technically speaking, the partnership was a success; they obtained eight patents in the United States and two in Canada. On the other hand, commercial success evaded them, because Technicolor and Cinecolor dominated the market; a niche for Opti-Color never materialized.

So far, García Moreno's inventions seemingly belong to the field of historical anecdote, since they were never industrially produced or used. However, that is far from true. The ample experience and knowledge García Moreno acquired during his Hollywood stint eventually led him to make invaluable contributions to the advancement of the Mexican film industry, as will be explained later.

In 1937, García Moreno's partnership with the Craig family underwent an important change: if formerly the engineer received a salary comparable to a medical doctor's, that provision was now suspended. He was not in the position to wait until Opti-Color became profitable, if it ever did, without a regular income. So, he was forced to ponder his options. He was not interested in a job at the film studios; instead he considered moving back to Mexico, where the film industry was rapidly progressing. Through his wife Hortensia, he met Mauricio Calderón, an influential music distributor in Los Angeles, and also a Bank of Italy board member. The Bank of Italy pioneered signature loans for film production, so Mr. Calderón had the shrewd idea of investing in film-related projects. Moreover, Mr. Calderón was interested in film production, not only because of his affiliation to the Bank of Italy, but through his brothers, José and Rafael Calderón, who were among the most powerful Mexican film distributors and exhibitors, based in Mexico and in the United States. The Calderón brothers had co-financed some Hollywood Spanish versions and many Mexican movies since the advent of sound.

García Moreno convinced them to invest in a film studio in Mexico City. The Calderón brothers were well aware that the existing studios were unable to keep pace with a constantly increasing number of film productions. As distributors and exhibitors, the brothers needed enough Mexican films for their clients and theatres, so they agreed to become financial partners in the new studio. Gabriel designed the facilities and chose the equipment to start operating. Thanks to his contacts and technical knowledge, he was able to buy second-hand machinery and accessories in excellent working condition on a limited budget (reportedly, the investment was fifty thousand dollars).

Only three film studios were working at full capacity in Mexico City in 1937: CLASA, Universidad Cinematográfica and México. They lacked enough facilities, as well as technical and human resources, to fill Mexican film industry needs. The Calderón brothers acquired a 22-acre property in Coyoacán, México City, large enough to provide space for eight sound stages, laboratories, and all the necessary facilities. At the end of 1937, García Moreno, his wife and their toddler daughter Raquel moved to Mexico City. He brought a technical team from Hollywood, in order to guarantee the quality of the work.

One of the engineers was banned by the Mexican union of film workers, UTECM, arguing his place should be occupied by a Mexican, albeit other foreigners were well-established in the film industry, like sound engineer J. B. Kroger.

The Estudios y Laboratorios García Moreno were ready to start operating in May 1938. Its partners had to face strong and bitter opposition from the corrupt leader of the film industry workers' union, Enrique Solís, who did everything he could to prevent the new studios from opening. Since he managed the Universidad Cinematográfica studios (which belonged to the UTECM) as a business of his own, Solís did not want a new competitor in the market. Eventually, Solís had to face the consequences of his crooked behavior—though only for the short term—and the Estudios García Moreno began operating. The studios offered new services and equipment inaccessible to Mexican film producers until then. Among them, there were:

1. The first re-recording equipment in the country, which meant a giant step in the making of movies in Mexico: at last, it was feasible to mix and combine audio elements (music, dialogue, special effects) to make optimal soundtracks. Before that, dialogue and music could only be married if the latter was performed while shooting. The equipment featured six-channel audio.
2. The first continuous motion picture film developing machine. The other studios developed film using an obsolete rack-and-tank system, which often resulted in prints of uneven quality.
3. An expert in the fields of still photography and cinematography, García Moreno introduced sensitometry to Mexico, unknown until then. This allowed filming and developing better-quality motion pictures, with optimal luminosity and avoiding undesired variations in contrast.
4. Back-projection equipment.

The García Moreno studios offered services of high professional standard, including 24/7 availability. Their goal was to allow producers to post-produce their films entirely in Mexico, instead of having to send material to Hollywood labs. Some months after opening the studios, the Calderón brothers searched for additional financial partners, in order to build all the planned sound stages (they had built only one). Then, Rafael took charge as managing director, forcing García Moreno to bow out. The next step was changing the name of the studios to Estudios Azteca (that name evoked the powerful Azteca Films, a major distributor of Spanish-language films in the United States, owned by the Calderón brothers and Alberto Salas Porras). García Moreno was not happy with the new state of affairs.

Finally, the Calderón brothers decided to include Enrique Solís and engineer Manuel Rivas as partners; the latter taking control of technical operations. García Moreno did not take that well and decided to leave the firm. After that, he opened his own laboratories on Rembrandt Street, and there he continued trying new inventions, and giving service to film producers and distributors. García Moreno was able to develop a new color film system, quite similar to Cinecolor, which he called Mexicolor. It was affordable and produced satisfactory results. At least two short subjects made with Mexicolor reached commercial exhibition. Lately, one of them surfaced, *Extravaganza mexicana,* an avant-garde musical, filmed with a camera leased from Eduardo Martorell. Painter and filmmaker Juan José Segura designed and directed it. Colors in the short faithfully reflect Segura's signature palette.

In January 1943, during a trip, García Moreno (still young and with many projects in the works) died after suffering from food poisoning. Before expiring, he told his friend Guillermo Calles that he had been purposely poisoned by someone. His assertion was never proved or even investigated. After his death, the García Moreno laboratories were dismantled and no trace of his equipment or tests have been found. Fortunately, one of his close associates provided Esperanza Vázquez with a precise account of García Moreno's activities, inventions and experiments in the last years of his life. Some of his later creations had indeed commercial use, mainly in the field of color and film developing.

García Moreno was an unassuming man, completely devoted to his work. He did not pursue applause or honors, notwithstanding the fact that he was a pillar of the Mexican film industry. For decades, his work was forgotten; his legacy as a filmmaker has been recognized at last, but his technical contribution to the industry is yet to be acknowledged. The authors hope their book, *Gabriel García Moreno: hombre de cine*, now in production, will contribute to that end.

Romualdo Tirado and the Pioneers of Spanish-language Cinema in Los Angeles

Alejandra Espasande Bouza

The birth and development of Spanish-language film production in early twentieth century Los Angeles, would not have been possible without the work of a group of pioneers whose life stories reveal both the institutional structures of production and the conditions of labor within them. In terms of understanding the history of Spanish-language film production and culture in Los Angeles, there is still much biographical groundwork to be done. This essay documents the professional trajectory of actor Romualdo Tirado Pozo (1880-1963), whose prolific entertainment career exemplifies the often itinerant nature of the profession, and more broadly, the working conditions for an army of actors, technicians and investors who were key in fostering the emergence of a Spanish-language cinema culture in Los Angeles. Like almost all of his colleagues, Tirado traveled between various Spanish-speaking countries, and found work in theatre and cinema wherever he could get it. This essay examines the development of Tirado's career from his native Spain to Latin America and Hollywood, highlighting the multiple roles of Tirado as child performer, zarzuela singer, actor, stage director, playwright, theatre impresario, filmmaker and motion picture exhibitor. It argues that the conditions of Tirado's life typified this sector, particularly once Tirado relocated to Los Angeles, where a growing Latino community and the beginning of sound film offered opportunity but also meant precariousness.

Romualdo Tirado Pozo, the son of Pascual Tirado and Juliana Pozo, was born in the town of Quintanar de la Orden, Toledo (Spain), on September 3, 1880. From early on, his life was shaped by often desperate conditions. Following the death of both of his parents, Tirado and his siblings were distributed among family members. The young Tirado was sent to an uncle in Madrid, where he began to earn a living by singing in the streets for coins, and where according to family accounts, he was recruited by the impresario of a circus troupe who paid 200 pesetas to his uncle.[1] Sometime later, at the age of eight, he joined La Compañía Infantil de Zarzuela, a performing company of children.[2] His debut performance took place at La Cadena Theatre in Madrid.[3]

1 "Romualdo's Story," Family biography. Private collection.

2 *La España Artística: Periódico de Teatros, Literatura, Política y Bella Artes*, Vol. II, No. 64, October 1, 1889, 3.

3 "Ecos y Noticias," *La Vanguardia*, January 23, 1931.

During the late nineteenth century, the success of the zarzuela, an autochthonous genre that consisted of musical dramas with spoken and sung dialogue, inspired the creation of zarzuela children's companies. These were embraced by the audience, but often criticized by the press for their exploitation of child labor. The presentations of La Compañía Infantil catered to adult audiences, whose curiosity was piqued by miniature song-and-dance performers, some as young as four years old.[4] While some of the child performers had caring parents, most were a source of income for their poverty-stricken households, and others, as in the case of Tirado, were orphaned and bound out to spend years on the road.[5]

In 1895, when Tirado was fourteen, a portion of the company was taken over by actor José A. Jiménez, who renamed it La Aurora Infantil, taking with him headliners and performers like Tirado, who played both a comic tenor and a *partiquino*, or chorus boy. Following a tour in Cuba, La Aurora Infantil began its zarzuela presentations in Mexico City, with the three-act zarzuela *El rey que rabió* (1891), under the umbrella of the renowned Teatro-Circo Orrín during a simultaneous engagement of the iconic British clown, Ricardo Bell—the beginning of an important professional relationship.[6]

In an 1895 publication, critic Enrique de Olavarría y Ferrari wrote about the ongoing presence of children's touring companies in Mexico and the potential for child performers to be exploited:

If you have attended a stage performance in the late hours of the night and have seen any of those child-actors surrendering tired and overworked into a sofa, chair or the heartless floor stage, and have seen the child being awakened with vulgar words and pushed and beat and kicked [...] If any of our readers has seen any of this, you will understand our repugnancy in dealing with Children Companies, because all there is of noble, and mannerly and decent in us, our humanity and piety, will rebel in dignity against such a barbaric and repugnant exploitation.

In contrast, Olavarría referenced a newspaper that highlighted what appeared to be the good treatment given to the child performers of La Aurora Infantil. After three months of presentations, the children had managed to win the hearts of the Mexican audience. A journalist who witnessed the company's departure from Mexico City, wrote:

Since 8 p.m., the train station began to fill with people that wanted to bade a last farewell to the charming children. When they arrived emotions peaked; the children were embraced, kissed, feted with gifts [...] Finally at 9:10 p.m., the train whistle was heard, and all the child artists popped their heads through the train windows exclaiming 'Hail Mexico!' to which the crowd replied 'Hail Spain! Hail the Children's Company!'[7]

---

4 *La España Artística* Madrid, Vol. III No. 95, May 3, 1890.
5 *La España Artística* Madrid, Vol. IV No. 143, May 23, 1891, 2.
6 *La Iberia*, Madrid, (April 16, 1895), 3; E. de Olavarría y Ferrari, *Reseña histórica del teatro en México*, Vol. 4, 1895, 555.
7 M.E. Fonseca Ávalos, *Amado Nervo: El periodista. Prólogo y recopilación de su obra periodística en El Nacional 1894-1898* (Mexico, 2008), 446.

The years Tirado spent with the children companies were key in shaping his onstage talents and ability to connect with audiences from all types of social and cultural backgrounds, but he could not remain a child performer.

In 1897, a Spanish newspaper announced the return to Spain of La Aurora Infantil with a cast of children that included "first baritone, Romualdo Tirado; 11 years."[8] It would not be the first time that Tirado, at the time 16, was listed with a younger age in print, because older children were thought less profitable. During this time, his voice began to change and the touring company he was with in Argentina, presumably the Aurora Infantil, abandoned him at the wharf *en route* to Paraguay. Alone and penniless, he experienced the hardship of life on the streets until the owner of a photo studio offered him a job peddling photographs.[9] At eighteen years old, he joined the Spanish merchant marines, with whom he traveled around the world, as far as South Africa where they joined the struggle of the Dutch Boers against the British, and back to Latin America, where they helped Spanish troops fight American soldiers in the Spanish-American War.

Around 1900, Tirado returned to Argentina where he joined Emilio Sagi Barba's zarzuela company. A native of Spain, Sagi had forged a successful career in Argentina. He started as choirmaster of a zarzuela company where he met, and later married, Concepción Liñán Pelegrí, comic headliner and dancer from Seville. Her sisters, Matilde and Filomena, worked as performers in the company. Tirado was struck by Matilde and began a two-year courtship.[10] In 1902, Concepción returned to Spain, and her sisters remained in Argentina, where they began performing with Tirado.

The three would become inseparable and embark on a multinational tour that would take them all over Latin America. Following an onstage marriage proposal, Tirado and Matilde married in 1907 in Guayaquil (Ecuador) and continued touring with Filomena. Newspapers noted the Tirado-Liñán partnership working in a variety of countries, including zarzuela performances in Santiago de Cuba (Cuba), in January of 1909, where they joined the traveling company of Colombian impresario and actor Alfredo del Diestro, who, like Tirado, would later find his way to Hollywood's Spanish-language productions.[11]

Later in 1909, the Tirados settled in Mexico City.[12] Shortly after their arrival, the Mexican Revolution erupted against the dictatorship of then President Porfirio Díaz. Once the Díaz regime was ousted, the stage became a focus of social and political commentary, exemplified by the work of leading female headliners, all of whom sooner or later would work with Tirado. From 1909 until his departure in 1919, he worked indefatigably as theatre impresario, stage director, actor, zarzuela performer and playwright, entertaining

8 *El Liberal de Tenerife*, Vol. VI, No. 1662, March 5, 1897.
9 Manuscript. Property of Matilde Tirado.
10 Family anecdote.
11 http://hemerotecadigital.bne.es/issue.vm?id=0003764339.
12 Florentino Hernández Girbal, Juan B. Heinink and Robert G. Dickson, "Romualdo Tirado," *Los que pasaron por Hollywood*, http://www.cervantesvirtual.com/obra-visor/los-que-pasaron-por-hollywood-0/html/ff1c4606-82b1-11df-acc7-002185ce6064_109.htm.

all types of audiences in theatres of the capital city and around the nation. In 1914, he branched out from zarzuelas into burlesque productions, an entertainment format that mockingly mimicked well-known plays.

On March 10, 1915, the Tirados found themselves at the Teatro Variedades in the coastal city of Veracruz with the staging of the Quintero brothers' one-act zarzuela *El amor que huye*. A review noted that Tirado "was received by the audience with a burst of applause that continued throughout the play."[13] Two years later, the zarzuela was adapted into a silent film, produced by Cirmar Films on location in Yucatan, *El amor que huye* (1917, Manuel Cirerol Sansores, Carlos Martínez de Arredondo). The film marked the first appearance of Tirado and Matilde on screen.[14] It opened at Mexico City's Teatro Principal in June of 1917. Although a review criticized the poor quality of the exhibited print, due to issues of film projection, the acting was commended.[15]

On June 15, 1918, the Tirados began a season of zarzuelas and operettas at Mexico City's Teatro Virginia Fábregas. The season's theme was to stage noteworthy works by Mexican playwrights, a groundbreaking endeavor considering the monopoly of Spanish works on the Mexican stage. Additionally, it was reported that "the revered comic actor and stage director Tirado" was going to join the guild of Mexican authors with the presentation of his operetta *La Reina Iris*.[16] His support of Mexican stage works was crucial during a time when the Sociedad de Autores Mexicana (Mexican Authors Society) was undergoing major restructuring.[17]

Tirado won the hearts of an audience that came to know him by the nickname «Cachipuchi.»[18] During their long stay in Mexico, the Tirados continued living in the company of Filomena, who, aside from working on their stage productions, was to devote the remainder of her life to caring for the Mexican-born Tirado children: Arturo Romualdo (1912), Miguel (1914), and Enrique (1917).[19] Were it not for the social upheaval caused by the Mexican Revolution, the Tirados might have settled in Mexico for good.

In preparation for their Mexico City departure, a pamphlet, dated February 7, 1919, promoted a farewell fundraiser to benefit Tirado. From August to October, the actor-impresario made a series of presentations with his company en route to the U.S., including stops at local theatres in Culiacán (Sinaloa) and Hermosillo (Sonora).[20] In October, both sides of the U.S.-Mexican border town of Nogales were sprinkled with brochures, announcing the arrival of the Companía de Opereta y Zarzuela Hispano-Mexicana Lle-

---

13 "Teatralerías," *El Pueblo*, December 3, 1915, 4.
14 Héctor Quiroga Pérez, *Iconografía del escenario mexicano (1909-1919). Part V.*
15 "La película *El Amor que Triunfa*," *El Pueblo*, June 25, 1917, 6.
16 "Chismes," *El Nacional*, June 15, 1918, 4.
17 Juan Felipe Leal, *El cinematógrafo y los teatros: Anales del Cine, Segunda parte.*
18 Margarita Mendoza López, *El Teatro de Ayer en mis Recuerdos* (Mexico: Editorial Porrúa, 1985), 78.
19 Birth certificate number 399, issued by a judge from the Civil Registry of Mexico City on September 11, 1912, indicates that Enrique Aristeo Arturo Romualdo was born as the legitimate child of the "artista lírico" Romualdo Tirado, from Quintanar de la Orden (Toledo-Spain) and Matilde Liñán, from Seville (Spain), on September 3, 1912 in the residence of his parents located at 43 Cinco de Mayo Avenue, Mexico City; Birth certificate number 138, issued by a judge from the Civil Registry of Mexico City, July 28, 1914, for Miguel Tirado, states that he was born on July 14, 1914 at the family house located in 19 Capuchinas Street; Form N-315. U.S. Department of Justice. Immigration and Naturalization Service. Declaration of Intention. Matilde Linan Tirado. May 16, 1945.
20 Brenda Judith Aguirre Fuentes, *Diversión y entretenimiento en Hermosillo (1902-1936): artículos y anuncios.*

randi-Soler, under the direction of Tirado, who made his way to the Arizona side on November 21, 1919.[21] A few days later, the company changed its name to Arte Nuevo and presented the three-act operetta *La casta Susana* in Tucson (Arizona). The audience on the U.S. side of the border did not always have the same tastes as audiences in Mexico. A writer for *El Tucsonense* scolded the local Spanish-language audience for having barely attended the recent presentations of touring companies. "Our 'pueblo' never fails to attend the carnival, even at the expense of having to pawn their 'metate' [grinding stone]." He concluded: ... "in due time the only companies that will visit us will be the circus, the minstrel shows, the carnival, and a boxer here and there. What do you prefer? The arias of a troubadour or the jokes of an American clown?"[22]

On February 28, 1920, the Los Angeles daily, *El Heraldo de México,* announced the upcoming arrival of a new troupe of artists under the direction of Tirado, who was described as "the best to have recently graced the Mexican stage."[23] Tirado's debut in Los Angeles took place at the Teatro Novel on Friday, April 23, 1920, where impresarios Dagoberto Campos and Luis Pedro Rivas hosted the staging of *The Merry Widow,* by his Gran Compañía de Opereta y Zarzuela Arte Nuevo, comprised of thirty-five performers and musicians that included the composer Ernesto González Jiménez, with whom he was to partner in a variety of projects and ventures.[24] A journalist noted that Arte Nuevo had been welcomed by an audience that had driven as far as thirty to fifty miles with their families. In his opinion, the Los Angeles audience could be classified in two ways: a sophisticated and cultured audience, comprised of "Mexican immigrants," familiar with the best of the Mexican stage, and the "genuinely Angeleno" audience, which made up a majority and was comprised of Mexicans who had lived too many years in Los Angeles to remember Mexico, or who lived in rural and mountainous areas, and experienced in Arte Nuevo a sample of high-caliber Mexican entertainment for the first time.[25] Yet, Tirado would also prove adept at speaking directly to this Angeleno audience.

Arte Nuevo's run at the Teatro Novel lasted from April to December of 1920. Its production output was hectic, presenting a new bill every day from Tuesday to Sunday, featuring a range of zarzuelas, operettas, *sainetes*, musical revues and stage plays. These included works authored by Tirado, such as the smash-hit production *De México a Los Angeles*. A reviewer noted that the play showed a "great spirit of observation" in its depiction of the trials and tribulations experienced by Mexican immigrants who come to Los Angeles, full of illusions but without knowledge of English. The plot centered on the misadventures of an old tailor from Mexico City who travels to Los Angeles with nothing but a notebook with a few English words. He is met with a crushing reality, disguised under a series of humorous scenes and musical acts. The stage sets were designed by Amador Arce and replicated Los Angeles' L.A.M. Co. Offices, the San Roman Restaurant, Venice Beach, and the interior of an Aztec palace. Some of the musical numbers included "Ice cream Soda," "Cow-Boys," a "Sirens and Beachgoers" act, "Tehuana," "Yucatecas," and "Mexicanas" acts, a "Chorus

---

21 *El Heraldo de México*, Nogales, Arizona, October 14, 1919, 6; U.S. Department of Labor Document. Per a U.S. Citizenship application, Matilde listed the date of entry as November, 20, 1919.
22 *El Tucsonense* ,Tucson, Arizona, January 3, 1920, 4.
23 "Pronto Tendremos Gran Temporada De Opereta, Zarzuela Y Comedia," *Heraldo de México,* Los Angeles, February 28, 1920, 8.
24 "Gran Temporada De Opereta Y Zarzuela En El Teatro Novel," *Heraldo de México,* April 18, 1920, 3.
25 "La Viuda Alegre," *Heraldo de México,* April 27, 1920, 2.

of Chinas," and a "Tapatío" duet. These titles reflect the mixing of the two cultures that shaped immigrants' lives.[26] Nevertheless, Arte Nuevo was dissolved later that year, a portion of the company traveling back to Mexicali with Tirado.

A newspaper from that time hinted at Tirado's incursion into motion picture production with the establishment of the Tirado Film Corporation.[27] This venture demonstrates the importance of stage and silent film antecedents for what would become independent Spanish-language film production. In 1921, Arte Nuevo returned to Los Angeles for a season at the Teatro Hidalgo. It offered the same type of quality and varied live entertainment expected by the now-familiar audience, but their shows increasingly included the exhibition of fiction and documentary silent films. During this period, Arte Nuevo began to produce adaptations of famous films, such as the staging of *Santa*, a novel by Mexican author Federico Gamboa which had been made into a silent film in 1918, and the staging of the Mexican silent film serial, *La banda del automóvil gris* (1919, Enrique Rosas). Additionally, Tirado continued writing and staging his own productions, which included *Tirado dentista* and *De todo un poco*.[28]

Later that year, the company moved to the Teatro Metropolitan (later Principal) where it hosted the premiere of the short film, *Revista Mexicana Arte Nuevo, N. 1.* The newspaper advertisement sheds light on its content: "You will see the repatriation of thousands of fellow countrymen and will see the presence of notable artists that presently live in Los Angeles. This is the first Mexican film of two reels that will be showcased to the public with the adaptation of music with national themes." The ad concluded, "Do not miss Tirado on film!"[29] This film, along with a film of his play *De México a Los Ángeles* (1921, Romualdo Tirado), seem to have been produced by his film company.[30]

As suggested by the subjects of these films, Tirado had a strong interest in the needs of his local community. On November 12, a newspaper article by Tirado announced an open call from his Companía Arte Nuevo for the submission of any type of work, which, if chosen, would be staged at the Teatro Principal. The authors would be compensated and anyone would be considered in the casting. Tirado wrote, "if through the efforts of those capable and enthusiastic we achieve the production of a work of real merit we would have met the need to awaken the sleepy brains of those unaware of their potential." The opportunity was revolutionary; Tirado, the powerful actor-impresario, had opened the way for local talent to flourish.[31]

Over time, his position in Los Angeles' Spanish-language entertainment culture was cemented. In his free time, he could be found teaching classes in Spanish diction, supporting local fundraisers and community events, or going on tour abroad or to local cities lacking Spanish-language entertainment.[32] Of a performance in San Diego, a journalist wrote, "I

26 "De México a Los Angeles En el Teatro Novel," *Heraldo de México,* November 28, 1920, 6.
27 "Fue Solemne La Inauguración Del Teatro "México" En Mexicali," *Heraldo de México,* December 28, 1920, 3.
28 Advertisements, *Heraldo de México*, May 3, May 22, 1921, 3.
29 *Heraldo de México*, September 30, 1921, 2.
30 "Beneficio del Actor Romualdo Tirado," *La Prensa,* Los Angeles, December 22, 1921, 5.
31 Advertisement, *Heraldo de México*, November 12, 1921, 3.
32 *La Prensa*, January 15, 1922, 5.

Romualdo Tirado in *La jaula de los leones* (1930, Fred J. Balshofer).

have seen 'favorites' of our English stage, but never before have I seen a whole audience rock with delight each time an actor reappears: let him be absent only five minutes from the footlights and at the first sound of his voice 'off stage' the applause will break anew."[33] As the decade advanced, many up-and-coming artists in his stage productions would establish themselves, including a young singer, Luz Reyes, in the drama *La Tirana* (1924), who would become the iconic singer Lucha Reyes.[34] Also in 1924, Los Angeles' cultural scene was rocked by the arrival of renowned Mexican playwright Guz Águila (Antonio Guzmán Aguilera), who began staging productions of his own plays at the Teatro Hidalgo.

In 1924-1925, Tirado the actor-impresario partnered with González Jiménez, and later with composer Lauro Urango, and the sisters Adelina and Angelina Iris, in the running of the Teatro Capitol. One of the highlights of the season included the staging of the play *El indio yaqui*, written by local playwright and *Heraldo de México* journalist Adalberto Elías González. The cast featured Mexican-born Hollywood actor and independent filmmaker Guillermo ("Indio") Calles. The day of the opening, among the audience was the cowboy actor Neal Hart, who went on to join Calles in the 1927 film version.[35] Another highlight included the premiere of the Mexican silent film *Atavismo* (1924, Gustavo Sáenz de Sicilia), which included an onstage prologue by Arte Nuevo, surely inspired by the lavish shows produced by showman Sid Grauman at his Egyptian Theatre in Hollywood.[36]

In 1925, the theatres on Main Street—the Hidalgo, Principal and Estella—were forced to address hygiene and fire safety issues that led the city to impose regulations which forcibly reduced the size of stock companies, making it impossible to stage large productions.[37] Tirado began having difficulties finding theatres to host his company, and instead had to go on tour. Finally, in September 1927, journalist and former silent film actor Alfonso Busson (*Santa,* 1918) announced the leasing of the Grand Opera House by Tirado, in partnership with González Jiménez and Arturo Pallais Jr. The approximately 1,300-seat theatre became the most stylish Spanish-language house in Los Angeles, re-opening as the Teatro México on September 15, with the staging of the Tirado-González patriotic-themed musical play *¡Mexicanos al grito de guerra!*[38] An editorial in *El Heraldo de México* commended the impresarios' efforts in securing such a highbrow and historic theatre, which had hosted artists of the caliber of Enrico Caruso, for the entertainment of their local Mexican audience, which they estimated to be over 150,000.[39]

---

33 *San Diego Union*, September 9, 1923, 15.
34 *Heraldo de México*, March 30, 1924, 8.
35 Rogelio Agrasánchez Jr., *Guillermo Calles: A Biography of the Actor and Mexican Cinema Pioneer* (Jefferson, N.C.: McFarland & Company, 2010); "Teatrales," *Heraldo de México*, September 5, 1924, 8.
36 *Heraldo de México*, September 30, 1924.
37 Nikolas Kanellos, *A History of Hispanic Theatre in the United States* (Austin: University of Texas Press, 1990), 100-101; *Heraldo de México*, June 11, 1925.
38 Advertisement, *Heraldo de México*, September 13, 1927, 6.
39 *Heraldo de México*, September 17, 1927, 3.

Despite this auspicious beginning, the local market for Spanish-language entertainment was about to undergo dramatic change. The Teatro México under Tirado combined live shows and motion picture exhibition until March 7, 1931.[40] According to the *Los Angeles Times*: "The reopening of the California Theatre some time ago as an international house, especially featuring good films in Spanish, has met with enthusiastic response from our own Quartier Latin, but it has resulted in the passing of the old Teatro México." Playwright Adalberto Elías González attributed the demise of the theatre to the 1929 Depression and subsequent deportations of the Mexican community in Los Angeles, accounting for a loss of audience. Although there was a brief attempt to bring zarzuela back to the Teatro México in 1932, the theatre was ultimately demolished in 1936.[41]

Another reason for the downfall of Spanish-language live theatre was the emergence of sound cinema. During the advent of film talkies, Hollywood was pushed to devise new ways of retaining a hold on its foreign markets by dubbing films, producing foreign-language versions of Hollywood films and original Spanish-language films. The demand for foreign-speaking talent brought an influx of Spanish-speaking talent that included large numbers of artists from Spain and Latin America, not to mention local Angeleno talent that ranged from already established Hollywood stars, such as Antonio Moreno and Lupe Vélez, to local stage actors, such as José Peña ("Pepet") and Romualdo Tirado. Parallel to the production of Hollywood's Spanish-language efforts, an independent and vibrant Spanish-language cinema culture was being produced by a group of enthusiastic investors, technicians and artists.

Rodolfo Montes' mark in the moviemaking business began in 1929 when he joined Cuban actor René Cardona in the production of what is considered to be the first Spanish-language talkie made in Los Angeles,[42] *Sombras habaneras* (1929, Cliff Wheeler). Montes went on to produce at least two more films, despite headaches with his first. He joined Spanish musician-caricaturist Xavier Cugat in the establishment of Hollywood Spanish Pictures Co. The first film, a Spanish-language musical directed by Cugat, *Gauchos, charros y manolas* (1930), featured Spanish-speaking artists from different countries and served as a showcase of Spanish and Latin American musical culture. To unify the musical numbers, a master of ceremonies, played by Tirado, was incorporated into the film. An article published by the *Los Angeles Times* (February 2, 1930) stated:

> An ambitious effort to provide Spanish talking pictures for 27,000 theatres in Spanish-speaking countries, and 100,000,000 persons served by these houses, is being undertaken by Rodolfo Montes and Xavier Cugat [...] The film has been produced in Los Angeles, as will future releases by the orga-

40 During 1930, the Teatro México screened: April: *Charros, gauchos y manolas* (1930, Xavier Cugat), *El Zeppelin perdido* (1929, Edward Sloman); May: *El león de la sierra* (1929, Miguel Contreras Torres); July: *Alma de gaucho* (1930, Henry Otto), *Dios y ley* (1930, Guillermo Calles); Aug: *La jaula de los leones* (1930, Fred J. Balshofer), *Así es la vida* (1930, George Crone); October: *El Charro* (1930, Guillermo Calles), *Serenata mexicana* (1930), *Sombras de gloria* (1930, Andrew L. Stone, Fernando C. Tamayo), *El águila y el nopal* (1930, Manuel Contreras Torres); November: *La fuerza del querer* (1930, Ralph Ince), *¡Aguiluchos mexicanos!* (1930), *Las campanas de Capistrano* (1930, Leon de la Mothe); December: *Una hija del amor* (1928, Candida Beltran Rendon), *El Charro* (1930), *Estrellados* (1930, Salvador de Alberich, Edward Sedgwick). See Jan-Christopher Horak's essay in this volume.

41 "La Vida Teatral En Los Angeles, Apuntes Históricos a Propósito de la Reciente Desaparición," *La Prensa*, San Antonio, Texas, October 11, 1936, 31-34.

42 José Bohr's *Sombras de gloria* (1930) is considered the second Spanish-language independent film.

> nization. About 400 persons, some seen on American screens, took part in «Revista Musical» *[Gauchos, Charros y Manolas]*, which is divided into three parts, one for Spain, another for México, and the last for the Argentina [...] The new Spanish screen revue will be changed for local release by including a Spanish actor [Romualdo Tirado], who is also credited in local talkies, as master of ceremonies. He will explain the three episodes."[43]

In 1930, Tirado was tapped by the brothers Joselito and Roberto Rodríguez to direct their three-reel independent production *Sangre mexicana* (1930), featuring Mexican soprano Celia Montalván. The film was filmed at Luna Park Zoo and showcased Montalván with animals. In all probability, the content may have been similar to the show the actress presented at Luna Park on May 5, 1931, as part of the Cinco de Mayo celebration. The *L.A. Times* announced that "Will Rogers is expected to be Master of ceremonies. At 5 p.m. Celia Montalván, film actress, will enter a cage confining five lions and give several song numbers." *Sangre mexicana* was different from other Spanish talkies made in Los Angeles in that its sound was recorded, employing the Rodríguez Bros. Sound Recording system. The Los Angeles newspaper *La Opinión* published a note explaining the invention:

> The invention of these two modest Mexican artists consists of a sound recording system variation, employed for the production of film talkies. The creation of a small receptor that makes it portable, much cheaper than the bigger ones [...] It can be run on a camera tripod and employed for the impression of sound film without the disadvantages of Movietone, which often sacrifices sound quality for image, or conversely. The apparatus of the Rodríguez brothers is already patented and its inventors look forward to starting to produce short films with it.[44]

Later that year, the Rodríguez Bros. Sound Recording system was employed to record the film *Santa* (1932), the first sound feature made in Mexico.

Tirado joined the independent film production business by forming a company named Ci-Ti-Go with his loyal partner, composer Ernesto González Jiménez, and impresario Mateo A. Cicero, who financed the film. Margarita Mendoza, in her book *El Teatro de Ayer en mis Recuerdos,* attributed a screening of Rodolfo Montes' *Sombras habaneras* at the Teatro México as the catalyst for Tirado to join the film production business. "Why not join the film business? ... [Maestro] Ernesto González Jiménez and the comic actor Romualdo Tirado ... convinced Mateo Cicero to be the financing partner [...] and following the last show at the Teatro México, each night part of the company went to Hollywood to film *La jaula de los leones*."[45]

---

43 John Scott, "Spanish Film Invaded: Local Group Plans Foreign Pictures Exclusively, Ambitious Effort Will Cater to 27,000 Theatres, First Production Soon to be Released Here," *Los Angeles Times*, February 2, 1930, http://www.proquest.com.
44 "Los hermanos Rodríguez y su invento que ha sido recibido con admiración," *La Opinión* , November 30, 1930.
45 Margarita Mendoza López, *El Teatro de Ayer en mis Recuerdos*, 80.

Ci-Ti-Go would produce only a single film. *La jaula de los leones* (1930, Fred J. Balshofer; alternate title, *La tragedia del circo*, 1931) was an adaptation of a Tirado zarzuela that had premiered at the Teatro México in 1927. It ran 74 minutes and featured performances by Tirado and members of the Bell family of circus performers, daughters of the clown Richard Bell, but famous in their own right by this time: Amelia, Alicia and Rosita Bell. The presence in Los Angeles of this circus family, whom Tirado had known since his time in Mexico, along with his recent experience working on the circus-themed *Sangre mexicana*, may explain his choice of the project. His son, Arturo, described the plot: "My father played a bum who joins the circus in order to eat, but he is given the job of feeding the elephants and the lions. In the final scenes, he is placed in the lion's cage and becomes one of the stars. In this picture, everyone got into the act. My mother plays a blind woman, whom my father befriends; my aunt [Filomena] and my sister [Matilde] also have a small part." Although the film was shot in a studio at night, the scenes with the animals were probably filmed at the Luna Park Zoo in Los Angeles.

The *L.A. Times* interviewed Tirado about his vision for Ci-Ti-Go: "This picture, Mr. Tirado claims, will eventually pave the way for American producing companies toward the selection of at least one type of story which appeals to Spanish-speaking people. This picture will be all-talking with incidental music by González Jiménez, well-known Mexican composer, and is being directed by an American photographic technician [Fred Balshofer] with Mr. Tirado directing the dialogue."[46] Some theatres in Los Angeles lacked sound systems for the playback of talkies; Ci-Ti-Go solved the problem of exhibiting *La jaula de los leones* by hiring the services of the Rodríguez brothers, whose portable sound system could also be used for playback.[47] *La jaula de los leones* was the first and only film made by Ci-Ti-Go. Like Rodolfo Montes, Mateo Cicero would also lose most of his fortune in the Depression. Regardless, both producers were key players in the short-lived expansion of independent Spanish-language film production in Los Angeles.

Simultaneous with his work on films produced independently by Latinos, Tirado became one of the most coveted character actors for Hollywood's Spanish-language films, appearing in over thirty films. In 1930, he was featured in at least four studio films: a talkie with Buster Keaton, *¡De frente, marchen!* (1930, Edward Sedgwick), whose premiere took place at the Teatro México on Friday, January 23, 1931, with the actors in attendance; another M-G-M film, *El presidio* (1930, Ward Wing), a Spanish version of *The Big House* (1930, George Hill) with actor José Crespo; a Universal Studios short with actress Lupita Tovar, *Only a Dream;* and a Paramount film, *The Texan* (1930, John Cromwell). In 1931, he worked on a film with his daughter Matilde, *En cada puerto un amor* (1931, Marcel Silver). When interviewed in 2007, the eighty-six-year-old Matilde recalled that, "He was asked at the studio if anyone looked like him. He brought Arturo, Miguel, Enrique, and when he took me, they said 'we want that one. She looks like her dad!' And, in a week I was there. They got me a school tutor [...] I had to be hidden behind something and he would come down from a ship and embrace me."[48] The multi-talented Tirado, who never learned to speak English, nor to drive a car, employed the assistance of his son Arturo to navigate

46 "Spanish film under way," *Los Angeles Times* (April 13, 1930), http://www.proquest.com.
47 Ibid, 81.
48 Interview with Matilde Tirado, 2007.

the studios and communicate. In a note to journalist Armando del Moral, Arturo noted the following: "I was the kid who assisted the director with translations. Can you imagine how many mistakes I must have made. The writers José López Rubio, Martínez Sierra and Poncela thanked me for the effort and favors like helping them with purchases and driving them and Catalina Bárcena to shops." Aside from continuing to work with the major Hollywood studios, during the mid-1930s Tirado also collaborated on productions by Reliable Pictures, *La última cita* (1936, Bernard B. Ray), and three films by Metropolitan Pictures: *De la sartén al fuego* (1935, John Reinhardt), *El capitán Tormenta* (1936, John Reinhardt) and *El carnaval del diablo* (1936, Crane Wilbur). In 1938, he worked for Jaime del Amo's Cantabria Films, appearing in *La vida bohemia* (1938, Josef Berne) and *Verbena trágica* (1939, Charles Lamont).

In 1938, Tirado joined Mexican star Tito Guízar in the cast of *Mis dos amores* (1938, Nick Grinde), produced by Ramos Cobián Productions, and distributed by Paramount. Another production was *El milagro de la Calle Mayor* (1939, Steve Sekely), a Spanish-language version of *Miracle on Main Street,* produced by Arcadia Pictures. Tirado culminated his screen career with *Tengo fe en tí* (1940, John Reinhardt), produced by Victoria Films, a partnership of Spanish actress Rosita Moreno, best known for her work in two Carlos Gardel films. These were among the last films made in Spanish in Hollywood during this period, as studios would increasingly turn to other ways to participate in the international Spanish-language film market.

Film prints of many of his early film appearances are considered lost or non-existent. Fortunately, the UCLA Film & Television Archive holds a number of studio films that feature his work, along with the two independent productions from Cantabria Films. They represent some of the few surviving films made by locals and immigrants who pioneered the production of independent Spanish-language cinema in a city, and an industry, dominated by mainstream English-language culture. These films are a treasure trove of comedies and tragedies that reflect the hopes and aspirations of the many artists who helped make Spanish-language film a reality in Los Angeles: an American cinema produced in Spanish that contributed to fostering Hollywood's on-screen diversity, the likes of which have not been seen again.

Romualdo Tirado passed away on October 17, 1963, in Los Angeles. A note published on October 22nd by *La Opinión* reads:

> Yesterday the remains of actor Romualdo Tirado were buried at Inglewood's Holy Cross cemetery, California [...] At 10 a.m. the funeral procession made its way to the cemetery. The entourage included a great number of artists who worked with him, and his most intimate friends. Tirado left a collection of writings that include a series of poems that reflected his religious fervor and his nostalgia for the motherland he never returned to. If a poem reflects the essence of his life, that poem is *El payaso (The clown)*, an excerpt of which reads:

Here lie the remains of a clown who passed away as he lived, not knowing how nor when, for some he was a great man, while for others he was... a clown.

Don't forget, dear audience, that you are the soul of the artist, who prefers your applause to worldly fantasies; they are all temporary, in this course of life. The truth is in the soul. Lucky those who guard it.

Carlos Gardel's Exito Productions, Inc. A Case of Hispanic Autonomy?

César Fratantoni

CARLOS GARDEL AT PARAMOUNT PICTURES

Cases of autonomy under the umbrella of a major studio are extremely rare in the Golden Age of Hollywood, the period ranging from the 1920s to the 1950s. Yet in 1934 Carlos Gardel arrived in New York and managed to control the production of four very successful Spanish-language films, using Paramount's production facilities and distribution network. Thanks to newly discovered documentation, and the survival of many of his letters, we have a rare look at the challenges a Hispanic producer would face if he tried to do business with one of the Big Five.

The four Spanish-language films Carlos Gardel made in New York open with the typical Paramount logo, but in Spanish: "Es un film Paramount" (It is a Paramount Film). Then comes the title of the film, and just below, the following line: "Producción de la Exito Productions, Inc." (An Exito Productions, Inc., production). Today it is not strange to see a Paramount film produced by an independent company, but in the 1930s, when the studio system was in its heyday, it was a rarity. In those days, the practice of large motion picture studios was to produce movies primarily on their own lots, with creative personnel often under long-term contract, and also to dominate distribution and marketing. Yet, these Gardel films made in New York are clearly an exception, with Exito Productions officially getting half the credit.

Why did Paramount make this unusual agreement with Carlos Gardel? It was undoubtedly the product of special circumstances. Paramount's very difficult financial situation, and the studio's record of Spanish-language productions, seems to indicate that there would have been no deal in 1934, had it not been for the extraordinary qualities of Gardel. It is true that with the coming of sound, the studio had decided that some foreign-language films had to be produced, to remain competitive around the world. In 1930, they took over the Joinville Studios near Paris, France, just for this purpose. But with the general public's growing acceptance of subtitles, support in Hollywood for producing foreign-language films had evaporated, especially in the case of a Paramount on the verge of bankruptcy. Paramount had stopped making Spanish-language films in France in late 1931,[1] and it was only when excellent box-office numbers for *Las Luces de Buenos Aires* (1931, Adelqui Millar), Gardel's first Paramount film, came in that the studio reluctantly considered making more films with Gardel and Imperio Argentina, the only other Spanish-language star who had delivered at the box-office. Two films were hastily made near Paris at the end of 1932, just before Paramount shut down its European operations altogether.

By 1934, the situation at Paramount hadn't changed ... They knew that some Spanish-language films could make money for the company, and were fully aware that a popular Spanish-language film would help them push their English-language productions in Hispanic markets, but things were so bad for the company that only a very attractive deal would overcome a general reluctance by the Paramount decision-makers to get involved in a foreign-language production once again.

The very attractive deal was Carlos Gardel himself. When he appeared in New York, hoping to renew his film career, he was already a well-known figure at the Paramount Office. In France, Gardel had participated as the star of three Paramount films, and two of them had been big box-office hits in the Hispanic world. This box-office record was very important, but there was something else about Gardel that interested the studio. When it came to making a Spanish-language film, Gardel had already proven himself in France as a reliable person who had informally led a group of Spanish-speaking people through the whole process. This was crucial in the 1930s, when it was extremely difficult for a studio like Paramount to deal with all the challenges associated with producing a foreign-language film. In preliminary conversations with the studio, Gardel seemed willing to take control of the process, and even use his own social network to import the Spanish-language talent needed. This was a relief for Paramount.

WESTERN ELECTRIC STEPS IN

There was still the key problem of funding. Paramount liked Gardel and was willing to work with him, but the studio could not commit resources, and the only way a deal could be made was if funding appeared from an outside source. This is probably what Gardel heard at the Paramount Building in New York ... and had been hearing since 1931. Trying to get independent funding for a film was not something totally new for Gardel. In a 1932 letter to his girlfriend during his European stay, he tells her that he is travelling to Spain to secure financing for a Spanish-language film.[2] Now in New York, he was forced to tackle the problem once again.

We don't know who encouraged Gardel to turn to Western Electric. It was probably the Paramount people themselves who suggested it, since it was no secret in New York that Western Electric, through its subsidiary, Electric Research Products Inc (E.R.P.I), was making loans to independent film producers. The decisive moment came in late March

1 Juan B. Heinink and Roberto G. Dickson, *Cita en Hollywood. Antología de las películas norteamericanas habladas en español* (Bilbao, España: Mensajero, 1990).

2 Rafael Flores Montenegro, *Gardel y el Tango, Repertorio de Recuerdos* (Buenos Aires: Ediciones de la Tierra, 2003), 230.

1934, when Western Electric agreed to finance two small-budget films that would be filmed in the U.S. and would feature Carlos Gardel. And if everything went well, another two would follow.

Why Western Electric? A subsidiary of AT&T, it had the mission of finding a way to invest large amounts of money that the parent company was still making, even during the Depression. On the other hand, as suppliers of filmmaking equipment for the studios, Western Electric was aware of the financial needs of the filmmakers. So, at 12% interest, they came up with the possibility of lending money to Fox and some independent filmmakers. Not directly, but through their subsidiary E.R.P.I., Fox, which had a relationship with Western Electric that went back to the 1920s, was ultimately loaned around $15 million. But there was also some money available for smaller productions, and this is where Gardel came in.

Once Paramount heard that Gardel had secured funding for two small-budget films—$71, 000 and $81,000 were ultimately received for the first two films—the company announced the unusual partnership with Carlos Gardel and went into action.[3] An apparently independent company, Exito Productions, was incorporated to produce the films, but using Paramount lawyers as officials and the Paramount Building in New York as the business address. This made Exito virtually a part of Paramount, but is seems clear that the big studio this time wanted to limit the risks of Spanish-language production and maybe avoid any scrutiny or criticism that could arise from its creditors.

The interesting thing here is that Paramount, which for financial reasons had mostly abandoned filmmaking in New York in 1932, turning over its Astoria Studios to Western Electric, would now, although under cover, be the dominant force behind the Gardel productions. But to the outside world, and even to the movie industry, Exito Productions, Inc. was an independent production company, and Carlos Gardel seemed to be running it with his aides. This is how he explained the agreement to his representative in a March 1934 letter:

> We have founded a production company that is called Exito's Spanish Pictures and of which I am the director. This company is financed by Western Electric and distributed by Paramount. For two pictures they will give me 25,000 dollars and 25% of profits and as I told you, I will have total control in my hands. The deal has already been signed by Paramount, Western Electric, and me [4]

THE PARTNERSHIP IN ACTION

Gardel would tap a long list of friends and contacts he had made in the entertainment world to come up with a script, find a suitable director, and recruit the actors at a very modest price. During negotiations, his team would argue that it was really a small com-

3 *Variety*, April 7, 1936, 4.
4 Letter from Gardel to Armando Delfino, April 23, 1934.

Carlos Gardel filming outside Astoria Studios, New York, for *El Tango in Broadway* (1934, Louis J. Gasnier).

pany with a small budget that was contracting them. When everything was ready to start filming, everyone gathered at the Eastern Service Studios in Astoria, Long Island. There, the group led by Gardel shot the movie in about two weeks, using Paramount's and Western Electric's equipment and technical personnel. Once the film was shot, the Paramount men really took over. They supervised the editing and, eventually, were in charge of distribution and marketing.

In their letters to Argentina, Gardel and his screenwriter, Alfredo Le Pera, initially complained of the difficulty they had attracting good actors.[5] This was probably because of their location, the small pool of Spanish-speaking actors, and the fact that they could not offer a lot of money. They also mention that in the editing phase—which they did not control—a lot of footage was cut from the picture.[6] Most of the complaints were related to the first two films made in New York. They seemed happier with the results of the third film, *El día que me quieras* (1935, John Reinhardt). One reason is that they had changed directors after the second film, letting go veteran French director Louis J. Gasnier, who was a difficult man to deal with, and contracting the younger and more easygoing John Reinhardt. But we can also imagine that by 1935, after the experience and financial success of the first two films, everyone felt more relaxed and Paramount's faith in Gardel had increased. In the two films made in 1935 by the partnership, everything seems to have run smoothly.

HISPANIC AUTONOMY?

We go back to the question: Was this a case of Paramount giving autonomy to its talent? Gardel and his collaborators ended up producing four films that were not too far from their original vision, using their own director and actors. So, in practical terms, the autonomy was granted. But true to the filmmaking culture of those days, Paramount did not relinquish control of the Exito films, which after all would carry the Paramount logo. The loans were given to Exito Productions, which was controlled and operated from the Paramount Building. The studio seems to have given Gardel a big say, especially when it came to suggesting actors and personnel to be hired, but all the crucial decisions and payments were probably made by the studio ... disguised, of course, as Exito Productions, Inc. Gardel sometimes admitted in his letters that key payments were made by someone else: "They have contracted Rosita Moreno, who costs 7,500 dollars for two films," he says in one of his letters.[7] We also know that when money had to be transferred to Argentina to make an advance payment to actor Tito Lusiardo, who was hired—like Rosita Moreno—for two Exito films, Paramount used its own branch in Buenos Aires to receive the wire transfer and eventually make the payment to Gardel's representative in that city, who in turn signed a contract with Tito Lusiardo. All this behind-the-scenes activity by Paramount seems to indicate that the studio was an active partner, working very closely with Gardel.

5 Enrique Espina Rawson and Alfredo Echániz, *Archivo Carlos Gardel* (Buenos Aires: Editorial Proa., 2013), 208.
6 Ibid.
7 Ibid.

As far as the characteristics of the products being made, we know that Gardel was allowed to choose the script and the people that were going to participate in his films. We don't know exactly what happened in the editing room, but we can examine the results. And here we can confirm that the films told stories that many Latinos could relate to, such as the problems of migration, social class differences, etc. In this sense, the autonomy given to Gardel's team clearly paid off. And most importantly, Latino audiences liked what they saw. The excellent Latino music was also a very strong point of the Gardel films, another positive result of autonomy. We should mention, however, that Gardel and his collaborators were wise and careful not to stray too much from the typical Paramount product of the era. And when the script seemed to go too far, Paramount's advisors were always there to bring things under control. We know from an interview given many years later, that the decision by Gardel and his screenwriter Le Pera to have four American women appear in bras and panties was changed presumably by the studio, possibly at the behest of the Hays Office, keeping them fully clothed... and asleep in the living room, while Gardel sleeps alone in his bedroom.[8]

THE RESULTS

By all accounts, the Gardel films were tremendous hits and gave Paramount and Exito substantial profits. They were shown around Latin America for years. Gardel claims in his private letters that the studio was delighted with him, and was eager to include him somehow in their regular English-language productions. He mentions that he was offered participation in an upcoming George Raft film, *Rumba* (1935, Marion Gering), but his serious problem with the English language discouraged the studio from going ahead with the plan. We have evidence that towards the end of 1934 Paramount filmed him doing two songs that would be included in the Paramount picture, *The Big Broadcast of 1936* (1935, Norman Taurog). This film was in post-production when the news of Gardel's surprise death in June 1935 arrived; with all future plans frustrated, Paramount decided to cut him from the film. But, the fact that he was officially part of this big musical project shows that in Paramount's eyes he was more than just an independent producer. In fact, all this interest Paramount showed has led some researchers to see the whole Exito experience as something Paramount set up, just to keep Carlos Gardel on board while the studio groomed him for roles in English-language Hollywood productions. The only obstacle was Gardel's need to improve his English. Whatever the future plans were, the Paramount-Gardel partnership remains a textbook case of how a big American studio could approach the difficult task of making films for the foreign-language market and achieve satisfactory results.

AFTERMATH

Since Gardel was Paramount's only card in Spanish-language filmmaking, his untimely death in June 1935 ended Spanish-language production there for three years. In 1938, a promising substitute for Gardel was found. This time the key figure was an East Coast

8 Arturo Yepez Pottier, *La lágrima en la garganta, La fascinante vida y extraordinaria vigencia de Carlos Gardel.* (San Juan, Puerto Rico: Producciones El Copihue, 2017), 82.

Italian-American, Dario Lucien Faralla. Faralla had made a name for himself in the corporate side of the business, rising to become treasurer of First National. He traveled to Hollywood in 1935, when he was offered and accepted a position to work as an assistant to Henry Herzbrun, then production executive at Paramount.[9] In Hollywood, Faralla gained some credibility as an associate producer, before bringing up the subject of a return to Spanish-language production. In 1938, he signed an agreement with Paramount that was in some ways similar to the Gardel deal, except that the star would be Mexican tenor Tito Guízar. Under the deal, Faralla left Paramount to become the head of Dario Productions, Inc., which was incorporated under California law.[10] Dario Productions, although staffed with English-speaking industry insiders, would concentrate on making Spanish-language films. Faralla, using his strong influence at Paramount, secured a contract committing the studio to distribute his new company's first four productions, all of them featuring Tito Guízar. There was obviously the hope that Guízar would deliver at the box-office, just like Carlos Gardel had done.

Once again, Paramount was not dealing with an untested actor. By 1938, Tito Guízar had already achieved enormous success as the singing cowboy of *Allá en el Rancho Grande* (1936, Fernando de Fuentes), a Mexican film distributed by United Artists. And like Gardel, Paramount was willing to introduce him to the mainstream market by giving him a small part in *The Big Broadcast of 1938* (1938, Mitchell Leisen). The box-office results of the Tito Guízar films may not have been satisfactory, because history says that Paramount did not extend the four-picture deal. Faralla would die only a few years later, in 1944. Rafael Ramos Cobián from Puerto Rico came close to achieving a similar arrangement, this time under the name Cobián Productions. He managed to make a picture with Guízar at Paramount, *Mis dos amores* (1938, Nick Grinde), before obtaining a distribution deal with 20th Century-Fox.[11] Unfortunately, only one picture was released under the agreement. A host of other producers, probably inspired by Gardel's success, tried their luck at Spanish-language production in the late 1930s. They never managed to make a second film.

There are probably many reasons why the Gardel-Paramount experience could not be repeated. The most obvious one is that Carlos Gardel had qualities that would remain unmatched for the rest of the century. He was simply one of a kind. But it is also fair to say that Gardel's enormous success had encouraged filmmaking in many Latin-American countries, and U.S. Spanish-language producers after 1935 found a degree of competition and maybe protectionism that had not existed just a few years before. Spain, one of the main Hispanic markets, had also been destroyed in the terrible Civil War. All these factors contributed to put an end to the "Hollywood in Spanish" era, but the films those years have left us will probably generate interest for a long time.

9 *Motion Picture Herald,* June 1, 1935, 63.
10 *Film Daily,* October 6, 1938, 2.
11 *Motion Picture Herald,* January 7, 1939, 14.

Guillermo Calles:
A Mexican Film Pioneer in California

Rogelio Agrasánchez Jr.

Leading his countrymen, Guillermo Calles became the first Mexican artist to appear in films made in California in the 1910s. Drawing on limited resources, he turned to producing and directing his own movies, which gained recognition among the Spanish-speaking public. In 1929, Calles completed one of the earliest Spanish-language movies with synchronized sound, beating other Mexican filmmakers in this endeavor. His work as an actor in more than a hundred pictures rounds out an amazing career that spanned half a century. In spite of all this, contemporary cinema historians are largely unaware of Calles's achievements, due in part to the unavailability of his silent productions. Missing from film archives are *El indio yaqui* (1927), *Raza de bronce* (1927), *Sol de gloria* (1928) and *Dios y ley* (1929), which represent his undying efforts to restore a positive image of Indians and Mexicans. In an age dominated by Hollywood stereotypes, this vision is quite exceptional. Also responsible for the scant interest in the work of Calles is a general tendency among scholars to focus on the so-called "celebrities" of Mexican cinema. This perception, regrettably, leaves out other less stylish, but equally important contributors to the medium.

I became aware of the importance of Guillermo Calles while researching the history of Mexican film exhibition in the United States. His name appeared frequently in the Spanish-language newspapers of Los Angeles. It surprised me that so much printer's ink went into discussing his career as an actor in Hollywood, as well as the films he directed in the 1920s and 1930s. His nationalist beliefs were evident when he answered a reporter: "I am going to make films that will amaze the world. When? I don't know, but I have to make them. Mexico has something unspeakable in the ruins of Mitla and in the Cruz de Palenque; nothing can compare to its majesty and I cannot let foreigners go in there and exploit these archeological treasures."

Calles partially fulfilled his ideal in 1932, making a feature-length travelogue of the towns and scenery along the Mexican Pacific Coast. With his own resources and the collaboration of a cinematographer, he was able to tour the highway that links Los Angeles to Mexico City. *Pro Patria* was the outcome of this venture, the last he undertook in the United States.

But who was Guillermo Calles? He was born in 1891 in Chihuahua, the youngest son of humble origins, part of the Tarahumara family. After his musician father passed away in 1893, the family began to struggle financially, and by the end of the decade Calles' strong-willed mother decided to move to a copper mining camp in Arizona. There, the family found an environment less than wholesome in every aspect. Guillermo worked as water boy for miners in an environment openly hostile to Mexicans. Still, the hardness of life in Morenci and Silverbell never deterred him from dreaming. He wanted to be an actor, as his brother and mentor, Pascual, once was. Guillermo used to write and stage plays with other children, already showing a vivid imagination, as well as leadership skills. Life in the Arizona mining camps was anything but uneventful during the time the Calles family lived there. They experienced a disastrous flood, labor unrest, the infamous orphan abduction of 1904, and the striking presence of Teresa, the "Santa de Cabora." Undoubtedly, all this contributed to feed his imagination and shape young Guillermo's mind.

In 1912, Guillermo Calles arrived in Los Angeles and soon after he began his career playing Indian and Mexican roles. In the early days, he procured a few relevant roles in films, but then mainly worked as an extra in movies, like *Joan the Woman* (1916) and other Cecil B. De Mille projects. In 1917, he joined the Vitagraph Studios, appearing in popular serials that featured William Duncan and other action heroes of the silent screen. Calles and other Mexican actors and extras were well appreciated, due to their talent and good disposition. Besides acting, Calles doubled for movie stars, performing dangerous feats. He was athletic, enjoying the stunts, though sometimes he ended up in pretty bad shape. At least twice, he landed in a hospital bed with little hope for recovery. But he was young and strong, and soon he was back at the film studios. Calles's talent and self-discipline led Vitagraph's executives in 1921 to offer him a position as film director, just when his five-year contract as an actor was to expire. In spite of the appealing offer, Calles refused, when he was told to become a citizen of the United States. He would not relinquish his Mexican nationality for any reason.

He left Vitagraph for a brief stint in Mexican cinema. His friend, Miguel Contreras Torres, who had been in Hollywood for a while, offered him a chance to co-write and co-direct his first movie, *De raza azteca* (1921, Guillermo Calles, Miguel Contreras Torres). Here he played the part of a noble and brave Indian who falls in love with a white girl and sacrifices himself for her sake and his best friend. Calles appeared in another Contreras Torres movie, *El sueño del caporal* (1922, Miguel Contreras Torres). If at any time Calles thought of remaining in Mexico to make a career there, he soon abandoned the idea. Producing movies in Mexico in those years was a real challenge. There was no established film industry, and the few film producers operating didn't consider their financial, technical or human resources to be viable.

So, in 1922 he returned to California and continued taking part in westerns, many of them starring Neal Hart and Roy Stewart. He went uncredited more often than not, and only by means of painstaking iconographic research have we at the Agrasánchez Archive been able to identify him in lobby cards and movie stills of a number of westerns. In 1926, Calles decided to pursue his old dream: to produce and direct his own movies. He worked hard at every job, even as a fruit picker, to fund his first project, *El indo yaqui,* released in 1927. While working on the film in 1926, he received a female American bull terrier, purportedly a gift from Rudolph Valentino. Calles trained the dog, named Águila, to do all sorts of tricks. With a career that spanned about a decade, Águila became the first dog star in Mexican film history.

Appearing in *El indio yaqui* were several Hollywood actors, such as Betty Brown and Walter Shumway. Other American actors who made cameos in the film were famous western players, as well as Calles's good friends: Neal Hart, Roy Stewart, and Joe Ryan. As in all of Calles's films, his dog Águila played an important part. Calles was good at casting. He usually mixed white and Mexican actors, some of them Indian. Among the Mexican players in *El indio yaqui* were Agustina López, an elderly Yaqui woman who played the Indian's mother; she was a respected supporting actress who had roles in several big productions, like *Redskin* (1929, Victor Schertzinger), starring Richard Dix, Juan Calles, and José Duarte (a very popular comedian from Yucatan, Mexico, who was known as "the Mexican Buster Keaton").

El indio yaqui premiered at the Teatro Hidalgo in Los Angeles. The film caught the attention of the public and Spanish-speaking critics, striking a sentimental chord among viewers who saw an Indian turned into a hero, a not-so-common occurrence in the cinema. This turnaround surprised (but also delighted) Spanish-speaking audiences, who were continuously bombarded by Hollywood's often derogatory depictions of Indians and Mexicans. Several film critics in Los Angeles praised the movie, saying "it will be the vindication of our race on the celluloid." Critics and colleagues also praised some special effects that Calles himself created. The prints were tinted, which shows the producer's determination to make an appealing film. He traveled the Southwest with *El indio yaqui*, and also embarked on an exhibition tour in Mexico. The film proved to be a complete success to the extent that it made Calles declare in an interview: "After a while, I got tired of earning money with that movie." So, the filmmaker became the first Mexican to thrive as an indie producer.

Though a few critics remarked that *El indio yaqui* was just a reversal of Hollywood's derogatory films, in this case stereotyping whites as villains, an analysis of the film's original script—actually the copy Calles used for editing—indicates otherwise. *El indio yaqui* features discrimination against Mexicans both in Mexico and in Arizona, but the film is devoid of the usual stereotypes. Several white characters are shown as good and kind, and there are Mexican villains, too. The story has plenty of autobiographical references and reflects Calles's lack of racial biases or resentments.

After this project, Rafael Corella, a well-known film exhibitor from Mexicali, hired Calles to direct and star in *Raza de bronce* (1927, Guillermo Calles), a movie about a Mexican Indian who disowns his race until he gets involved in the defense of Mexicali against one of the filibuster invasions; witnessing his motherland at peril awoke his patriotism. The participation of battalions of the Mexican Army in war scenes made a great impression on spectators. This film was also a critical and commercial success. Calles's nephew, José Domínguez, was a revelation as a movie villain. He took part in all Calles productions and later had a prolific career in Hollywood as a supporting actor.

Like Calles, Rafael Corella was interested in offering a positive image of Mexico and its citizens on the silver screen. Corella had already produced a documentary, *Baja California* (1926, Rafael Corella), showing the territory's industry, nature, and people, as a response, among other things, to William Randolph Hearst's newspapers constant attacks against Baja California and Mexico in general.

One year later, in 1928, Calles produced, directed and starred in another feature-length film: *Sol de gloria*. He again played an Indian who is brave and sacrifices his life for a virtuous woman. Using striking ads, the Teatro México launched an effective campaign to promote the film's premiere. Alluring graphics and sensational phrases tipped off the public: "The best Mexican picture in which the main attractions are love, intrigue, mystery, ferocious animals, executions and thrilling scenes of great excitement." *Sol de gloria* was shot mainly on location, as were all of Calles's films; in this case, they went as far as Nayarit and Mexico City, the tight budget notwithstanding. Guillermo Calles and Carmen la Roux starred in the movie, while his sister, María de Jesús, his brother, Juan, his nephew, José Domínguez, and the famous composer and orchestra director, Carlos Molina, had relevant roles. Ernie Smith, a nephew of Albert Smith, Vitagraph's founder, was in charge of the cinematography. A few years, later Smith collaborated with Calles in the making of *Pro Patria* (1932, Guillermo Calles). There was plenty of adventure in *Sol de gloria*. One more time, Calles himself was the Indian hero. Here, he works as a diver for two brothers who are pearl dealers. Unbeknownst to him or the brothers is the fact that he is also a relative, since he is their late father's love child. The villain knows it and tries out of envy and hatred to destroy him, which leads to chases, bandits battling the Army, and a crocodile attack.

So successful was this film that Calles remade it in 1938 in Mexico as *Pescadores de perlas*. Shot mostly on location in Acapulco, the film's climactic scenes took place in the historical San Fernando Fort. However, Calles only wrote and directed the movie, while the hero was a Mulatto, rather than an Indian. *Pescadores de perlas*, although made in the same style as the silent version, did not meet commercial success.

In 1929, Calles made another silent film in California, *Dios y ley*. A year after its release, he added dialogue and music to half of its footage. *Dios y ley* therefore became the first movie with synchronized sound made by a Mexican. Unfortunately, like his previous films, this one is considered lost. Whatever we know about it comes from contemporary newspaper reviews. In *Dios y ley*, the romantic couple was played by Carmen Guerrero and Guillermo Calles. The film featured landmarks in Los Angeles County, such as Casa de Adobe and the Mayan Revival portal at the Southwest Museum of the American Indian, as well as places like San Gabriel. Miss Guerrero later appeared in Spanish versions of Hollywood films, e.g., *Drácula* (1931, George Melford). Several members of the Calles family took part in *Dios y ley*: his mother, Anatolia Guerrero, his sister María de Jesús, her son, José Domínguez, and a few of his nieces. *Dios y ley* was as successful as Calles's earlier films. He traveled the Southwest screening it and made a tour in Mexico. For many, watching a Mexican movie with sound was an exciting experience.

Not much is known about *Dios y ley*'s plot. However, judging from available sources, including numerous stills and lobby cards, he is an Indian hero who falls in love with a girl at a convent boarding school or orphanage. When the hero confronts the bad men in the story, they torture him, but it doesn't prevent him from saving his sweetheart. The torture scenes, in which the Indian hero's eyes are burnt, were perhaps the most striking in the film. Also arresting was the sequence portraying the 1900 eruption of Colima's volcano. One moviegoer complained that the movie, with some scenes set in the Isthmus of

Guillermo Calles. Courtesy of Agrasánchez Film Archive.

Tehuantepec, featured *charros*. According to him, there were no such characters in the Mexican Southeast. However, the incensed spectator was wrong; actually there were, and still are, *charros* in that region.

Calles produced his movies on very little money. Nevertheless, he was the only Mexican filmmaker living in California who achieved commercial success in those days. A few fellow citizens attempted to make profitable feature films in California, some of them even before Calles did, like Manuel Ojeda, Chano Urueta, and Miguel Contreras Torres, but none of them reached their goal. Calles once declared: "For a picture that costs $50,000, I have been forced to make it with only a quarter or a fifth of that amount." Undoubtedly, his long experience in the Hollywood studios proved instrumental in learning how to make the best use of resources, and how to promote films.

Needless to say, the inception of sound made things more difficult for independent producers. Calles was not the exception. In 1930, he made *El charro*, an obscure medium-length film, believed to be silent. The only evidence of its existence is a pair of ads in Spanish-language newspapers, as well as the lobby cards and movie stills that the Calles family preserved. As usual, Calles was the leading man in this film. Angelita Salcedo, his wife, was the female star. According to surviving images, the movie seemed to be a romantic story.

In the same year, Dorita Ceprano and Enrique Areu, theatre players and impresarios, appointed Calles to direct *Regeneración* (1930), an urban melodrama, starring both of them. J. H. Hoffberg distributed the film, and Ceprano and Areu kept a print for screening during their theatrical tours. Times were difficult after the Great Depression and Calles and his wife were forced to accept parts as extras in all sorts of films. Even if he had good connections in the industry, production had dwindled and furthermore his Mexican accent made it difficult for him to get Indian character parts in sound films. Many a time, Guillermo and Angelita had to take part in scenes shot on location under extreme weather conditions. On several occasions, *La Opinión* reported their being ill with pulmonary and bronchial diseases, because of their work.

But no illness or bad times could make Calles give up. Despite all, Calles set out in 1932 to make *Pro Patria,* a film that showed Mexico's Pacific Coast. It happened to be the first feature-length sound travelogue (part optical, part synchronized) made by a Mexican. Arthur Reeves, with his Artreeves system, was in charge of sound. Calles secured logistical support from the Mexican Army, thanks to Consul Enrique Ferreira's intervention. Ferreira was an influential diplomat and also former President Plutarco Elías Calles's brother-in-law. At the time, high-ranking Mexican officials were in charge of the Mexico-Los Angeles highway construction, and they were eager to support a film that would portray Mexico's modernization. Though the film had a budget of a mere 2,000 dollars, Calles and his team were able to cover a lot of territory traveling by car for about two months.

In January, Calles and his companions—his wife Ángela, cinematographer Ernie Smith, and his dog Águila—embarked from Los Angeles on their journey. It started with a short interview with Mayor John C. Porter, who entrusted Calles with a letter for Mexican President, Pascual Ortiz Rubio. They crossed the border at Nogales, Arizona, where they were authorized to film immigration officers doing their job. Given that the highway linking Los Angeles and Mexico City was still under construction, the team had a strenuous trip; with no bridges to cross the numerous rivers along their path, their automobile at some points had to be carried by ferry boats. Since they traveled in winter, conditions were often harsh. Sometimes, they were forced to spend the night in the car. Calles and his team visited several military camps set up for the highway construction. There, he met General Pablo Rodríguez, Colonel Filiberto Gómez—who was in charge of the highway works—and many other relevant military officers, politicians and entrepreneurs. Most of them made brief appearances in *Pro Patria*. Calles drove his Cadillac (acquired in the times his movies were hits) all the way from Los Angeles to Mexico City. Wherever they made a stop, the crowds cheerfully greeted and attended them. Undoubtedly, the Mexican Government and Army's support was instrumental in making their journey more pleasant and their work easier. Indigenous people are seen in many sequences of *Pro Patria*, always shown in a dignified manner, like some fishermen with their butterfly fishnets in a wonderful view of Lake Pátzcuaro, in the State of Michoacán. After more than a month, Calles and his companions reached the capital of the Republic. At the Castle of Chapultepec, the Mexican presidential residence, they met the Mexican Head of State, Pascual Ortiz Rubio, to whom Calles handed Mayor Porter's letter. Calles was allowed to take several views of the Castle and surrounding areas.

It is worth noting that Calles made a peculiar—and quite interesting—travelogue. For instance, he reenacted some of the adventures he and his team ran into during their journey, such as encountering wild animals, or the time a bull pushed him to the ground. Calles also took the liberty of altering the chronological/geographical sequence of two stages of the trip, in order to make the film more appealing. Along the journey, the scenes were shot silent, with synchronized narration added later. Gabriel Navarro, renowned Mexican journalist, composer and playwright, wrote the script and read it. Navarro had published a few of Calles's long letters sent from his expedition and was quite enthusiastic about *Pro Patria*.

Pro Patria premiered in Los Angeles at the Teatro México in July 1932, meeting great success. Diplomats, Calles's Hollywood friends and some celebrities attended. Reportedly, there was a universal exclamation of joy among the audience, while watching the opening three-minute sequence of a waving Mexican flag in Technicolor. Later on, Calles toured several cities exhibiting *Pro Patria*, starting in El Paso, Texas, and ending in Mexico City. The documentary was praised by numerous critics. The film's last public showing was in 1933; after that, it fell into oblivion.

Knowing that he had no more to do in California, Calles finally decided to move back to Mexico. His wife chose to stay in Los Angeles, working for Steve Clemente, the renowned Yaqui knife-thrower. Calles had a very good reputation as a skillful filmmaker. So, in Mexico City, producer and actor Ramón Pereda engaged him to direct his two first productions, both made in 1933. In *El vuelo de la muerte* (1934), Calles personally shot the aerial scenes from a plane, using a device he designed for holding the camera. The other film, *El héroe de Nacozari* (1934), was based on a true story about a Mexican locomotive driver who sacrificed himself to avoid the explosion of a train in town. The film is still screened each year, on the anniversary of the hero's deed in Nacozari, Sonora.

Calles directed a few more films in Mexico but met with discrimination in his own country. When he, one of the founders of the Mexican filmmakers guild, was to direct a series of films in the 1950s, other directors firmly opposed the idea. Calles's return to the megaphone was not to be, in spite of a much publicized hunger strike. He continued his career as a supporting actor until passing away in 1958, and his movies were forgotten. Only a few authors and scholars knew about his films until the publication in 2010 of *Guillermo Calles: A Biography of the Actor and Mexican Cinema Pioneer.*

Recently, one of his movies came to light: *Pro Patria*. It surfaced again thanks to a dedicated movie collector, film archivist, and Grammy-winning music producer, Alan Boyd. Now Dino Everett, head of the Hugh Hefner Archive at the University of Southern California, is in charge of its photochemical and digital restoration, while the author is working on the editorial restoration. Extant are nine reels of nitrate picture negative and four reels of track negative. Missing are five reels of track and the Technicolor sequence. USC received a National Film Preservation Grant, which is paying most of the costs for the photochemical restoration. Editorial restoration will consist of rewriting and re-recording the missing narration. Rewriting is already in process, based on the aforementioned letter-journal Calles sent Gabriel Navarro. Film prints (35mm) and 4K digital versions will be subtitled. An additional digital version with only the original narration (four reels) will be kept for historical purposes. With the restored version, we will learn more about the work of this pioneer of Mexican and bi-national cinema, and will also be able to see Mexico as Guillermo Calles and Ernie Smith saw it.

José Mojica: The Tenor from Jalisco, Mexico, Who Conquered Hollywood

Rosario Vidal Bonifaz

- *With love for the "patidifuzo"*

INTRODUCTION

After years of being practically forgotten, Hispanic cinema has more recently become the object of study for researchers recuperating the careers of those Hispanic artists who passed through 1930s Hollywood, making films in California or Joinville, outside Paris. Publications include: Juan B. Heinink and Robert G. Dickson's *Cita en Hollywood: antología de las películas norteamericanas habladas en español* (1990), Florentino Hernández Girbal's *Los que pasaron por Hollywood* (1992), with interviews with film professionals who worked on these productions, Jesús García de Dueñas's *¡Nos vamos a Hollywood!* (1993); Álvaro Armero's *Una aventura americana: españoles en Hollywood* (1995), Ruth Vasey's *The World According to Hollywood, 1918-1939* (1997), and Lisa Jarvinen's *The Rise of Spanish-Language Filmmaking: Out from Hollywood's Shadow, 1929-1939* (2012). In the case of the Fox Film Corporation, there's Aubrey Solomon's *The Fox Film Corporation 1915-1935. A History and Filmography* (2011).[1] Nevertheless, it remains ironic that a pioneering book about the subject, *The Rise and Fall of Spanish Talking Pictures* by Mexican Gabriel Ramírez (1985), remains unpublished and without an editor interested in taking on the project.

As is known, Hispanic cinema is linked to the 1930s Hollywood studios, which filmed versions of a movie in several languages at the same time. This studio production project aimed to conquer the Hispanic film market by attempting to understand and assimilate different linguistic communities, filming foreign-language versions of the English original in French, German and Spanish. Initially, European producers did have the technical infrastructure to develop their own sound movies. Hollywood's Hispanic productions had consequences in the mid- and long-term for Hollywood, but also contributed to the

1 Juan B. Heinink and Robert G. Dickson, *Cita en Hollywood* (Bilbao, España: Mensajero, 1990); Florentino Hernández Girbal, *Los que pasaron por Hollywood* (Madrid: Editorial Verdoux, 1992); Jesús García de Dueñas, *¡Nos vamos a Hollywood!* (Madrid: Nickel Odeon, 1993); Álvaro Armero (ed.), *Una aventura americana. Españoles en Hollywood* (Madrid: Compañía Literaria, 1995); Ruth Vasey, *The World According to Hollywood, 1918-1939* (Madison, WI: University of Wisconsin Press, 1997); Lisa Jarvinen, *The Rise of Spanish-Language Filmmaking: Out from Hollywood's Shadow, 1929-1939* (New Brunswick, N.J.: Rutgers University Press, 2012); Aubrey Solomon, *The Fox Film Corporation, 1915-1935. A History and Filmography* (Jefferson, N.C.: McFarland & Company, 2011).

constitution of several cinema industries, such as those in Mexico, Argentina and Spain (since every country has its own idiosyncrasies, slang and accents), and also helped to set the basis for a star system in those countries.

This production strategy was implemented at big studios, like Metro-Goldwyn-Mayer, Paramount, the Fox Film Corporation, United Artists and Warner Bros., as well as at medium-size studios like Columbia and Universal, and independents like Hal Roach;[2] all were based in Hollywood and surroundings. Following the formula that was already a Hollywood tradition, most of these companies based their films on the star system, hiring actors like Antonio Moreno, who didn't have an exclusive contract at first, but later collaborated mostly with Fox. Stan Laurel and Oliver Hardy (known in Mexico and other countries as "El Gordo y el Flaco") worked for Hal Roach. Buster Keaton made two films for Metro-Goldwyn-Mayer. José Mojica had an agreement with the Fox Film Corporation, while Carlos Gardel's Exito Productions were released exclusively through Paramount Pictures.

BIOGRAPHY OF JOSÉ MOJICA

José Mojica was born on the sugar and coffee farm Cerrito Colorado, in San Gabriel, Jalisco, Mexico, at 4 AM on September 15, 1896,[3] and died in Lima, Peru, on September 20, 1974. He was the son of Dr. J. Jesús Chavarín Vázquez[4] and Virginia Mojica.[5] Considered what then was called a "natural child," he only carried his mother's last name. When he was five years old, he learned the first letters of the alphabet with his teachers Petra and Josefa Covarrubias; the latter also taught him Church history. In 1902, he was enrolled in the elementary school Escuela Primaria Oficial de Niños, overseen by Evaristo F. Guzmán, and located in the San Gabriel area. In 1906, he moved with his mother, who played the guitar, to Mexico City, where they stayed at the Continental Hotel. Years later, Mojica concluded his basic studies at Saint Marie College. He later went to Escuela Elemental Número 3, and the San Carlos Academy, with the idea of studying painting and drawing. For four years he attended the National School of Agriculture and Veterinary Science, but was unable to finish his studies due to the Revolution, starting in Mexico in 1910, which caused the school to close.[6] He then took singing lessons with teachers José Eduardo Pierson and Alejandro Cuevas, enrolling at the National Music Conservatory. He started as a soloist in opera at the Ideal Theatre, and finally, on October 5, 1916, made his debut at the Arbeu Theatre[7] as first tenor in Rossini's *The Barber of Seville*.[8]

---

2 Heinink and Dickson, 23.

3 Registro Civil, 1895, Jalisco, Acta número 393.

4 *México bautismos, 1560-1950, accessed at https://mexicangenealogy.info/find-your-mexican-ancestors-using-mexican-catholic-church-records/*

5 *México bautismos, 1560-1950.*

6 In 1913, when the "Decena Trágica" happened, San Jacinto closed its doors, before the arrival of Villa's and Zapata's troops to Mexico City. Many agronomists abandoned school in 1914 and joined various revolutionary factions. In 1914 the school was closed. See Alejandro Tortolero Villaseñor, *De la coa a la máquina de vapor. Actividad agrícola e innovación tecnológica en las haciendas mexicanas: 1880-1914* (Mexico City: Siglo Veintiuno Editores – Colegio Mexiquense, 1995), 71. Some of the impact that the revolutionary movement left on José Mojica's memory was represented in a sequence of the film *Yo pecador* (1959, Alfonso Corona Blake), a biographical film about the actor, from the book of the same title.

7 Now the Miguel Lerdo de Tejada Library.

8 Cf. José Rogelio Álvarez (ed.), *Enciclopedia de México* (Mexico City: Enciclopedia de México, 1977), 109-110.

With this artistic background, Mojica traveled to New York, where he started working as a dishwasher, but soon managed to get supporting roles in an opera company. He was employed at the Metropolitan Opera House, rising to fame when he sang with Mary Garden in *Pelléas et Mélisande* by Claude Debussy. During the next nine years, Mojica sang at the Chicago Opera. Sponsored by Enrico Caruso, he was selected to sing one of the main roles in the 1921 world premiere of *The Love for Three Oranges* by Sergei Prokofiev.[9] Mojica managed to learn English, Italian and French, play the guitar, practice dancing and several sports. Next, Edison hired him exclusively to record opera music and Mexican songs.[10] Later, he had an exclusive contract with RCA Victor. He became famous, receiving a great amount of correspondence from his fans; the press noted that he had to hire a full-time secretary to answer his letters.

In 1928, Mojica traveled from Chicago to Los Angeles to perform screen tests at several studios, where he sang in Spanish and English. However, only Fox sent a representative to visit Mojica in Chicago, offering him a contract for forty weeks and about $80,000.[11] The eleven films produced by Fox between 1930 and 1934, with impressive performances by the talented singer from Jalisco, were outstanding examples of the importance of Hollywood's Hispanic movie industry: *El precio de un beso* (1930, James Tinling and Marcel Silver),[12] *Cuando el amor ríe* (1930, David Howard, William J. Scully), *Hay que casar al príncipe* (1931, Lewis Seiler), *La ley del harem* (1931, Lewis Seiler), *Mi último amor* (1931, Lewis Seiler), *El caballero de la noche* (1932, James Tinling), *El rey de los gitanos* (1932, Frank Strayer), *La melodía prohibida* (1933, Frank Strayer), *La cruz y la espada* (1933, Frank Strayer), *Un capitán de cosacos* (1934, John Reinhardt) and *Las fronteras del amor* (1934, Frank Strayer).

The incredible box-office success of *El precio de un beso* encouraged Fox to begin producing Spanish-language original films. From 1930 to 1931, Fox made between seventeen and eighteen films in Spanish, fourteen of them produced simultaneously as English versions; many scripts from 1920s silent movies were used. From 1932 to 1935, Fox produced twenty-two movies in Spanish, twenty of them from English versions. As far as we know, all of José Mojica's films were released in Spain and Uruguay, and six with some success in Mexico and eight in Peru. Below is a chart that will allow us to assess the distribution of these films in those markets.

9 Gabriel Pareyón, 2006.

10 Álvarez, *Enciclopedia de México*, Vol. 9 (1977), 109-110.

11 Jarvinen, 121-124.

12 His first film was an English musical, *One Mad Kiss*, with Antonio Moreno and Mona Maris, a story based on the Lola Montes case. Director Marcel Silver didn't work out, so the producers remade part of the material shot by James Tinling, filming in Spanish at the same time; this was the first Hispanic movie from Fox. See Heinink and Dickson, 99; Lisa Jarvinen, 121-124.

Film	Mexico	Uruguay	Peru	Spain	Portugal
El precio de un beso English: *One Mad Kiss*	Palacio, September 4, 1930	Renacimiento, July 27, 1933	Princesa, March 26, 1932	Barcelona: Capitol, September 6, 1930 Madrid: San Miguel, November 17, 1930	
Cuando el amor ríe		Rex, March 21, 1931	Iris, September 27, 1933	Barcelona: Capitol, January 2, 1931 Madrid: Royalty, January 5, 1931	February 1, 1932
Hay que casar al príncipe		Colonial September 9, 1931	Cine Teatro Municipal de Lima, November 10, 1932	Madrid: Callao, Sept. 21, 1931 Barcelona: Fantasio, October 17, 1931	March 9, 1932
La ley del harem		Colonial, Grand Splendid, May 11, 1932	Iris, November 30, 1933	Barcelona: Kursaal, November 26, 1931 Madrid: Avenida, February 23, 1932	
Mi último amor English: *Their Mad Moment*		Rex, November 23, 1932	Iris, Capitol, May 5, 1934	Madrid: San Carlos, September 26, 1932	November 2, 1932
El caballero de la noche		Rex, March 23, 1933		Barcelona: Capitol, December 21, 1932	May 3, 1933
El rey de los gitanos	Teresa, Granat, Venecia, Parisi-ana, Rívoli, March 3, 1934	Ariel, March 21, 1933	Excélsior, July 13, 1935	Barcelona: Kursaal, May 23, 1933	December 12, 1933
La melodía prohibida	Teresa, Granat, Venecia, Parisi-ana, Rívoli, June 23, 1934	Colonial, March 14, 1934	Excélsior, September 10, 1935	Barcelona: Capitol, December 21, 1933	May 28, 1934
La cruz y la espada	Goya, Teresa, Odeón, Rialto, Monumental, Granat, Edén, Venecia, Parisi-ana, Rívoli, May 3, 1934	Ariel, May 4, 1934	Excélsior, May 4, 1935	Barcelona: Cataluña, February 26, 1934	May 18, 1934
Un capitán de cosacos	Palacio, February 7, 1935	París, March 29, 1935		Barcelona: Cataluña, September 28, 1934 Madrid: Capitol, October 8, 1934	December 6, 1934
Las fronteras del amor	Palacio, August 15, 1935	Azul, June 13, 1935		Madrid: San Carlos, December 24, 1934	February 13, 1935

José Mojica and Anita Campillo, in *La cruz y la espada* (1934, Frank R. Strayer, Miguel de Zárraga).

Other documented screenings in Latin America included: *El precio de un beso,* Buenos Aires: Renacimiento, August 14, 1930; *Cuando el amor ríe*, Havana, Cuba: Neptuno, February 8, 1931; Buenos Aires, April 14, 1931; *Hay que casar al príncipe*, Havana, Cuba: Rialto y Prado, September 7, 1931; *Un capitán de cosacos,* Buenos Aires: Renacimiento, August 29, 1934.

José Mojica's films met with considerable success in the Spanish-language North American market. All eleven of Mojica's Fox films were screened in Los Angeles's Mexican theatres, including *La cruz y la espada*, which was reprised more than eight times between 1934 and 1941. In this regard, it is also interesting to note that six of Mojica's early titles are not known to have been screened in Mexico City, although one of them, *La ley del harem,* also enjoyed eight runs in Los Angeles between 1931 and 1938, many at the old Hidalgo Theatre.[13]

A CASE STUDY: *LA CRUZ Y LA ESPADA*

A good example of the cinematography in these movies is *La cruz y la espada,* which we will analyze below. Directed by Frank R. Strayer, the film starred Mojica and Anita Campillo (the good girl from *Cuesta abajo*), a California-born actress with Spanish heritage. It is one of a small number of films from the Hispanic film production that has been preserved. Made with the participation of director Miguel de Zárraga, the plot can be considered very Latin, due to its religious background, and the noticeable confrontation between good and evil.

Brother Francisco (José Mojica) has taken holy orders due to a love deception, and now educates children, takes care of the sick, and supervises wine production, produced by Native Americans in a California Franciscan monastery. The friar's best friend is a passionate young man, José Antonio (Juan Torena), whose main goal in life is to find gold and be able to get married to his girlfriend, Carmela (Anita Campillo), since he cannot ask her to share his poverty ("she deserves the best of the world"). Francisco is concerned the hunt for gold may bring trouble to his mission. Mónica, Carmela's aunt, is against the relationship between her niece and José Antonio, who goes searching for the gold that will allow him to buy Las Flores property for his bride to be, hire servants, and purchase a buggy. On the other hand, Francisco is worried, because the bandit called "El Mestizo" and his gang are hiding near the monastery. Francisco, dressed as a civilian, joins a crew carrying flour for farmers and witnesses the gang's attack on the village. With a group of Indians he manages to save the beautiful Carmela from "Mestizo," who is released upon the condition that he return to the holy mission. The bandit swears revenge. Carmela calms down, since "she's not used to get kidnapped." She is grateful to Brother Francisco, and develops a great admiration for his fortitude, his courage and love for life, and she doesn't understand how he could give up the secular world. Francisco confesses he "got tired of life," because of a woman, singing, she was "full of grace, like Hail Mary."

13 See the contributions of Violeta Núñez Gorritti and Jan-Christopher Horak in this volume.

The melody was inspired by a poem of Nayarit native Amado Nervo, which had been one of Mojica's musical successes for RCA. This sequence seems to be an allusion to the famous painting *Retrato de Joaquina Candado,* by Francisco Goya, one of a series of iconographic references to classic Spanish paintings.[14]

Later, Francisco brings groceries to José Antonio and his mates at the mine in the heart of San Blas. He reports that "El Mestizo" has emptied the village's cantina, and was about to take Carmela; he also delivers a letter from Carmela, explaining her side of the story. In the village's celebrations, Brother Francisco leads a *jota* dance and sings a song ("Así nació California, flor de México y España"). Afterwards, the friar sees Carmela dancing, his eyes reflecting his illusions, but regretfully walks away, when he realizes the older women of the village are eyeing him, as had the monastery's abbot, who realizes everything. Confused and alone, Francisco sings to Carmela and sees her reflection on the water; now she looks like the Virgin Mary, making him have doubts about his religious vocation. Worried, Carmela's aunt reproaches her for her relationship with Francisco, but the young woman stands up for herself, saying she is only grateful to him since he saved her life.

Returning to the monastery after visiting the mining camp, Francisco hides in a cave to escape a storm. This is an excellently filmed sequence: in the dark, his own torso appears over his shoulder, perfectly lit from below, showing his baser instincts. His torso says: "Fool! Punish yourself like this, you are a man, be a man!" He then remembers his encounters with Carmela, when he saved her and had her in his arms: "I should have kissed her, she is beautiful, lovable, she could be yours." He questions his vows of poverty, obedience and chastity, but then finds gold in the cave.... Besides several El Greco paintings, this sequence takes us directly to the genius of Francisco de Zurbarán, who captured the apostles and monks at the moment of being tempted by the devil. The rain, symbol of nature and instincts, stops. Francisco leaves, praying to God to keep him away from temptation. He sings as bright clouds shine on him. A beautiful landscape of rocks and clouds, sky and earth seem to reconcile the future priest.

Back at the monastery, Francisco's letter tells José Antonio where the gold is. José Antonio, who never gets Francisco's letter, comes back triumphantly carrying the gold, but stares with suspicion at Carmela, who he believes has cheated on him with his best friend. José Antonio stabs Francisco in the hand, and the friar asks to be stabbed "in the heart." José Antonio realizes that it all has been a misunderstanding and that his beloved has never cheated on him. Carmela arrives with the two men pretending nothing has happened, saying José Antonio had come to ask Francisco to sing at their wedding. In the last excellent sequence, we see how order returns. José Antonio and Carmela get married, while Francisco sings "Hallelujah" for them and for himself, showing his conscience is quiet and at peace.

14 The author thanks painter Carlos Vidal for his help with the accurate identification of paintings referred to in some key scenes in *La cruz y la espada*.

Although the film is in many ways conventional, we have to acknowledge its aesthetic achievements, thanks to the previous experience of the director, Frank R. Strayer (Altoona, Pennsylvania, September 21, 1891- February 3, 1964, California), creator of silent films, like the dramatic thriller *The Lure of the Wild* (1925), produced by Columbia Pictures. He also directed the comedy *Just Married* (1928), starring James Hall, Ruth Taylor and Harrison Ford, produced by Paramount Pictures. Strayer, who had directed Mojica on three previous occasions (*El rey de los gitanos, La melodía prohibida* and *Las fronteras del amor*), took advantage of *La cruz y la espada* to demonstrate an extraordinary visual sense: several shots reveal elaborate compositions, e.g., the celebration of Mass, the encounter of Francisco with Carmela that utilizes the religious symbolism of the "Hail Mary", or the mountain landscapes (recalling some paintings of Joaquín Mir, Daniel Vázquez Díaz, Benjamín Palencia and Ignacio Zuloaga, capturing a clear pantheistic perspective), the skies and palms surrounding the monastery, the robbery of the village by "El Mestizo" and his gang, and Carmela's kidnapping. In keeping with the musical genre, the plot allows the leading man to sing whenever he has the chance; that was what the audience wanted from him. As noted, Mojica's role presaged real life, when years later he became a priest in the Franciscan Order.

The influence of co-director Miguel de Zárraga is seen in the staging of a Spanish environment, e.g., the wine harvest which recalls paintings like *La vendimia* by Francisco de Goya, or *Vendimiando Jerez* by Joaquín Sorolla; the special care in sowing the soil, the *jota* dance which references *El baile de los magos* and *La gallina ciega,* both by Francisco de Goya, or *Grupo de Lagarteranos, Jota de Aragón* and *El baile* by Sorolla; the bar, which doesn't allow indigenous Randull to enter (a critique of racism). Furthermore, the emphasis on the heroism of Franciscan priests, who civilized the indigenous people of California, without oppressing them.

Mojica became one of the big four Mexican stars of Hollywood cinema, next to Dolores del Río, Lupe Vélez and Ramón Novarro. He competed in the Hispanic musical cinema with Carlos Gardel, the famous "Zorzal criollo", who filmed eight successful pictures in those same years. Hispanic movies from the Fox Film Corporation owed a big part of their success to Mojica, who continually appeared on the top lists of male stars, whether the actor played a highwayman in London, a Cossack in Russia, a prince of Arabia, the bandit Turpin or a priest. Besides, the Mexican actor wrote several songs for his movies, with the purpose of having a more "genuine" Mexican flavor for the Hispanic audience they were meant for.

About *La cruz y la espada*, Mojica would say he was overwhelmed by "the sympathy of lots of people who didn't see him as a movie actor. In Mexico, where a hard fight for religious freedom was being waged, this movie was taken very well."[15] The film premiered in ten cinemas in Mexico City in early May 1934, the most tumultuous period of the Cristero Rebellion, which ended in 1938, once the Lázaro Cárdenas government was installed. It seems that Strayer's film had no major repercussion in Mexico City, where it was only

15 See José Mojica, *Yo pecador* (Mexico, D.F.: Editorial Jus, 1956).

screened for a week, but Mojica's success increased in cinemas across Mexico, where religious beliefs had more influence, and the rebellion had a more negative impact than in the capital city.

In conclusion, we can point out that Hispanic films starring Mojica presaged his later Mexican films. They gave the Jalisco native singer the opportunity to develop his histrionic and musical talents: *El capitán aventurero* (1938, Arcady Boytler) and *La canción del milagro* (1939, Rolando Aguilar). By that time, Hispanic cinema was in decline, while Mexican cinema was on the rise, due to World War II restrictions and the acceptance of Hispanic audiences. In other words, Mojica was one of the many talented actors who would help Mexican cinema achieve its status as the most solid and influential cultural industry in the Ibero-American world.

Conchita Montenegro in Hollywood: Reception and Performing Style

Núria Bou

The Spanish actress Conchita Montenegro starred in ten Spanish-language film versions and took part in seven original Spanish-language titles in Hollywood from 1930 to 1935. Hailed as the Spanish Greta Garbo, she was one of the few actresses who, after working in the world's film mecca in the first years of the sound era, pursued a career in French and Italian films and finished her film career back in Spain. She starred in her last film in 1944, and disappeared without explanation from the public eye shortly afterwards, imitating the mysterious retirement that Garbo herself had pulled off three years earlier.

Conchita Montenegro is also remembered for her nude scene in the French production *La femme et le pantin* (1929, Jacques de Baroncelli), for being the first Spanish actress to triumph in Hollywood, and for starring in some of the most significant films of the Franco era. My analysis in this essay will focus on the first part of her filmography: from the silent period through to her Hollywood sound films (1929 to 1935). In particular, I will examine Conchita Montenegro's acting style in the films she starred in, beginning with *La femme et le pantin*[1] and including the seventeen pictures she made in Hollywood. By means of a textual and comparative analysis, I will tease out how the American performing style influenced the actress' filmography. Parallel to this, I am also interested in exploring the effect this influence had on the reception of the star in Spain.[2]

Surprisingly, the film *La femme et le pantin* was screened in Spain in January 1931 (under the title *La mujer y el pelele*), while the country was still under the dictatorial government established by Primo de Rivera. The picture was promoted as a "cultural film," but as it was a silent film, it went unnoticed among the new "talkies." It received very little publicity, no newspaper or film magazine making mention of the actress' nude scene. Nothing was written about the eroticism of the scene, in which Conchita Montenegro appears first as a shadow, dancing suggestively, until she moves into the light to reveal her breasts and buttocks. At the end of the scene there is even a full-frontal nude

1 Prior to this film, she had acted in very small roles in the Spanish films *Rosa de Madrid* (Eusebio Fernández Ardavín, 1927) and *Sortilegio* (Agustín de Figueroa, 1927).

2 This research has been supported by a Salvador de Madariaga grant from the Spanish Ministry of Education, Culture and Sports. This grant covered the cost of a stay in Los Angeles, to do research at the UCLA Film & Television Archive and the Margaret Herrick Library. The article is part of the Ministry of Economy and Competitiveness research project *"El cuerpo erótico de la actriz bajo los fascismos: España, Italia y Alemania (1939-1945)"* ["The Erotic Body of the Actress under Fascism: Spain, Italy and Germany"] (CSO2013-43631-P).

shot reflected in a bottle of champagne, while she continues to dance for an all-male audience. After such a daring performance, how did Conchita Montenegro end up becoming one of the female icons of Francoism? There can be little doubt that *La femme et le pantin* was not released in the United States because of the nude scene, which was far too explicit. How did Hollywood producers channel the sex appeal of this actress in a pre-Hays Code era characterized by efforts to suppress the depiction of sexuality?

I will show here that the promoters of Spanish cinema facilitated an erasure of the actress's "indecorous" beginnings, despite the fact that Hollywood producers had signed her to represent temptation, seduction and female sensuality in English-speaking films, in roles depicting Latinas or extroverted European women. As David Bordwell suggests, eroticism in the films of classical Hollywood cinema was constrained by a principle of "decorum"[3]. For this reason, its producers cast foreign actors to portray characters that could be more sexually provocative. From Pola Negri to Marlene Dietrich, from Rudolph Valentino to Maurice Chevalier, the characters played by these European actors could be more erotically daring because they came from very different cultures, and in their ethnic/racial "otherness" they could subtly transgress the moral limits that the censors had begun imposing[4]. Although Conchita Montenegro embodied a feminine sensuality that only foreign women could portray, the Spanish actress did not greatly "dramatize" her characters in her spoken roles in English: there was very little exaggeration in her performances, in contrast with other European actors who normally represented "otherness:" "their difference from their American counterparts has frequently been expressed in terms of an overtly 'theatrical' performance style"[5]. Conchita Montenegro could represent sensuality, but—adopting an American acting style—she toned down her performances in Hollywood to mitigate the eroticism she had embodied in *La femme et le pantin*.

THE AMERICAN PERFORMING STYLE

Restraint is what characterizes classical cinema, especially in the films of the 1930s. Representations of sexuality, violence, and certain social issues could only appear on screen, if they were presented to the spectator indirectly. Metaphorical language took over classical cinema. On the other hand, as David Bordwell shows, the narratives of the films of these years were very clearly and precisely structured. Telling a story well and as transparently as possible was the main objective of most Hollywood films. Just as this "classical transparency" theoretically erases the director's signature, the actors, ruled by the objective to appear realistic—and to avoid obscuring the meaning of the plot—steered clear of melodramatic gestures. Moreover, Bordwell demonstrates that with the arrival of sound, the speaking of the actors resulted in performances that were "less mobile; in using voices to signal the characters' feelings, [the actor] plays down facial expression and bodily movement"[6].

3 David Bordwell, Janet Staiger and Kristin Thompson, *The Classical Hollywood Cinema: Film Style and Mode of Production to 1960* (London: Routledge, 1988), 3.
4 Alastair Phillips and Ginette Vincendeau (eds.), *Journeys of Desire: European Actors in Hollywood* (London: BFI, 2007), 15.
5 Ibid.
6 Bordwell, 542.

The American (or classical) performing style, which according to Roberta E. Pearson[7] began to be established in D. W. Griffith's films from 1908 to 1913, shifted away from the theatrical expressiveness that drew from the catalogue of gestures popularized by François Delsarte in the 19th century. Griffith needed to define a *realist code* in contrast to the melodramatic poses that looked too histrionic on the movie screen. Nicole Brenez astutely notes that this "American performing style seemed to France's first avant-garde to be an example of simplicity, truth and freshness, which Louis Delluc and Jean Epstein contrasted with the academic theatrical style of French actors".[8]

It is obvious that Jacques de Baroncelli was familiar with the American style when he directed *La femme et le pantin*. Although the film included Expressionist and European elements in the *mise-en-scène*, it also took the Hollywood classical system into account: the close-up shots of Conchita Montenegro—with a studio lighting typical of the glamorous close-ups of Hollywood's first great actresses—reflect the influence of this style, while also highlighting the indisputably photogenic qualities of the Spanish starlet. The historians René Jeanne and Charles Ford, in their book *Le Cinéma Français*, define Jacques de Baroncelli as a director with "French spirit and culture" who liked to surround himself with "international elements."[9]

What I find interesting here is that in *La femme et le pantin,* Conchita Montenegro exhibits one of the most widespread practices among actors in classical cinema: expressive restraint at the most dramatic moments. A noteworthy example of this is the scene in which Don Mateo (Raymond Destac) discovers his lover Concha Pérez (Montenegro) dancing naked, and marches up to her in a rage: the actress is shown in close-up, holding Don Mateo's gaze almost without blinking, with no effort to portray surprise, bewilderment or fear in her facial expression. Similarly, there are moments in the film when Conchita Montenegro behaves—and is filmed—in a manner typical of a Hollywood star. For example, she wanders through the gardens of Don Mateo's great mansion in a style evocative of Greta Garbo, with highly restrained gestures and an extreme elegance, glamorously displaying her dress with a low-cut back.

Montenegro also reveals a more playful use of gestures in the scene in which she visits Don Mateo's house and reacts like a little girl amazed by the luxurious rooms of the great mansion: the comic nature of this reaction recalls the charm of Hollywood silent film actresses like Marion Davies or Clara Bow. This shouldn't surprise us: as Titty Soila suggests, stardom enters into a dialogue with modes of representation and European cinematic styles imitate—or distance themselves from—the great Hollywood system[10]. Even in France, Conchita Montenegro had already begun flirting with the American style; but it would be in Hollywood—with the roles she played in multiple-language version films—that she would finally embrace a classical acting style.

7 Roberta E. Pearson, *Eloquent Gestures: The Transformation of Performance Style in the Griffith Biograph Films* (Berkeley: University of California Press, 1992).
8 Nicole Brenez, "Retos disciplinares, politicos y ontológicos del gesto: poética del actor," in Fran Benavente and Salvadó Glòria (eds.), *Poéticas del gesto en el cine europeo contemporáneo* (Barcelona: Intermedio, 2013), 299.
9 Charles Ford and René Jeanne, *Histoire Encyclopédique du Cinéma: Le Cinéma Français 1895 1929*. Vol. 1 (Paris: Robert Laffont, 1947), 386.
10 Tytti Soila (ed.), *Stellar Encounters: Stardom in Popular European Cinema* (New Barnet: John Libbey Publishing, 2009), 3.

Photograph by Hal Phyte

CONCHITA MONTENEGRO

Conchita Montenegro, portrait in *The New Movie Magazine,* December 1931. Photo by Hal Phyfe.

THE CLASSICAL PERFORMATIVE MODEL IN THE MULTIPLE-LANGUAGE VERSIONS

With the arrival of sound, Hollywood producers feared losing their non-English speaking audiences and signed actors from various different countries to make multi-language versions based on English-language originals. This was how Conchita Montenegro began her career in the world's film industry mecca: imitating American actresses, internalizing the *restrained* classical style. The Spanish star performed in five Spanish-language versions in Hollywood:[11] *Sevilla de mis amores* (1930, Ramón Novarro), *¡De frente, marchen!* (1930, Edward Sedgwick), *En cada puerto un amor* (1931, Marcel Silver), *Marido y mujer* (1932, Bert E. Sebell) and *Dos noches* (1933, Carlos F. Borcosque). Below, I will analyze the films *En cada puerto un amor* and *Marido y mujer* in relation to their respective original versions, *Way for a Sailor* (1930, Sam Wood) and *Bad Girl* (1931, Frank Borzage).[12]

In both Spanish-language films the scenes follow the same order as the original versions,[13] using the same dialogues translated directly into Spanish. The sets, props, costumes and music are also identical to the originals. The sequencing is not replicated exactly, although the same extreme close-ups and even many of the same wide shots are inserted. The two films are thus very close to their respective originals. However, the final effect is not the same. In both cases, these films were shot in fewer days; the lighting is weaker and the sound less even; the dialogue is not well adapted and the phrasing often sounds theatrical and unnatural.[14]

As far as the performances are concerned, most of the Hispanic actors[15] in these two productions imitate the gestures of their American counterparts. It is obvious that the performers were given very precise instructions on how to play the scene. In this respect, it is interesting to note that Conchita Montenegro not only reproduces the more obvious gestures of Leila Hyams in *Way for a Sailor* and Sally Eilers in *Bad Girl,* but even mimics certain little details of their performances: in *En cada puerto un amor,* for example, she imitates subtle movements like pressing the palms of her hands together or nervously patting down her dress.

---

11 Apart from these Spanish-language versions she also starred in two remakes: *Su última noche* (Carlos F. Borcosque, 1931), a remake of *The Gay Deceiver* (John M. Stahl, 1926), and *Hay que casar al príncipe* (Lewis Seiler, 1931), a remake of *Paid to Love* (Howard Hawks, 1927).

12 Copies of the films are available at the Archive Research and Study Center, the UCLA Film & Television Archive, and Filmoteca Española. According to Heinink and Dickson (1990), *En cada puerto un amor* was filmed in November and December of 1930 at the M-G-M Studios, and *Way for a Sailor* was released, according to IMDb, on 1 November 1930. The production dates for the M-G-M production *Bad Girl* were 1 June to 4 July 1931, while *Marido y mujer* didn't begin shooting until October 1931, shortly after the release of the English-language version on 13 September 1931.

13 In the case of *Marido y mujer,* the film omits one initial scene that serves as a kind of prologue, and shortens three scenes, where in the English-language version some children appear playing with the protagonist in the street. In *En cada puerto un amor* the number of scenes is the same.

14 For a detailed exploration of the dialogues and accents of the different actors who performed in the Spanish-language versions, see Lisa Jarvinen, *The Rise of Spanish-Language Filmmaking. Out from Hollywood's Shadow, 1929-1939* (New Brunswick, N.J.: Rutgers University Press, 2012). A critical reading of the playwrights who worked on these versions can be found in José Antonio Pérez Bowie, *Materiales para un sueño: En torno a la recepción del cine en España, 1896-1936* (Salamanca: Librería Cervantes, 1996) and Manuel Rotellar, *Cine español de la República* (San Sebastián: Festival Internacional de Cine, 1977). See also Román Gubern, *Raza :Un ensueño del General Franco* (Madrid: Ediciones 99, 1977).

15 In a supporting role in the film *Marido y mujer,* Rosita Granada tries for a comic register with a variety of popular Spanish expressions that bear no relation to the original character played by Minna Gombell in *Bad Girl.* She is an exception in these two films, although actresses like María Fernanda Ladrón de Guevara, Catalina Bárcena and Rosita Díaz Gimeno tried to inscribe a more genuinely Spanish oral and physical style in the Spanish-language films they made in Hollywood.

In keeping with the American film production standards, Conchita Montenegro employed the classical style with its restrained use of gestures. In some scenes, she even tones down the dramatic level of her emotions more than the original actress. For example, in *En cada puerto un amor*, Montenegro reacts in anger when the handsome sailor kisses her unexpectedly, but her rage is less visibly expressed than that of Leila Hyams: while the American actress, on opening the front door for him to leave, points with a tense hand towards the threshold, Montenegro moves towards the same door without expressing her anger with any other body movement.

Moreover, at the end of the same film, when the female protagonist watches anxiously while her beloved rushes off to an act of suicidal heroism on the high seas, we see Conchita Montenegro unwaveringly impassive in a single medium shot that is repeated four times: her suffering is made explicit through the analytical editing, with a neutral gaze and no specific facial expression. Because she knows that the American editing style requires expressive restraint, Montenegro does not reproduce the emotion with theatrical grimaces of pain: her performance here is even slightly more neutral than Leila Hyams.

The reduction of facial expressions and physical gestures is a constant throughout both these Spanish-language versions, as is the total suppression of the actress' sexuality. Significantly, in *Way for a Sailor* the only moment of sensuality portrayed by Leila Hyams is in a scene in which she is walking with the protagonist (played by John Gilbert) to the sea. The sailor walks behind her and stops for a moment to look at her. Leila Hyams, standing slightly above him, turns around and sees him contemplating her body. The wind presses her dress against her, blowing the fabric sensually around her groin, and in reaction to his admiring comment ("What a figure!") she covers the lower part of her torso with her hat. The scene still has a subtly erotic flavour: the setting, the wind, the flowing hair, the dress billowing around the female body and their poetic conversation all serve to generate the amorous chemistry typical of classical cinema. In the Spanish version, however, this scene is quite different. The seaside setting is replaced with a public park that is anything but bucolic, and there is no wind. The character played by José Crespo gazes at her in the same way and makes the same admiring comment, but the scene is cut down to an exchange of phrases that, without the wind or the sea in the background, prove utterly ineffective in expressing the mutual attraction between the protagonists.

Film historian Lisa Jarvinen suggests that most foreign-language versions were more daring than their English-language counterparts. The producers allowed the films targeting foreign markets to be more sexually explicit, transgressing the classical canon established by the domestic censors. But this does not appear to be the case for the surviving Spanish-language versions featuring Conchita Montenegro, as in these films she portrays women who are domesticated, chaste and morally irreproachable.

SPANISH RECEPTION

The Spanish-language versions made in Hollywood by Conchita Montenegro received no attention in Spanish film magazines, nor did her Spanish-language productions with original scripts, the exception being *Sevilla de mis amores*. None of the star's other films received as much publicity as this picture. Montenegro's face appeared on the cover of an issue of the magazine *Popular Film* (1931), which also contained a full-page photograph of the actress. In the same magazine, nearly a month later, the reporter Mario Arnold continued praising the film and interviewed the star in a two-page promotional spread with three photographs. The film was publicized as "the first Spanish film on a Spanish subject and with Spanish characters, spoken in our language and written in Andalusian" (*La Vanguardia*, 1931). Taking into account that film production was almost non-existent in Spain in 1930 and 1931, it is not surprising that the film would be so highly acclaimed.

But critical praise in Spain for Hollywood's multi-language versions gradually dried up. It is evident that Conchita Montenegro's subsequent films were not welcomed by promoters of Spanish cinema, who were concerned about the state of their local industry. In *Hay que casar al príncipe, En cada puerto un amor* and *Marido y mujer*, the actress portrayed a Parisian, a Londoner and a New Yorker, in Hollywood plots that erased the actress' nationality. Spanish critics wanted films and actors that contributed to the construction of a Spanish imaginary[16]. Conchita Montenegro's American performance style was at odds with the cinematic ideology of the moment. This explains why, after the "homage to Spain" (*La Vanguardia*, 1931) that was *Sevilla de mis amores*, Montenegro all but disappeared from the Spanish film industry press, with one notable exception being Mario Arnold's article in *Popular Film* in April 1932, repeating rumours circulating in the press: "Conchita Montenegro doesn't want to be Spanish", a headline that introduced an article containing sensational statements like "Conchita Montenegro renounces her homeland [...] renounces her mother."

AMERICAN RECEPTION

In the United States, Hollywood's Spanish-language productions were generally relegated to the background, deemed of interest only to Spanish-speaking markets. However, *Sevilla de mis amores* was publicized in American magazines. *Picture Play* (1931) dedicated an entire page to the star, with two photographs: one of her in Sevillian dress, but with tight shorts, and another—much bigger—wearing futuristic underwear that had very little to do with Ramon Novarro's film. The article began with the phrase: "CONCHITA MONTENEGRO! There's zip and fire, lure and languor in that name!"

One month later saw the release in the United States of *Strangers May Kiss* (1931, George Fitzmaurice), starring Norma Shearer, with Montenegro shining in a supporting role, thanks to a dance in which she introduces flamenco gestures over tango music. The sensuality of the actress' dancing and the way she approaches the male lead—embracing him despite the fact they have never met—introduces a type of foreign character that was permitted such eccentricities. In *Never the Twain Shall Meet* (1931, W. S. Van Dyke), *The Cisco Kid* (1931, Irving Cummings), *The Gay Caballero* (1932, Alfred L. Werker), *Laughing at Life* (1933, Ford Beebe), *Hell in the Heavens* (1934, John G. Blystone), and even in her supporting role in *Handy Andy* (1934, David Butler), she continued to portray daring, uninhibited young women who would dance and easily seduce the male protagonists.

16 Marta García Carrión, *Por un cine patrio: Cultura cinematográfica y nacionalismo español (1926-1936)* (Valencia: Publicacions de la Universitat de Valencia / PUV, 2013).

American magazines praised the actress' beauty and sensuality that the Spanish-language versions had suppressed. In this same era, she was publicized in photographs where she posed in skimpy clothing. Paradigmatic examples include the snapshot of Montenegro dressed as a Mexican woman that filled a whole page in *The New Movie Magazine* (1931) and her picture on the cover of *Picture Play* (1932): in the first, she is wearing a very open blouse and looking defiantly at the camera; in the second, she has on the same blouse and a pair of tight red shorts.

Indeed, her photographs were more daring than her films. Although she embodied the Latina or European woman as a "sexualized other," her appearances were restrained and exhibited none of the daring of *La femme et le pantin*. There was, however, one exception: *Never the Twain Shall Meet*, released in Spain in 1933 under the title *Prohibido* ("Forbidden"). In *Never the Twain Shall Meet*, Montenegro portrays Tamea, a native Pacific Islander presented in revealing outfits and with a long mane of hair, playing an accordion while singing animatedly on the roof of a boat. Leslie Howard portrays the businessman from the big city who falls instantly for Tamea's beauty and spontaneous manner. This spontaneity generates comedic value in the scene where the girl arrives at the businessman's mansion with an attitude rather similar to that described above in *La femme et le pantin:* Tamea enters the house of Dan (Leslie Howard) and, amazed by the modern wonders that surround her, begins fondling the objects in the house with great amusement. Dressed in loose-fitting clothes, she plays the accordion and moves her hips to the sound of a celebratory song: Conchita Montenegro, without theatrical exaggerations, is able to convey the childish nature of a character who repeatedly attempts to smother the male protagonist in kisses.

The comic qualities of the character do not mitigate the intensity of a subsequent scene in which the protagonists kiss, revealing to the spectator the profound attraction they feel for one another: the close-ups of Tamea before the first passionate kiss between them—with lighting that softens the excitement in the actress' eyes—demonstrate that Conchita Montenegro had mastered the melodramatic romanticism of Hollywood classicism perfectly.

Between comedy and melodrama, Conchita Montenegro portrays the most daring role of her Hollywood filmography in this picture, not only because of her risqué wardrobe but above all because of the vampiric relationship she has with her lover (which again recalls the role she portrayed in *La femme et le pantin*). Far from exposing the full-frontal nudity of her French film (but with a notably more intense eroticism than the restrained sexuality of her roles in other English-language films), *Never the Twain Shall Meet* led one critic for the *Motion Picture Review* (1931) to warn: "It is likely, however, that adolescents would be too much affected by its sensual appeal at the expense of the moral involved." Conchita Montenegro exhibited her sex appeal as a foreign woman with significant success in the Hollywood press in *Never the Twain Shall Meet* and *The Cisco Kid*. However, although she received more critical acclaim in the United States than in Spain, her later titles were not as warmly received, and in 1934 she stopped acting in English-language films in Hollywood.

RECLAIMING A NATIONAL STAR

Surprisingly, in 1934—in the period known as the Conservative or "Dark Biennium" (*bienio negro*) of the Second Republic—Conchita Montenegro unexpectedly began receiving recognition as a Spanish success abroad. This was surprising because at the time Spanish critics were promoting the films that would begin the so-called "Golden Age of Spanish Cinema." At the end of 1933, the Spanish film scene began to change, thanks to the box-office success of local productions, and the star power of the actress Imperio Argentina. For the first time in the history of Spanish cinema, audiences were flocking to domestic productions that offered familiar stories set in their own country. Conchita Montenegro had obviously remained outside these developments, which the Spanish press was so keenly celebrating and praising. The actress's sensuality in France and Hollywood could not be celebrated in the conservative and religious context of commercial cinema under the Republic, as Román Gubern has noted.[17] Moreover, Montenegro's performing style was completely at odds with the attempt to build a uniquely Spanish cinematic tradition. And yet, in the magazine *Popular Film* (9 August 1934), a two-page spread was dedicated to the actress, with photographs and the headline "A Spanish Woman in Full Triumph." The article affirmed that Spaniards were proud of her successes in Hollywood and that it didn't matter that Conchita Montenegro had wanted to become Americanized, because "she could never forget her homeland." Suddenly, within a few weeks, other magazines would be acclaiming the actress as the elegant Spanish woman who had triumphed in Hollywood. In the magazine *Cinegramas* (September 1935), her upcoming wedding to Raúl Roulien was announced. The article also mentioned that she would be returning to Europe. A week later, in the same magazine, Montenegro would declare in relation to her marriage: "in our love there are no affairs or scandals. Everything is upright, proper and honest. It's a Spanish-style wedding." In this way, the new acclamation of Conchita Montenegro promoted her as a strait-laced "human star," conservative and morally irreproachable.

However, as the report in *Cinegramas* illustrates, her sex appeal was completely elided. Under the headline "The Star, Her Mother, and Her Husband" (1935), Montenegro is shown wearing an elegant suit jacket, in a totally sexless pose, representative of how she would be shown in her later films in the Franco era. The reporter makes no reference to any films, or to the actress's work, and certainly not to her "American" acting style. The story is the triumph of the domesticated woman off-screen.

None of the other stories published about her at this time make any mention of the nude scene in the French film or the praise she had received for her sensuality in Hollywood. Their sole focus was on applauding the fact that "Spain" had conquered Hollywood. The "Dark Biennium" paved the way for a new image for Conchita Montenegro, which the Francoist film industry instrumentalized after the Civil War. The extroverted and self-assured attitude she had displayed in her more daring Hollywood films would disappear; however, paradoxically, in her Francoist films she would continue to use the basic American performing style that she had learned in the Spanish-language versions.

17 Gubern, Román, *El cine sonoro en la II República (1929-1936)* (Barcelona: Lumen, 1977).

Antonio Moreno: The Star Who Returned to Spain without Leaving Hollywood

Mar Díaz Martínez

In June 2014, I arrived at the Cinematic Arts Library of the University of Southern California, where archivist Ned Comstock told me I was the first person to ask about Spanish actor and director Antonio Moreno. This was not the first time I had heard that. Ned had prepared seven previously unopened boxes for me. When I saw their content, I was overcome with tears: there, were the original scripts of *The Benson Murder Case/El cuerpo del delito* (1929), *The Bad Man/El hombre malo* (1930), *The Cardboard City/La ciudad de cartón* (1934), *The Cat Creeps/La voluntad del muerto* (1930), *Those Who Dance/Los que danzan* (1931), *One Mad Kiss/El precio de un beso* (1930), *Primavera en otoño* (1932), *Rosa de Francia* (1935), *Storm Over the Andes/Alas sobre el Chaco* (1935), *¡Asegure a su mujer!* (1935) and *Señora casada necesita marido* (1933). All lost movies, except the last three. There were the scripts of the first two Mexican sound films, directed by Moreno: the mythical *Santa* (1932), starring Lupita Tovar, and *Águilas frente al sol* (1932). As far as I know, they are the only originals that exist. There also was the script of *Maria de la O* (1936), the only project Antonio worked on in Mexico. I have never found original materials from this film. Furthermore, I found his personal scripts, annotated, underlined, with notes on costumes, drawings, the pages bookmarked with envelopes with his address. Why had no one ever asked for Antonio Moreno? How is it possible that the achievements of this professional had been buried for so long, despite working five decades, having made 150 films, and being a true pioneer? Let´s review his career:

Antonio Moreno was born in Madrid, Spain, on September 26, 1887. In 1910, Moreno began acting in theatre repertoire companies, touring the United States. He was twenty-three years old, had lived in the United States for eight years, was very attractive and did well in small roles. He learned fast and from the best: he performed alongside Maude Adams, Mrs. Leslie Carter, Constance Collier, Tyrone Power Sr., and many more. He even played Shakespeare with E.H. Sothern and Julia Marlowe. But one day Antonio had a problem with a director, because he mispronounced a word. He was fired and tried his luck at the movies, a new medium that would not require an impeccable accent. His looks were perfect for the camera, which clearly fell in love with him. He started as an extra with director D.W. Griffith, no less. Among his first shorts, filmed in 1912 and directed by Griffith, are *The Musketeers of Pig Alley,* considered the first gangster film, and *An Unseen Enemy,* a melodrama starring the Gish sisters. In both, we can distinguish the handsome Antonio perfectly among the extras. In 1915, he was already a leading man in dozens of films at Vitagraph, becoming famous. At the end of the decade he starred in several serials, keeping up an incredible work schedule. The most famous was *The House of Hate* (1918, George B. Seitz), sharing stardom with Pearl White. Shooting at full speed, doing totally irrationally risky scenes, playing the most varied characters, Antonio grew in popularity. By 1921 he was fed up with serials and wanted to star in feature films. He demanded that Vitagraph release him from his contract and decided to work freelance forever: he would never again be tied to a studio by a draconian contract.

The 1920s were amazing. Antonio was the first Latin lover, the romantic heartthrob who played sophisticated Europeans, rude cowboys, alluring swordsmen and melancholic aristocrats with equal mastery. His Latin origin didn't mark him for roles, but it did exert a fascination in the press of the time, which always emphasized his deep black eyes and his olive skin, with headlines like "The Modern Don Juan," "The Spanish Cavalier," "Tony Toreador."

He starred in *My American Wife* (1922, Sam Wood) with Gloria Swanson, *The Spanish Dancer* (1923, Herbert Brenon) with Pola Negri, *Mare Nostrum* (1926, Rex Ingram) with Alice Terry, *The Temptress* (1926, Fred Niblo) with Greta Garbo, *Beverly of Graustark* (1926, Sidney Franklin) with Marion Davies, *Madame Pompadour* (1927, Herbert Wilcox) with Dorothy Gish, and in 1927 he received his most definitive qualifier: Elinor Glyn, the writer who invented the term "It," said that the only actors who had "It" in Hollywood were Clara Bow and Antonio Moreno, so Paramount right away produced a film with that title, *It* (1927, Clarence Badger), starring the couple. On the personal side he couldn't do better: In 1923, Antonio married the heiress of an oil magnate, Daisy Canfield, who was educated, sophisticated and belonging to California high society. Together, they built a mansion high on a hill near Silver Lake, rivaling the golden couple of Pickford and Fairbanks as hosts of Los Angeles' most desirable parties. Antonio was at the top. What could go wrong?

I spoke at the beginning of Antonio's erasure from cinema history. I have come to the conclusion that one reason is the simplified way in which his career has been described with two oft-repeated but false notions: (1) Antonio Moreno was one of many Latin lover types, imitating Rudolph Valentino, and (2) His career ended when sound arrived, due to his accent. Regarding the first, we have seen that when Valentino became famous in 1921, Antonio already had many years of fame and dozens of films behind him. With regard to the second, there is much to say. There are many factors to consider: his age at that moment, his professional motivations, the accent (but for the opposite reasons), his unfulfilled dream, the enormous changes that the industry suffered and, of course, the arrival of cinema spoken in Spanish. Let's see how a career that was solidly established changed convulsively and definitively in just five years.

In 1930, Antonio turned forty-three years old. His appearance had changed. He had been in front of the cameras for eighteen years, playing all sorts of characters, and needed new challenges. He was ambitious, creative, always seeking to experiment, to grow. Tired of being the romantic protagonist, he wanted to go deeper. He wanted to play other characters, be the antagonist, explore new ways of performing. He was aware that younger actors were more likely protagonists and he would soon play only supporting roles. But there was something else: Antonio had a dream: to direct. He felt that he should appear less before the camera and express his creativity in another way. Directing was his next goal.

Is it possible that, as has been said, Antonio had a Spanish accent so strong that it condemned his career? I don't think so: Antonio was born in Madrid in 1887 and lived in Andalusia (in the South of Spain) during his childhood and adolescence. He went to the United States when he was only 15 years old, so by 1930 he had been speaking English for twenty-eight years. Language impacted Antonio, especially in the 1930s. In this important career moment, he decided to participate in Spanish-language film productions. Antonio was a poor emigrant who triumphed, an illiterate child who fulfilled the dream of becoming a Hollywood star, someone who embodied the American Dream. The emigrant always remains a bit nostalgic, so he just couldn't say no to working in Spanish. Between 1930 and 1932, more than 100 films were filmed in Spanish in Hollywood. That required a large number of Spanish speakers at all levels of production, precipitating a migration of professionals from Spain and Latin American countries. Antonio Moreno played a crucial role, because he knew everybody in Hollywood, functioning as a cohesive force. At the same time, Antonio's fame made him a sure-value box-office draw. In addition, being bilingual, he could play the same role in English and Spanish versions.

Antonio received offers to star in the first Spanish versions of four studios: Warner, Fox, Universal and Paramount. For Paramount, in March 1930 he filmed *El cuerpo del delito* (1930, Cyril Gardner), the Spanish version of *The Benson Murder Case*, a film based on one of the Philo Vance detective novels. Antonio played the murderer, his role taken by William Boyd in the English version. The film was very popular, but Antonio was criticized for speaking Spanish with a strong American accent, although his performance was highly praised.

In his first Fox film, Antonio had a great opportunity. *One Mad Kiss* (1930, Marcel Silver), filmed in April, was based on the story of Lola Montes with a script by Dudley Nichols. The protagonist in this successful musical was José Mojica, while Antonio was billed third in credits, again playing the villain. Antonio, according to Juan B. Heinink and Robert G. Dickson in *Cita en Hollywood*, also worked as an adviser for director Silver. But this first step went wrong. The filming was suspended because Mojica had to fulfill his contract as a singer at the Chicago Opera. The director was fired, while Fox waited for the return of Mojica months later before reshooting with another director, James Tinling. It was a tremendous blockbuster. The Spanish version, *El precio de un beso,* was filmed with the same actors, allowing Fox to reduce costs. But the critics hated the different Spanish accents: Mexican (Mojica), Argentine (Mona Maris), Castilian Spanish (Moreno). Baltasar Fernández Cué, who was preparing *El hombre malo* (*The Bad Man*, 1930, William McGann), adapting the dialogue into Spanish for Warner Bros., wrote about Antonio in *World Cinema* in July 1930:

> Moreno is today one of the most attractive figures among all the actors who work on the screen in Spanish. According to him, however, that debut was one of the hardest tests of his artistic career: "Do you want to believe that I was afraid to speak to the microphone in my own language?" Antonio

> Moreno told me naively. Antonio was studying his own language with Spanish advisers, but in *El hombre malo* Antonio had to play a Mexican bandit, dressed as a charro. He took the opportunity to explain that "I made the bad man speak in a language that, while revealing the humble origin and the Mexican character of the role, presents him in a form that cannot but please the sensible Mexicans and will not displease non-Mexicans." Antonio Moreno has already put himself in the hands of a Mexican instructor to learn the accent with which he must say his role.

Despite all the warnings, *El hombre malo,* directed by William McGann in May 1930, was a sad example of how little Hollywood producers understood the intended market for these films, according to Lisa Jarvinen in *The Rise of Spanish-Language Filmmaking;* they succeeded in offending a lot of cultural sensibilities, although the film was a box-office success.

In July and August 1930, Universal's first Spanish-language production was filmed: *La voluntad del muerto* was directed by George Melford at night, while Rupert Julian directed the English version, *The Cat Creeps,* by day. Antonio Moreno and Lupita Tovar starred, beginning a very close friendship. Lupita recalls in her memoirs that "I was especially excited to meet Antonio Moreno. He had not practiced his Spanish for a long time and always looked at me when his dialogue was difficult." In August-September 1930, Moreno made *Los que danzan* (*Those Who Dance*) for Warner-First National, directed again by William McGann, with Spanish dialogue by Baltasar Fernández Cué. Antonio got very good reviews.

Here, we come to a turning point in Antonio's career. Juan de la Cruz Alarcón, distributor of Universal films in Mexico, decided to produce the first Mexican sound film. His choice was to adapt the novel *Santa* by Federico Gamboa. Together with journalist Carlos Noriega Hope and others, he founded the National Film Production Company and proposed the lead role to Lupita Tovar. She accepted and when they talked about finding a director who had experience and spoke Spanish, the name of Antonio Moreno arose and Lupita approved it. Antonio was very popular in Mexico, so that was a great promotion for *Santa*.

The proposal he had been waiting for had finally come. It was a good moment. It seemed that Hollywood was never going to give him the opportunity to direct, so he said yes right away. But conditions were a challenge: Antonio did not intervene in the script, written by Noriega Hope, nor in the casting. When he arrived in Mexico City, he found that the studio where he was to shoot was an old silent film operation with glass walls and ceilings, thus without any soundproofing; they had to put mattresses and blankets up to cushion against outside noise. The sound equipment was a prototype designed by Mexican engineers, the Rodríguez brothers; there was no budget for props or costumes, so actors brought from home what they could. But everyone on the crew was aware that they were making history. Antonio was under a lot of pressure and he had to shoot at full speed for less than a month, with many human and technical limitations.

The story of *Santa,* a poor young woman, seduced and abandoned by a soldier, who ends up working as a prostitute in Mexico City, finally expiating her sins with a pious death, was a great success. Supported by an immense publicity campaign, orchestrated by Carlos

Trade advertisement for *El precio de un beso* (1931, Marcel Silver, James Tinling) with José Mojica, Antonio Moreno, Mona Maris.

Noriega Hope, who was the director of *El Universal Ilustrado*, a Mexican literary journal, *Santa* premiered on March 30, 1932, with the President of the Republic in attendance. Called "the first national film," it was the beginning of a whole subgenre in Mexican cinema.

Antonio immediately began shooting another film, which was the opposite of *Santa*. *Águilas frente al sol* (1932) was written by Gustavo Sáenz de Sicilia, one of the owners of the National Film Production Company. The plot followed the line of *Mata Hari* (1931, George Fitzmaurice), which had recently premiered, and other American films involving sophisticated and exotic locales with sexy international spies. Shot quickly and released on July 13, the cosmopolitan atmosphere did not attract attention, so the film failed at the box-office. Before the premiere of *Águilas*, Antonio had already returned to Hollywood. He was in Mexico for only six months, but left a great mark.

Antonio did not work in Hollywood until December 1932, when Fox decided to make Spanish-language movies with original scripts. During 1933, 1934 and 1935, a new Spanish-language film was released in New York every week. The Hispanic machinery worked to the max. Antonio chose *Primavera en otoño* (1933, Eugene Forde), written by Gregorio Martínez Sierra and José López Rubio, starring Catalina Bárcena. Then they would make more movies together.

In February 1933, Daisy and Antonio decided to separate for a time and five days later Daisy died in a traffic accident. Antonio was greatly affected by Daisy's death. He did not return to work until October for Fox's *La ciudad de cartón* (1934, Louis King), with a plot by Gregorio Martínez Sierra, adaptation by José López Rubio, and again starring Catalina Bárcena. It received very good reviews. The Fox films of these years were remarkable; Fox was the only studio to still trust its Spanish department, fighting on for a long time, even with difficulties.

The two films Moreno next filmed with Fox are the only ones that survive; both are sophisticated comedies, without Latin connotations. The first, *Señora casada necesita marido* (1935, James Tinling), utilized the same lead actors as his previous film. Antonio was described as an "excellent actor" in *Cine-Mundial* and the film was highly praised. The second film was adapted by Jardiel Poncela; *¡Asegure a su mujer!* (1935, Lewis Seiler) is a delightful sex comedy.

At the beginning of 1935, all staff at Fox saw their salaries reduced by half, according to Lisa Jarvinen. The Spanish department was eliminated that summer when, due to financial problems, Fox and Twentieth Century merged. *Rosa de Francia* (1935, Gordon Wiles) was the last film made in Spanish by Fox. Adapted by José López Rubio, the script offered a mordant view of some royal characters in Spanish history. The cast was headed by Rosita Díaz Gimeno, Julio Peña and Antonio Moreno.

After Fox ended Spanish productions, others continued. Universal produced its last double version: *Alas sobre el Chaco/Storm over the Andes* (1935, Christy Cabanne), a film set in the war between Paraguay and Bolivia, in which Antonio worked again with his friend Lupita Tovar, playing the same character in both versions.

Finally, Spanish-language cinema in Hollywood came to an end. Antonio got a part in a movie, *The Bohemian Girl* (1936, James W. Horne, Charles Rogers), starring Stan Laurel and Oliver Hardy. Before the production wrapped, the actress Thelma Todd died; the film shows very clearly that her disappearance affected the narrative, especially with regard to her character and Antonio's. When the producers called Antonio to shoot new scenes to try to save the film, he wasn't available, damaging his standing in the film.

But Antonio had a new contract, traveling to far-off Spain. Director Francisco Elías was determined that Spanish cinema achieve international rank, hiring López Rubio to write the script for *María de la O* (1936), with José Luis Salado, based on a play and a very popular song of the same title. They decided to hire a Hollywood star and Antonio said yes. The role was perfect for him: an Andalusian painter who falls in love with a gypsy and marries her. The gypsy family kills her and, after killing the murderer, he disappears. Years later, he returns an elegant, rich man who has made his fortune in the United States. This was actually the only character in Antonio's career whose accent was exactly his.

Shot in Andalusia, Antonio enjoyed the bullfights, visited his mother, and befriended the great dancer Carmen Amaya, who played his daughter. His stay in Spain was an event; since his arrival in January 1936, the press had followed him everywhere. But filming was a disaster. The first day of production in Barcelona, a fire destroyed the studio; when they arrived in Seville, the river overflowed. Antonio was struck by appendicitis, returning to the United States in May, after finishing filming, just a few weeks before the Civil War began. The film could not be released until November 1939, and didn't receive good reviews. Antonio never returned to Spain.

Hollywood had changed, and nothing was as he knew it. He felt displaced and did not work for a while. In 1938, he made a semi-Hispanic film for Monogram Pictures, *Rose of the Rio Grande* (William Nigh), which premiered in Spain eight years later as *El nuevo Zorro*. Once again, playing the villain who dies at the hands of the hero, Moreno received third billing.

Antonio's decline can be measured by viewing the drop in his wages during the years he made films in Spanish Hollywood: for *El cuerpo del delito,* he earned $6,000 for less than two weeks of work. For *El hombre malo* he earned $2,000/week for four weeks of filming. In the mid-30s, in the Fox original productions, his salary was already below $1,000. And finally, *Rose of the Rio Grande* earned him $750/week.

According to Lisa Jarvinen, Antonio made his transition not from silent actor to talking actor, but from silent actor to Spanish film actor. This transition almost ended his career. His roles in the films he made between 1939 and 1944 are forgettable. In most he had a line or two and usually played a Mexican or an Indian. In some films, his character disappeared on the editing room floor.

In 1945, he returned to Mexico and announced that he had a contract with Clasa Films Mundiales for five films: three as an actor and two as a director. His plans were frustrated again: he only made *Sol y sombra* (1946, Rafael E. Portas), in which he played an old

Andalusian bullfighter turned cattleman in Mexico. He returned to Hollywood to work as a supporting actor in good adventure films, like *The Spanish Main* (1945, Frank Borzage), *Captain from Castile* (1947, Henry King) and *Dallas* (1950, Stuart Heisler).

The 1950s came and with them the rebirth of Antonio's career. Hollywood's most interesting directors demanded him: Richard Brooks in *Crisis* (1950), Anthony Mann in *Thunder Bay* (1953), Jack Arnold in *Creature from the Black Lagoon* (1954), Raoul Walsh in *Saskatchewan* (1954) and John Ford in *The Searchers* (1956).

He played small but important roles, the films benefitting from the performance of Moreno, who aged well on the big screen. A 1953 *Thunder Bay* story said: "Older viewers will be thrilled to see Antonio Moreno, the beloved idol of the silent screen, playing his role with real authority. Moreno is still handsome, still a great actor and one wonders why he has not been seen more often on the screen."

In John Ford's *The Searchers*, Antonio and John Wayne meet in a bar and share a toast in Spanish. The dialogue is not in the script, so it's easy to imagine that they improvised the lines.The same toast is said in his last film by his best friend, Gilbert Roland. It's a movie that can only be seen in two American archives. It was filmed entirely in Cuba in 1958 by a production company that went bankrupt, before it could be released. In *Catch Me If You Can* (1959, Don Weis) Antonio plays Roland's mentor, the man who taught him everything, which was the case in real life.

Antonio didn't act again. He died in 1967 in his Beverly Hills house, at age seventy-nine. In the history books, Antonio Moreno's name always appears as a marginal note. But, if we collect all the mentions of Antonio, joining them patiently, as in a puzzle, the results are impressive. Sometimes you have to get off the beaten path and look at what has been left in the margins of the history of cinema. There are many treasures to discover, like Antonio Moreno.

An intertitle introducing Antonio's character in *The Spanish Dancer* (1923), says: "Spain knew Don César as a daredevil and carefree noble for whom gold was made to play with, and life was nothing more than a stage for the impulsive adventure."

I like the quote for Antonio. His life was really a great adventure, he was a pioneer in many respects, making his way through the dead ends that arise in cinema's complicated path. If we look at his career from that perspective, running through the history of cinema from 1912 to 1959, it is of importance. Its two very distinct phases, hinged at the moment when his homeland brought him his mother tongue, the language of his childhood; as an émigré who missed his country of birth, he could not help but accept it with all its consequences. This part of his life is kept in some boxes in a library in Los Angeles, forgotten dreams of lost movies that deserve to be known. Antonio Moreno: The star who returned to Spain without leaving Hollywood.

Competing against Hollywood: A Case Study, *Contrabando*

Eduardo de la Vega Alfaro

I.

Towards the end of June 1929, pioneer Guillermo ("Indio") Calles—originally from a Sonora family related to the famous politician/soldier Plutarco Elías Calles—began production of *Dios y ley* (1930, Guillermo Calles) in Hollywood, later adding sound elements.[1] The film represented maybe the most meaningful case of a strategy of Mexican filmmakers looking to take advantage of Hollywood's production facilities, in order to establish a national cinema, once the most violent phase of the Mexican revolution had ended. The film's plot was located in southeastern Mexico, so the California locations had to resemble as much as possible typical sites in Oaxaca, where the love story between a native (played by Guillermo Calles) and a beautiful young woman of Latin ancestry takes place. It was one of the paradoxical ways Mexican cinema tried to compete against Hollywood, which had almost total control over Hispanic screens, given the lack of film industrial development in Latin American countries.

According to *Cita en Hollywood,* by Juan B. Heinink and Robert G. Dickson, the overwhelming presence of Hollywood cinema on Spanish-speaking screens reached its apex in 1931. During that year, Hollywood studios completed a total of forty-three Spanish-language features, one medium-length film, and five short films. Their clear commercial strategy was to combine various themes and genres, creating a Spanish "Star System" that included numerous actors from Spain and Latin America. In retrospect, the sheer quantity reveals that producers of so-called "Hispanic" cinema were confident about the acceptance of their films in Spanish-speaking countries, because these had traditionally been their "natural markets."

At the beginning of that peak year for Hispanic cinema, the California Theatre in Los Angeles started to exhibit a series of six one-reel documentaries, titled *Viajes de Bernal a México* (1930), which accompanied the releases of Hollywood's Hispanic films: *La llama sagrada* (1931, William McGann), *El último de los Vargas* (1930, David Howard), *Don Juan diplomático* (1931, George Melford), *La carta* (1931, Adelqui Millar), *Los que*

1 To find about the life and work of this particular person, consult Rogelio Agrasánchez Jr., *Guillermo Calles. A Biography of the Actor and Mexican Cinema Pioneer* (Jefferson, N.C.: McFarland & Company, 2010), 185.

danzan (1931, William McGann) and *El valiente* (1931, Richard Harlan). We can assume that the California Theatre specialized in releasing Spanish-speaking films, funded by big Hollywood companies, such as the Fox Film Corporation, Paramount Pictures, Universal and Warner Bros.[2] On the other hand, the short films, exhibited between January 30 and March 6, 1931, had been produced and directed by Mexican filmmaker and journalist Alberto Méndez Bernal. According to an article in the *Los Angeles Times* (March 6, 1931), the short films formed a "journey documented by a photographer from Metro-Goldwyn-Mayer, showing a route through some of the most interesting cities from Mexico." Méndez Bernal apparently collaborated with the aforementioned Hollywood studio or took a cameraman employed by them. Quoting the film's advertisement in *La Opinión* (February 20, 1931), *Viajes de Bernal a México* was a "colorful journey," and at the same time "the chronicle of Mexico's evolution," that included images of a "pilgrimage to the sanctuary of Our Lady of Guadalupe," revered by Mexican Catholics. In an interview with the author, Mrs. Helena Buelna, daughter of a famous revolutionary soldier for Francisco Madero and Pancho Villa, Rafael Buelna Tenorio, stated that she had seen the films, defining them as "very pleasant and enjoyable documentaries," which most likely were used to promote the beauty of Mexico's landscapes and traditions, especially in the southern United States. *Viajes* was in fact similar to other travelogue shorts, like *México, país de romance* (1929, Gustavo Sáenz de Sicilia) or *Así es México* (1931, Germán Camus), the latter even being screened for General Pascual Ortiz Rubio, the President of Mexico.

The success of those short films, both touristic and testimonial, probably opened an opportunity for Alberto Méndez Bernal to get involved in a more ambitious project, a full-length film. Assisted by his cousin, Fernando Méndez García (both were from Zamora, Michoacán, and related to the cinema pioneers Pedro and Francisco García Urbizu),[3] Bernal started filming *Contrabando* (1932, Alberto Méndez Bernal, Raymond Wells) in August 1931, with locations in Tijuana (including the Casino and Agua Caliente racetrack), Rosarito beaches, and some other locales. According to later press reports, and some surviving location stills, we can deduce that the footage was of insufficient quality, so many sequences were filmed again, during the first days of March 1932. It is also possible that the production had to be suspended in August 1931, before resuming a half a year later. The fact is that in mid-June 1932, *La Opinión* and other publications in the Mexican capital began publicizing the film's upcoming release.

Indeed, *La Opinión* (September 11, 1932) published an image, taken when the film's production wrapped. In the picture, we can see among members of the crew and staff, actors Dorothy Sebastian, Ramón Pereda, Don Alvarado, and Virginia Ruiz (the last three were outstanding performers of Hispanic films), in addition to Alberto Méndez Bernal and Fernando Méndez García. At the center of the picture is General Agustín Olachea Avilés (1890-1974), who had taken the position of Governor of Baja California Norte, just before the release of *Contrabando*. In a note accompanying the image, some of the plot was revealed: ... "based on historical events [...] a group of foreign conspirators in Baja California try to raise a rebel army; the plans go well, until a 'Love' matter gets in the

2 See Jan-Christopher Horak's essay in this volume for a history of the California and other Mexican cinemas in Los Angeles.
3 Cf. Eduardo de la Vega Alfaro, *Fernando Méndez (1908-1966)* (Jalisco: Universidad de Guadalajara, 1995), 237ff .

way, and then things start to take a different direction [...]." Also announced in the same publication was the fact that "all of Tijuana's garrisoned troops [...]" had participated in the filming, and that the film showed "how an attempted rebellion against the government was foiled, before the government could end the affair!"

According to Mrs. Helena Buelna, who met Fernando Méndez García shortly before the filming of *Contrabando,* and married him after working as script girl on the film, General Avilés was one of the financial investors. Today, it seems clear that he was probably the film's real promoter, because of the part he had played in squashing the rebellion, led by José Gonzalo Escobar in March 1929, against the interim government of Emilio Portes Gil, following the 1928 assassination of Álvaro Obregón who had been elected President again. Olachea Avilés had previously participated in the famous Cananea Strike of 1906, considered a precursor to the 1910 Revolution that overthrew the dictatorship of Porfirio Díaz Mori. He also signed the Plan de Hermosillo, published on March 3, 1929, in the capital of Sonora. That document reviled Plutarco Elías Calles, who had become the strongman of national politics after Obregon's assassination, and who in the Plan de Hermosillo document was identified as "the Jew of the Mexican Revolution." He had supposedly placed "one of his puppets, one of his instruments, one of the members of his entertainment world," into the Presidency by establishing what would become the Partido Nacional Revolucionario (PNR), the distant predecessor of the current Partido Revolucionario Institucional (PRI).

Genral Olachea Avilés was ordered by the federal government to the town of Naco, Sonora, where he signed the Plan de Hermosillo, which was also signed by a number of important soldiers and politicians who were not happy with the possible re-election of Obregón; they believed in the feasibility of a new dictatorship, like that of Porfirio Díaz Mori, which lasted for thirty years until 1911. Actually, the *escobarista* rebellion started just when the PNR was holding its constituent assembly in Querétaro. However, the armed revolt of approximately 30,000 men proved to be disorganized and erratic, which is why some of the leaders and promoters, including Olachea Avilés, decided to betray the cause and remain loyal to the federal government. As a reward for his faithfulness, Olachea Avilés was promoted to Brigadier General and, furthermore, designated the Governor of Baja California Norte on November 7, 1931, a position he held until September 6, 1935, except for the brief interlude of two weeks—from August 18 to September 8, 1932—during which Arturo M. Elías had provisional authority over the area.

Thanks to the film's script, preserved for many years by Fernando Méndez's family, to which I had access, we can deduce that the film had a typical love story and not a few family melodrama elements, besides political intrigue and armed conflicts. The story begins with the reading of a letter, in which the provisional President Emilio Portes Gil requests that the American authorities stop trafficking arms over the border, thus benefitting the rebels, led by Escobar. In the film, the villain is named Hernández, a character clearly inspired by the brilliant politician Gilberto Valenzuela, an Escobar agent in the United States, whom Escobar himself had planned to promote to the Presidency, in case the attempted coup actually managed to overthrow the government. According to the film's biased perspective, the diplomatic relations between Mexico and United States were in harmony, which wasn't totally true in those days; a climate

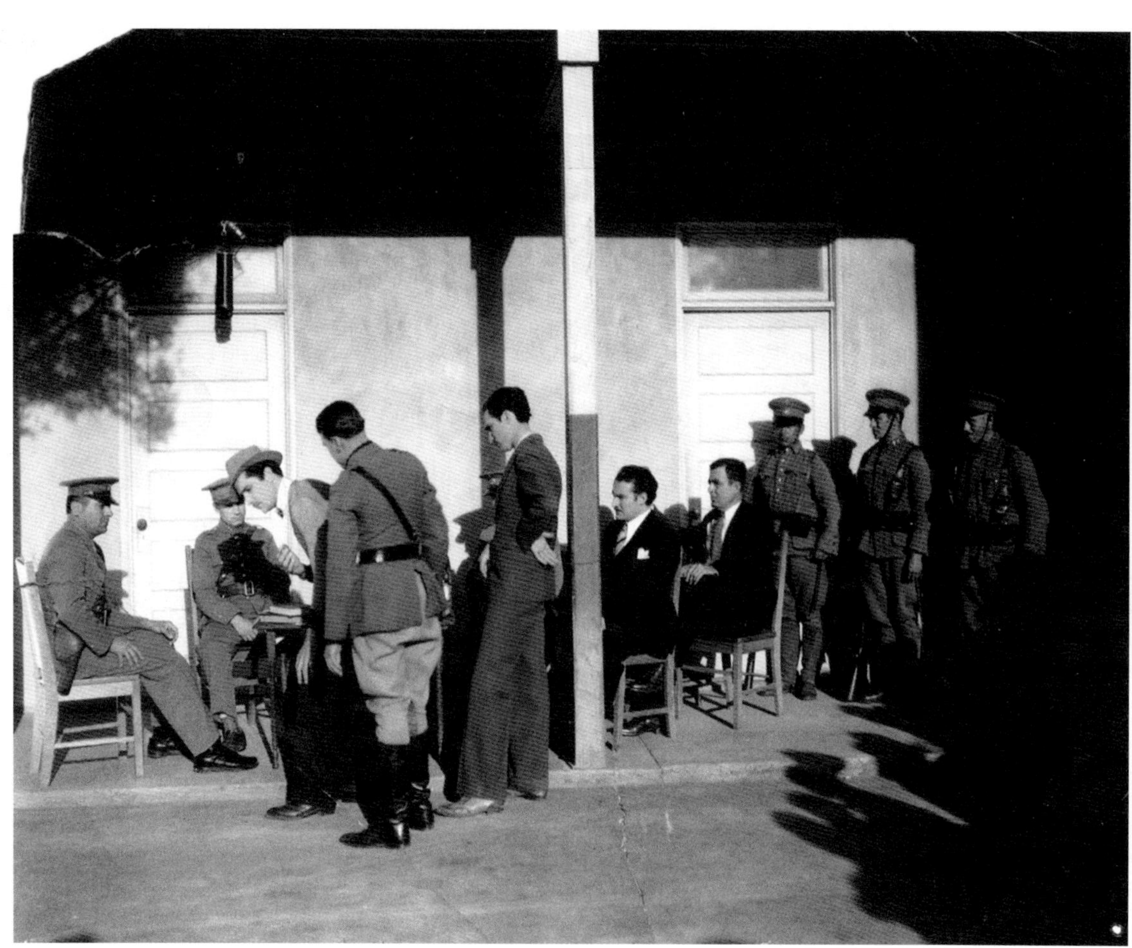

Don Alvarado (with a hat), actor, Fernando Méndez, Ramón Pereda and others during production of *Contrabando* (1931-1932).

of strong political tension existed in 1932, due to the violent expulsion of a large number of Chinese from Mexican territory, many of whom crossed the border to go to California, Arizona, Texas and New Mexico.

Thanks to the film's script, we know that *Contrabando* consisted of six parts. The adaptation and the dialogue are attributed to Fernando Méndez, direction to Raymond Wells, cinematography to Jack Foqua and directing assistance to Robert Farían. Previously, Wells had directed at least seven films, among which we can highlight the four released sequentially in the Mexican capital, starting in April 1918: *El terror* (1917, *The Terror*), *La llama del amor* (1917, *Love Aflame*), *El héroe del día* (1917, *The Hero of the Hour*) and *Mr. Donald en Nueva York o El campeón* (1917, *Mr. Dolan of New York*), produced by Universal Films through their Red Feather Photoplays subsidiary.[4] For the making of *Contrabando*, Bernal hired someone with previous experience who was known as director in Mexico. On the other hand, we know that the film's sound system was rented by Dwain Esper, future filmmaker of exploitation films, like *Maniac* (1934) and *Marihuana* (1936), both today considered cult films. Fernando Méndez collaborated as a make-up artist on the latter titles; he then became a director of excellent Mexican horror films, like *Ladrón de cadáveres* (1956) and *El vampiro* (1957).

II.

According to incidents mentioned in the script, we can reconstruct the film's plot: An honest young man, Carlos, who works as a bellboy at the Hotel Casino in Agua Caliente, is unfairly accused of trafficking arms to anti-government rebels. Carlos works hard, barely sustaining his blind mother, Doña Mariquita, and fulfilling the desires of his girlfriend, Lolita, a "good-looking, flirtatious" girl with whom he sometimes walks on the beach. José, Lolita's brother and Carlos's friend, intervenes so that Carlos is cleared of involvement in the arms deal. A report from a repentant José, who had actually participated in the arms trafficking, allows the capture and death of the rebels, led by Hernández, who was interested in Lolita and had originally accused Carlos.

Several testimonies published about *Contrabando* point out that the film was made in two versions, Spanish and English. The film script has numerous directions for camera angles, shots of objects, hands, faces, etcetera, with only a few lines of dialogue; it is a typical film treatment, primitive in sound and production. Thanks to surviving documents and testimonies, we can deduce that Don Alvarado played Carlos and Ramón Pereda played the important role of Hernández. Dorothy Sebastian played the part of Lolita for the English version, while Virginia Ruiz (or Zurí) starred in the Spanish one. Grace Wells (mother of Raymond Wells?) played the old lady portraying Carlos's mother in the English version, while Spanish actress Artemiza Cabezud played the same part for the Hispanic market. Press notes indicate that Alberto Méndez Bernal directed the Spanish version or was co-director of one or both films.

4 See María Luisa Amador and Jorge Ayala Blanco, *Cartelera cinematográfica 1912-1919* (Mexico, D.F.: UNAM, 2009), 108ff.

Contrabando was screened at the Teatro México in Los Angeles on September 14, 1932, which Alberto Méndez Bernal rented. The premiere date was chosen to coincide with the commemoration of Mexican independence (September 16), probably to encourage Mexican nationalism among those who immigrated to the United States. Agustín Olachea Avilés and his political staff were present for this "solemn act." Celebrity guests included José Mojica ("famous Mexican star"), Antonio Moreno ("famous film star", who had already filmed *Santa* and *Águilas frente al sol*, two pioneering movies from Mexico), Dorothy Sebastian ("American movie star"), William Boyd ("acclaimed screen actor"), Don Alvarado, Catalina Bárcena, Paul Ellis, María Calvo, Hilda Moreno, Julio Peña, Raúl Roulien, Carlos Villarías, Juan Torena and Mona Maris, many of them leading stars or minor performers in Hispanic films, who may have wanted to prove with their presence their support for cinema made south of the border.

As we certainly know, the death of Obregón and the defeat of the Escobaristas allowed the consolidation of Plutarco Elías Calles as strongman of the Mexican Revolution, a movement that was considered legitimate, despite frequent power struggles. For its implicit condemnation of the rebels headed by Escobar, *Contrabando* sympathized with the system called "Maximato callista," in which a strongman had power, even above the President and the Union Congress.[5] In making the film, Olachea Avilés apparently wanted to please Calles and all he represented. But both the historical facts and the production of *Contrabando* allow us to consider a different reading: before placing his signature on the Plan de Hermosillo, Olachea had been a spy, an agent for the government who infiltrated the very core of the Escobar organization, contributing to its destruction from within. These maneuvers were ethically questioned in the novel *La sombra del caudillo*, originally published in 1929 by Martín Luis Guzmán. In 1960, the book was adapted for an eponymous film, directed by Julio Bracho. As President of the Partido Revolucionario Institucional between 1956 and 1958, and previously Secretary of National Defense, Olachea Avilés opposed the film, promoting its censorship, so that it remained banned for thirty years, although it was secretly seen by at least a few people.[6]

Thanks to an interview given by Méndez Bernal, published in *La Opinión,* we know that during its two-week release at the Teatro México, *Contrabando* was seen by about 20,000 viewers in Spanish, while the English version was meant to travel to other places in the United States where there were fewer Latinos. This relative success possibly occurred because the film visualized an historical incident on the border between Mexico and the United States that somehow involved the governments of both countries.

During its release in Los Angeles, *Contrabando* shared the Teatro México's screen with a five-part documentary in Spanish, *Lo que vio mi cámara,* which included beautiful "landscapes of the life in Baja California Norte, in Sonora, in Torreón, in Mexico, in Aca-

5 For the sophisticated and complex mechanism of power, see Tzvi Medin, *El minimato presidencial: Historia política del Maximato 1928-1935* (Mexico City: Editorial Era, 1982), 176ff; and, especially, Arnaldo Córdova, *La Revolución en crisis. La aventura del maximato* (Mexico, D.F.: Editorial Cal y Arena, 1995), 552ff.

6 For a full analysis of the process of censorship for this film, consult Eudardo de la Vega Alfaro, *La Revolución traicionada. Dos ensayos sobre literatura, cine y censura* (Mexico, D.F.: UNAM, 2012), 81ff.

pulco and in many other places of our country" (*La Opinión,* September 14, 1932). On a different note, *La Opinión* published an article the following day by author Ernán de Sandozequi, which detailed specific places seen in the film:

> Mexicali, Ensenada, Isla de Guadalupe, Torreón, San Diego's fort in Acapulco, Taxco, Lago de Coyuca, a military stop in the capital of the country, some shots of the Colegio Militar and a final anthem with scenes of a great festival at the national stadium. Dances, songs, *charros, chinas* and... *el jarabe tapatío;* a view of the national pavilion with its tri-color flag waving at the stadium's highest point, under a tropical sky full of light.

The article ends with the recognition of Alberto Méndez Bernal as the film's producer. A different article, published the following day by the same paper, said that the film had been synchronized by the same filmmaker from Michoacán. It is therefore not absurd to assume that *Lo que vio mi cámara* was a re-edited version of *Viajes de Bernal a México,* possibly complemented with footage from a quick incursion into Mexican territory by Méndez Bernal and his cousin Fernando. Indeed, *Contrabando* represented an abundance of cinematic nationalism in the heart of Los Angeles, screened on an appropriate date.

The Spanish version of *Contrabando* was released in seven movie theatres in Mexico City, before February 22, 1933, apparently without the accompanying *Lo que vio mi cámara.* Contrary to its Los Angeles release, it was a complete failure, despite its controversial political nature, which would have resonated with local public opinion. It is still unknown where the English version was screened. It is clear, however, that *Contrabando* followed the formula of Hispanic films by hiring actors who had been outstanding performers in Spanish-version films. Making two versions allowed them to capture a wider market, as opposed to what happened to *Dios y ley.* In that sense, it could compete — despite fewer resources—against Hollywood's Spanish-speaking cinema in the Mexican domestic market. Of course, by 1932 Hollywood Hispanic cinema was in decline, while Mexican film production was just starting up, as it was in other countries, like Spain and Argentina. During 1933, only eleven Hispanic films were produced, plus two short films, which made evident the crisis of this commercial strategy in the Mecca of Cinema.

In conclusion, we can mention the fact that, according to testimony given at the time by Fernando and Rafael Méndez Buelna, the sons of Fernando Méndez García, the latter stored a copy of *Contrabando* for many years. It was supposedly screened in many places in the United States, maybe before García started collaborating with Dwain Esper in 1934. But screenings may have occurred in the mid-1970s, at a point when the recently founded Filmoteca de la Universidad Nacional Autónoma de México already existed, since they had a copy, probably the only one that survived the passing of time. That copy was apparently severely damaged, and subsequently destroyed. But it is fair to say, given all that has been discussed in the previous pages about this irreparable loss, that *Contrabando* has a special place in the history of early Mexican and Latin-American sound cinema.

The Frustrated Career of Celia Villa

Bernd Hausberger

Celia Villa's career is no more than a footnote in film history, but it highlights the possibilities and limitations open to a Mexican woman in the movie industry in the mid-1930s. This essay relies mainly on information found in the daily press, allowing us to get a picture of the representation in the United States of Latina women and Mexican history, but not the real Celia Villa.

Celia Villa was born on January 25, 1915,[1] the result of one of the ephemeral marriages of the Mexican revolutionary, Francisco ("Pancho") Villa. Not much later, her mother, Librada Peña, died. When Villa made peace with the government in early 1921 and retired to the hacienda of Canutillo, near Parral in southern Chihuahua, he brought seven of his children from different liaisons, among them Celia.[2] She never ceased talking about her happy days in Canutillo. She had many friends, private teachers, employees, cars. Pancho was a loving father who took his children to ride horses or to swim, played hide-and-seek with them, and fulfilled all their desires.[3] One of them was going to the cinema in Parral, as Elías J. Torres, one of Pancho's confidants later reported. Her father foresaw a movie career for Celia, since "in all the newspapers that come here, the first thing she looks for are the portraits of the artists and the announcements of pictures."[4] Celia remembered especially her father's farewell when he left for Parral, where he was assassinated on July 20, 1923: "He told us all goodbye and said, 'If I don't see you any more in this world, I'll see you in the next one'."[5]

Celia's idyllic times ended with the death of her father. She first lived with her uncle, Hipólito Villa, in Chihuahua, and on his farm in El Fresno.[6] Later, she lived with some aunts of Villa's mother, then moved to El Paso, Texas, with the wife of Hipólito, where she worked as a maid.[7] Celia was 18 when her life took a new direction. In those days, newspapers reported extensively on the Metro-Goldwyn-Mayer project *Viva Villa!* (1934, Jack Conway, Howard Hawks), probably the first Hollywood production to be filmed in

1 Death certificate issued by the US Consulate in Madrid, www.ancestry.com (consulted 25/05/2015).
2 Katz, Friedrich, *The Life and Times of Pancho Villa* (Stanford: Stanford University Press, 1998), 740; Taibo II, Paco Ignacio, *Pancho Villa: una biografía narrativa* (México City: Planeta, 2006), 694.
3 "Daughter of Pancho Villa gets marriage proposals," *El Paso Herald-Post*, 28 November 1933.
4 Elías J. Torres, "Hijos y esposas de Villa", Mixcoac, 25 February 1935, *El siglo de Torreón*, 3 March 1935.
5 "Daughter of Pancho Villa looks for job in El Paso," *El Paso Herald-Post*, 10 November 1933.
6 Ibid.
7 "Villa's daughter visits New York," *New York Sun*, 9 April 1934; Interview by Eugenia Meyer, 12 July 1973, Archivo de la palabra, PHO/4/10, Dirección de Estudios Históricos (DEH), Instituto Nacional de Antropología e Historia (INAH), México City, 17-18.

Mexico. Shooting started in October 1933, but faced a great deal of resistance, because it was seen as a *gringo*-incursion into Mexican national history. After an alleged offense during a military parade by actor Lee Tracy in early November, filming could only continue after M-G-M publicly apologized and Tracy was dismissed.[8] Due to delays, Jack Conway replaced Howard Hawks as director, while a good part of the cast was also replaced.

At the same time, a young reporter discovered Celia Villa living in El Paso and published an article about her in the *El Paso Herald-Post* (November 10, 1933). The story and her photo were reproduced in newspapers all over the USA. Celia received by mail many declarations of love and offers of marriage. When Irving Pichel, one of the actors who left the *Viva Villa!* project, arrived in El Paso on his way back to the USA, he was asked about a possible movie career for the Mexican girl: "'Miss Villa has the looks,' observed Mr. Pichel. He suggested that Miss Villa be present at the premiere of *Viva Villa!* in Los Angeles three months from now."[9]

The young woman definitely aroused M-G-M's interest. During the film's pre-production, the company sought the participation of Hipólito Villa, Pancho's brother, as well as one of his widows.[10] Plans got more concrete with Agustín, the eldest son of the "Centaur of the North," but they did not come to fruition, due to the young man's mental problems.[11] In the face of difficulties already mentioned, M-G-M resorted to Celia, inviting her to attend the premiere of their film in New York.[12] This publicity stunt turned the orphaned, "jobless and forgotten," "penniless" girl into a short-term celebrity.

However, Celia attracted the attention not only of Hollywood and the press, but also of U.S. Immigration authorities; since she had no legal status, she was deported to Juárez. It took M-G-M several months to arrange her legal re-entry into the USA, signing her up to promote the premiere of *Viva Villa!* in New York and other cities.[13] Her contract gave her a relatively small salary of $35 a week, plus $4 a day for expenses, clothing and transportation, and the incentive to enter the world of film, as M-G-M representative E. B. Coleman pointed out.[14] But, suddenly Celia disappeared, and the rumor spread that she had signed another contract with a border office employee who planned to present her in Los Angeles. The matter was settled after M-G-M slightly improved its offer.[15] It was possibly only a fight about the profits Celia was promised, a "pot of gold that lies at the end of the rainbow;"[16] her disappearance may have been a trick to force the stingy company to shell out more money.[17] Later, it would be said that M-G-M had plotted a

---

8 Louis B. Mayer telegram to President Abelardo L. Rodríguez, Los Angeles, 22 November 1933, in Archivo General de la Nación, Abelardo L. Rodríguez, 545-4, reproduced in the main newspapers of Mexico City.
9 "Villa's daughter gets fan mail, offers of job," *El Paso Herald-Post*, 27 November 1933.
10 *Variety*, 22 August 1933, 63.
11 "Son of famous Mexican rebel chief in films," *Los Angeles Times*, 29 September 1933; "Villa son committed to Norwalk Hospital," *Los Angeles Times*, 2 November 1933.
12 "Villa's daughter gets movie contract," *El Paso Herald-Post*, 31 March 1934.
13 See information in *El Paso Herald-Post*, 10 November 1933, 28 November 1933, 2 December 1933 and 31 March 1934.
14 See details of contract in "Celia Villa spurns offer of $35 week," *El Paso Herald-Post*, 4 April 1934.
15 Later, it was said that Celia had received $50 a week. "Aunt of Celia Villa wonders where she is," *El Paso Herald-Post*, 28 July 1934.
16 Dr. B. U. I. Conner, "The Fence," *El Paso Herald-Post*, 4 April 1934.
17 "Celia Villa goes East on Theatrical Tour," *El Paso Herald-Post*, 6 April 1934.

kidnapping to increase Celia's advertising value,[18] that the whole affair emanated from "a fit of temperament,"[19] or that it was an attempt of "some Mex" to take advantage of Celia's great career about which they fantasized.[20]

Anyway, Celia arrived punctually for the premiere at the Criterion Theatre in New York, on April 10, and then toured Philadelphia, Baltimore, Washington, and several Texas cities, including San Antonio, Wichita Falls, Paris, Austin, Fort Worth, and Amarillo.[21] Celia was involved in a media turmoil whose scope she still had to learn how to handle. When arriving in New York, she was described "as timid as a mouse."[22] "... A reporter came and gave me a lot of publicity," she recounted in retrospect, and "I was so young and scared [...] and they hired me for that *Viva Villa!* movie."[23] At the reception on April 31 at the Willard Hotel in Washington D.C., a reporter showed sensitivity to what that experience must have meant to her:

> [...] a pensive and slightly bewildered young woman completely surrounded by a milling crowd of motion picture executives, newspaper photographers, press agents, radio personalities, news reporters, a few of laity, and here and there a smattering of dramatic editors. [...] Her lack of an enraptured and complete comprehension of the situation might easily be accounted for by the fact that she speaks and understands only a few words of English. Being plumped down into a room full of foreign strangers falls something short of affording the utmost in mental and physical exhilaration, as anybody who has undergone the experience will tell you. [...] she herself stresses the fact that unlike her country women Lupe Vélez, Raquel Torres, Dolores del Rio and the rest, she is neither a singer nor a dancer. She is, however, entirely willing to submit to a public introduction and one suspects nurtures an overweening ambition to become a star of the cinema.[24]

At the end of her contract, however, Celia took destiny into her own hands, deciding not to return to Mexico, but rather to seek her luck in American show business. Celia had some success presenting Mexican songs, notwithstanding the fact that she later would say her nerves prevented her career from prospering: "They just said that I was Pancho Villa's daughter, and I was all nervous and could not sing."[25] After being featured on Rudy Vallee's popular radio show in 1934,[26] she performed the following years in different clubs in New York and other cities.

18 "Celia Villa 'Kidnapping' stunt seen," *El Paso Herald-Post*, 9 April 1934.
19 George Tucker, "Some hot tamale," *The Evening Tribune*, Albert Lea, Minnesota, 18 April 1934.
20 "Along the Rialto with Phil. M. Daly," *Film Daily*, New York, 10 April 1934.
21 "Celia Villa Starts Tour," *Motion Picture Daily*, New York, 28 April 1934, 3; "Releasing *Villa* April 27," *Film Daily*, New York, 24 April 1934.
22 "Bandit Villa's daughter timid as wee mouse," *Indiana Evening Gazette*, Indiana, PA, 12 April 1934.
23 Eugenia Meyer interview, 1973, 18.
24 Nelson B. Bell, "Pancho' Villa's daughter, Celia, is feted in capital," *Washington Post*, 1 May 1934.
25 Eugenia Meyer interview, 1973, 18.
26 Jo Ranson, "Radio Dia-Log," *Brooklyn Daily Eagle*, 2 August 1934.

In contrast, her film career was rather short. On December 28-29, 1934, she participated in a sketch with Carlos Gardel in Paramount's successful revue, *The Big Broadcast of 1936* (1935, Norman Taurog), filmed at Astoria Studios in New York. Gardel was the superstar of the Hispanic cinema and his inclusion in the revue was to introduce him to an English-speaking public, while Celia was a Latino woman with some appeal to that target group.[27] Celia's singing, as director Norman Taurog stated, was one of the ingredients the movie needed, "that strike with pleasure on the general ear."[28] The musician Terig Tucci later remembered that Manuel Peluffo and Carlos Spaventa also participated in the skit. Because Spaventa had to kiss Celia, Gardel played a prank on the young woman, instigating the director to make them repeat the scene five or six times, to the amusement of the staff; clearly there was a lack of today's gender sensitivity.[29] Between the end of January and the beginning of February 1935, Celia participated in another Gardel movie, *El día que me quieras* (1935, John Reinhardt), also filmed in New York and distributed by Paramount. But her part was very small, while her scene in *The Big Broadcast of 1936* was cut before it was released, shortly after Gardel's death in June 1935.[30] So, her movie work ended after a little more than one month.

In 1935, Celia tried to break into the Mexican entertainment industry. Her return to Mexico was far from triumphant. She was hired by the Politeama Theatre Company to present songs and dance numbers that she had famously performed, as was announced with some exaggeration, in the stellar theatres of the United States.[31] What she actually did in Mexico cannot be reconstructed with certainty. It's documented that she took part in *El tesoro de Pancho Villa* (1935), which Russian Arcady Boytler directed. In El Paso, Texas, where Celia had been spotted, film impresario Rafael Calderón promoted the film with her participation.[32] In fact, Celia was not in the movie. Its producer, Felipe Mier, only invited her—along with the whole cast—to a barbecue at a ranch outside Mexico City, where she sang several songs, accompanied on guitar by the popular comedian Arturo Ernesto Manrique Elizondo, alias "el gordo Panseco."[33] But a few days later she left her native country, according to a Mexican daily, disillusioned with her lack of success.[34] American media published another version. They described Celia's return to New York as a relief, after experiencing threats, anonymous letters, and turbulences, all related to her father's controversial legacy.[35] While some applauded her, others saw her as a danger; the government tailed her. The old Villistas allegedly asked her to lead a new revolution, but Celia Villa did not want to be a "Mexican Joan of Arc:"[36]

---

27 Documentation about the production only lists ten musicians and "six extra people," one of them possibly Celia: Letter, Ted Reed to Fred Leahy, Production Manager, New York, 26 December 1934, Margaret Herrick Library, AMPAS, Paramount Pictures production records. 28 f.327: *The Big Broadcast of 1936*.

28 Idwal Jones, "A camera goes a-roving," *New York Times*, 7 July 1935.

29 Terig Tucci, *Gardel in New York*, quoted in Simón Collier, *Carlos Gardel. Su vida, su música, su época* (Buenos Aires: Plaza & Janés Editores, 3rd ed., 2003), 188.

30 *The Film Daily*, 23 January 1935 and 11 February 1935; Collier, 2003, 188-190. Photo of Celia Villa with Gardel, in "Straight from Hollywood," *Boston Daily Globe*, 20 May 1935. The scene remained in the Spanish version, *Cazadores de estrellas*, of which no complete copy has been preserved.

31 "La hija del célebre guerrillero Pancho Villa," *El Nacional*, México City, 12 May 1935.

32 "Celia Villa gets Movie Contract," *El Paso Herald-Post*, 3 July 1935. For Rafael Calderón, see Michelle Vogel: *Lupe Vélez. The Life and Career of Hollywood's "Mexican Spitfire"* (Jefferson, N.C.: McFarland & Company, 2012), 103-104.

33 Hugo del Mar, "Luces y sombras del cine nacional," *Revista de revistas*, México City, 2 June 1935.

34 Luis de Gal, "Noticiario cinematográfico," *El Excelsior*, 29 May 1935.

35 "Had hectic time," *The Evening News*, North Tonawana, N.Y., 20 November 1935.

36 "Report Celia Villa given revolt offer," *El Paso Herald-Tribune*, 6 December 1935.

I went to Mexico simply as a traveller [...]. I didn't know that my father still lived so intensely in the memories of his people—that to many he is yet a god and to a few a devil. I never dreamed of becoming a girl Pancho but some thought that was my purpose. They believed I had come to unite the old Villistas and lead them as my father has done. It was ridiculous.[37]

Back in the USA, Celia went to the Canadian National Exhibition in Toronto, hired by Mexican impresario J. G. del Pozo, along with a group of dancers and singers, to represent the "glamour and the romantic surroundings of Old Mexico."[38] She continued to sing in clubs. In 1939, she performed with her half-sister Alicia (or Panchita) Villa, at the Embassy in Philadelphia.[39] In 1941, she was elected at the Pick Hotel in Youngstown, Ohio, as "the most beautiful warbler to appear in Youngstown within the past year."[40]

In the 1940s, she finally came to Hollywood. After the United States had entered World War II, Celia appeared in March 1943 in a photo with French actor Charles Boyer and Jackson Leighter, a contributor to the Office of the Coordinator for Inter-American Affairs,[41] identified as "a recent goodwill visitor in Hollywood, seeking to improve the already excellent relations between her native Mexico and the United States."[42] Her intentions, however, were to "get into the movies", as she noted in 1973.[43] She pursued casting director Ferdinand A., alias Fred, Datig, a 52-year-old widower,[44] who didn't give her work but married her. The wedding took place on September 6, 1943,[45] but in April the following year, Celia requested the divorce.[46] Her disappointment was still evident in 1973: "He was a casting director of Metro-Goldwyn-Mayer, [...] he was the one who chose the stars for the movies. Of course, he could have helped me a lot, right? But he said, no." She claimed to have lived with Datig until his death in 1951,[47] but Celia probably returned to New York, where she lived at 17 West 64th Street, just one block from Central Park.[48] She possibly acquired her flat as part of her separation agreement with Datig.

News about her continued to appear in the press. On one of her trips in 1944, she stopped in El Paso, where she announced that apart from working in films and nightclubs, she planned to write the "the story of her life that ranges from Mexican farm girl to basking in the lights of New York and Hollywood."[49] She never realized the project, perhaps because the public preferred the adventures of her father, a bandit-revolutionary, to those of his daughter. In September 1949, she appeared in New York together with Al Seigal in a pro-

37 Gordon Gordona, "Mexico too exciting for daughter of Villa," *Berkeley Daily Gazette*, 26 November 1935.

38 *Official Souvenir Catalogue & Programme*, Canadian National Exhibition, Toronto, 23 August – 3 September 1935, 21; "Villa's daughter visits Canada," *Niagara Falls Gazette*, 23 August 1935.

39 "New attractions offered in Phila. Night Clubs," *Philadelphia Inquirer*, 21 July 1939.

40 *Youngstown Vindicator*, Youngstown, Ohio, 4 September 1941.

41 About this organization, see Gisela Cramer and Ursula Prutsch (eds.), *¡Américas Unidas!: Nelson A. Rockefeller's Office of Inter-American Affairs (1940-46)* (Frankfurt/Madrid: Vervuert/Iberoamericana, 2012).

42 *The Milwaukee Journal*, 29 March 1943.

43 Eugenia Meyer, 1973, 18.

44 U.S., World War II Draft Registration Cards, 1942, www.ancestry com (consulted 27/03/2015).

45 See, for example, "Pancho Villa's daughter weds," *New York Sun*, 8 September 1943; "Daughter of Pancho Villa wed," *New York Times*, 9 September 1943.

46 "Pancho's daughter divorces movie mate," *Long Beach Independent*, Long Beach, CA, 4 April 1944.

47 Eugenia Meyer, 1973, 19. Datig died on 11 December 1951; see the *New York Times*, 13 December 1951

48 U.S. Entry document, Laredo, TX, 8 March 1947, www.ancestry.com (consulted 25 March 2015)

49 "Celia Villa visits E. P.," *El Paso Herald-Post*, 21 October 1944.

gram.[50] Later, she wanted to write a book about her father. She always had made statements in defense of him, although only later would she dare to express her displeasure with *Viva Villa!* Her father was "a happy, jovial man. He was not a caricature like, say, the way Wallace Beery played him in the movies."[51] In 1946, a Spanish newspaper announced that three daughters of Pancho Villa, María del Carmen, Alicia and Celia were collecting material for a book entitled *Vida íntima de Pancho Villa*, to clarify the truth about their father and to rectify his bad reputation."[52] In 1948, it was reported that Celia had written a story about Pancho Villa, to be serialized by a Mexican newspaper.[53] It was not until 1955 that Elsevier Press, Houston, announced the publication of Celia's book in English as *My Father Pancho Villa*.[54] The volume was said to be the product of a collaboration between Celia and Oren Arnold, who in 1952 had written a few pages on Pancho.[55] Newspapers cited Celia, saying she hoped to be able to tell "a little of the truth" about her father, whose character had been far from clarified in previous writing and filming.[56]

The revived interest in Celia again originated with a new fiction film about her father, *The Treasure of Pancho Villa* (1955, dir. George Sherman).[57] Unfortunately, Celia's book was not released, due to Elsevier Press's withdrawal from the U.S. market.[58] In 1979, Celia's co-author, Oren Arnold, published *The Mexican Centaur. An Intimate Biography of Pancho Villa*,[59] mentioning Celia only as an informant. In June 1960, Celia was referred to as the author of *Pancho Villa Was My Father*, when she sought—with other relatives of Pancho Villa—to petition the Mexican President to erect a monument to the late revolutionary.[60] In 1973, she summarized her decades-long wish to tell her version of her father's story, testifying to his fight for the people, and against injustice, because "he was of such poor origins, he saw how people suffered." Those plans seem not have been completely idle talk, because she had collected primary sources about the Mexican revolutionary and his struggle.[61]

By then, Celia had become a real New Yorker, as columnist Mel Heimer commented. She taught dance at a Central Park South Studio and worked three hours a day as a hostess at Arthur Maisel's restaurant on Herald Square.[62] She supported her older sister Micaela,[63]

50 Earl Wilson, "It happened last night," *The Delta Democrat-Times*, Greenville, MS, 22 August 1949.
51 Mel Heimer, "My New York," *The Vidette Messenger*, Valparaiso, IN, 28 October 1955; Eugenia Meyer, 1973, 21.
52 Rafael Martínez Gandia, "La hijas de Pancho Villa van a escribir un libro en defensa de su padre," *Los sitios de Gerona*, 17 September 1946.
53 Cholly Knickerbocker, "Ill Pooch Delays Vows," *San Antonio Light*, 17 August 1948.
54 "Hija de Pancho Villa es mesera en Nueva York," *El Tusconense*, Tucson, Arizona, 29 July 1955.
55 Oren Arnold, *Thunder in the Southwest. Echoes from the Wild Frontier* (Norman, OK: University of Oklahoma Press, 1952), 219-226.
56 Heimer, 195.
57 *Premiere*, 10 October 1955.
58 *Publishers' Weekly*, Vol. 172 (1957), 36.
59 Oren Arnold, *The Mexican Centaur. An Intimate Biography of Pancho Villa* (Tuscaloosa, AL: Portal Press, 1979).
60 "Kin of famed Mexican bandit seek monument," *Corpus Christi Times*, 4 June 1960.
61 Eugenia Meyer, 1973, 20-21. See also Guadalupe Villa and Rosa Helia Villa, *Pancho Villa. Retrato autobiográfico, 1894-1914* (Madrid, Spain: Taurus, 2004), 33.
62 Heimer, 1955.
63 Personal information, Dra. Guadalupe Villa Guerrero (17 December 2014).

Celia Villa posing in April 1934

who having divorced in 1952, had moved to the United States with her three children. She also acquired American citizenship.[64] Finally, she moved for what are unclear motives to Spain, where she knew Ernest Hemingway.[65] She died in Madrid on April 20, 2001.[66]

CELIA VILLA AS A PUBLIC IMAGE

Celia Villa was always represented as an exotic other, framed in terms of specific historical, ethnic and female stereotypes. She was defined through her father, whether in her language, the songs she sang, the clothes she wore on stage. It is true that in 1934 Celia hardly spoke English, the American press almost never failing to highlight it:[67] "She knows just one English word. It is 'Okay.'"[68] "She speaks no English, but understands a few words, such as 'love' and 'kisses' and 'okay.'"[69] "In fact, her English vocabulary seems to be limited to a pensive 'hello' and a quiet 'goodbye.'" But in her native tongue, she was perfect."[70] These ironic comments not only mark difference, but also a hierarchy. In addition, they limited her professional possibilities in the United States.[71]

The fact is Celia Villa could not escape being associated in the United States with her father, with all the negative signifiers attached to his actions in the Mexican Revolution, especially his attack on Columbus, New Mexico, in March 1916, and the punitive expedition of General Pershing. Newspapers always defined Celia as the daughter of Pancho Villa, whose figure evoked memories and promised spectacle, action, crime and even sex, because the press regularly emphasized the many wives that he had during his life.[72] Villa was characterized for the readers mostly as a "bandit," "bandit chieftain," "terrorist" or "rebel," thus highlighting his violence and minimizing his political role. Although it seems that later characterization as a revolutionary became more common, the insistence of Celia on the merits of her father could provoke sarcasm in 1955: "Senorita Villa declares Old Pancho was really a Robin Hood and not, as we've been led to believe, a robbin' hood."[73]

Curiously, Celia's ethnicity, although Latina, occasionally placed her close to African-American culture. At the beginning of her *Viva Villa!* promotion tour, Celia visited the preacher Rosa Artimus Horn in Harlem, who in 1929 had founded the Pentacostal Faith Church of All Nations, and in 1934 began to broadcast a much-heard religious radio program for African Americans.[74] In September 1934, Celia performed with the Bama

64 Certificate of Naturalization, 5 December 1955, New York; see Petition No. 666732; www.ancestry.com (consulted 24 March 2015).
65 Howard Jacobs, "Remoulade. Daughter of Villa surfaces in Orleans," *Times-Picayune*, New Orleans, 16 May 1974.
66 Report, U.S. Embassy, Madrid, UU.; http://www.ancestry.com (consulted 25 May 2015).
67 *El Paso Herald-Post*, 31 March 1934; "Celia Villa disappears", *El Paso Herald-Post*, 2 April 1934; George Tucker, "About New York," *Evening Leader*, Corning, N.Y., 11 April 1934; "Some hot tamale," *Evening Tribune*, Albert Lea, Minn., 18 April 1934; Carl Eastwood, "Washington Newsletter," *Evening Tribune*, Albert Lea, MN, 8 May 1934.
68 "Daughter of Villa sees Bandit Film," *Syracuse Journal*, 6 May 1934.
69 "Bandit Villa's daughter timid as wee mouse," *Indiana Evening Gazette*, Indiana, PA, 12 April 1934.
70 "Viva Celia Villa is cry of Wichita Falls," *Wichita Daily Times*, 22 May 1934.
71 "Celia Villa called 'find'," *El Paso Herald-Post*, 18 August 1934; "Celia Villa broke now," *El Paso Herald-Post*, 2 February 1935; "Celia Villa gets job in pictures," *El Paso Herald-Post*, 16 March 1935.
72 For example, "Daughter," *New York Sun*, 9 April 1934.
73 William Ritt, "Your're telling me," *Tyrone Daily Herald*, Tyrone, PA, 2 August 1955.
74 "Pancho Villa's daughter in New York," *Baltimore Afro-American*, 5 May 1934. For Rosa A. Horn, see Antony Appiah and Henry Louis Gates (eds.), *Africana. The Encyclopedia of the African and African American Experience, Vol. 3* (Oxford: Oxford University Press, 2nd ed., 2005), 236-237.

State Collegians (from Alabama State College, Montgomery) at the Harlem Opera House, where in 1935 Ella Fitzgerald would make her first public appearance. Strikingly, of the four times that I found her father identified by newspapers as a revolutionary or patriot between 1933 and 1935, two were in African-American publications (*Baltimore Afro-American*, and *The New York Age*), and one refers to Celia's performance in the Latin club El Gaucho, possibly using the language that its managers used.[75] The Columbus invader had a better reputation in ethnic minority cultures than among white Anglos.

Despite her ethnic affiliation, her participation in the Spanish-speaking films of Carlos Gardel or her performance at the Latin cabaret El Gaucho, Celia Villa usually performed for white audiences, whose expectations of her public persona she had to meet. Celia was, above all, pretty. The first mention of her says: "Celia has a radiant smile, pretty brown eyes, and dimples. She is a brunette and only eighteen."[76] Later she is described as "dark and handsome with a young-mature beauty."[77] An observer in Wichita Falls, Texas, gave the most comprehensive description:

> It's difficult to tell about the senorita. She isn't what is termed beautiful, but she is mighty, mighty attractive. She possesses that what-it-takes-to bring the press to a speedy attention. Her hair is coal black and her eyes are even blacker. They sparkle like black diamonds. She weighs 126 pounds—so she said—and she is around five feet six inches tall. [...] Her dress was—well, it's difficult to remember what it was or what it was like, but who would want to look at her dress when her eyes could be enjoyed.[78]

Celia could in fact be irresistible, as the reporter noted about the reception given to her: "The mayor of the city was not present to present the keys of Wichita Falls, but keys wouldn't be necessary for that girl for those eyes would open any door."[79] Her ethnic ascription was related to a discourse on gender. Consequently, her tongue was erotized and feminized, as Celia spoke in "soft cadenced Spanish"[80] or "soft, throaty Spanish."[81] Her image was saturated with all the elements, sometimes contradictory, of stereotyped women, in general, and Latina women, in particular. Celia was beautiful and exotic, young and shy, she could be used as symbol of fertility,[82] but also be dangerous, like her father. "If there is such a thing as a 'masher' left hanging around the stage doors of New York, they would do well to let Senorita Celia Villa pass with the usual ogle. Her photographs look too much like her father to offer encouragement. Fresh young men are likely

---

75 "Bama State Collegians in Return Engagement at Harlem Opera House," *The New York Age*, 1 September 1934; "This'n' That," *Huntington Daily News*, Huntington, PA, 5 October 1934; "Night Club Notes," *New York Times*, 18 April 1936; also Jonathan Gill, *Harlem. The Four Hundred Year History from Dutch Village to Capital of Black America* (New York: Grove Press, 2011), 242-245, 290-292, 323-326.

76 *El Paso Herald-Post*, 10 November 1933.

77 Heimer, 1955.

78 *Wichita Daily Times*, 22 May 1934.

79 Ibid.

80 "Daughter," *New York Sun*, 9 April 1934. About the western inclination "to project the non-Occident as feminine," see Ella Shohat, "Gender and Culture of Empire: Toward a Feminist Ethnography of the Cinema," in Matthew Bernstein and Gaylyn Studlar (eds.), *Vision of the East. Orientalism in Film* (New Brunswick, N.J.: Rutgers University Press, 1997), 23ff.

81 Maynor D. McGee, "Villa was enemy of saloon," *The Laredo Times*, 19 April 1934.

82 See her photo in Marjorie Van de Water, "Is the human race on its way out?," *Hattiesburg American*, Hattiesburg, MS, 1 April 1935.

to end up as stuffing for bologna."[83] In this way, Celia was constructed as a sweet or dangerous object of desire and conquest, facilitating her entrance into society. A final question asked in Wichita Falls, therefore, was not innocent: "What about this American sweetheart you want? You do want one, don't you?' [...]. 'Yes, I want a big, strong what-you-call brunet or maybe a blond. I think I like an Irishman, the best. Handsome, you know."[84]

Nor was it innocent when, in 1955, she was asked to account for her love life: "You ask Celia the logical question and she answers logically, 'Well, I would say Mexican men are more romantic—but American men make better husbands.'"[85] Assuming that Celia had enough experience to answer, the question plays with the idea of the erotic debauchery of non-whites.[86] But if we can believe the story, Celia had learned to handle the situation. She gave the "logical" answer that white American men of the 1950s (officially) wanted to hear.

Celia's stereotypical image was not exactly hostile. Being marked as Latina limited some possibilities, but gave her others, which some Latinos tried to exploit. For example, half-German Mexican actress Paula Marie Osterman adopted her mother's surname, Raquel Torres, to exploit her Latin potential. Joseph Krantz, a Viennese Jew, adopted a Latin identity, in order to have a career as Ricardo Cortez.[87] In the days of Dolores del Río, Rudolph Valentino and Ramón Novarro, Latino origins determined identity, but were hardly fatal. Everything depended on adapting to hegemonic expectations. As Celia experienced it in 1936, this required some art. When she was invited to participate in the centennial celebrations of Texas independence, Celia considered this in bad taste; Mexico was in mourning, so Mexicans in the United States were asked to boycott the celebrations.[88] Her statements immediately annoyed the American Legion, an organization of American veterans. In El Paso, Commander Davis Green demanded identification with the country that gave her work. He also criticized the Mexican consul's permission to celebrate Cinco de Mayo at El Paso High School Stadium. "We feel this is un-American. [...] We believe our grounds should be used for American holiday celebrations."[89]

This episode notwithstanding, Celia represented a reconciliation between Pancho Villa, the violent revolutionary and aggressor in Columbus, and the American public. After Villa's death, his memory was de-historicized and stereotyped by making an American fiction film, in keeping with President Roosevelt's good-neighbor policy.[90] Celia's submission to the rules her role imposed on her strengthened that process. Symbolically, Celia presented "a torch song" at the Château Moderne in 1936, while actor Lee Tracy was in the audience; his career had suffered a severe setback after the *Viva Villa!* scandal, while

83 Harry Carr, "The Lancer," *Los Angeles Times*, 18 April 1934.
84 *Wichita Daily Times*, 22 May 1934.
85 Heimer, 1955.
86 Shohat, 1997, 41-42.
87 Clara E. Rodríguez, *Heroes, Lovers, and Others: The Story of Latinos in Hollywood* (Austin/New York: Oxford University Press, 2004), 15-20. Others preferred to anglicize their names, e.g., Margarita Carmen Cansino became Rita Hayworth.
88 "Celia snubs Texas Centennial Fete,"in: *El Paso Herald-Tribune*, 21 April 1936.
89 "E. P. Legion post Criticizes Celia Villa Texas Clash," *El Paso Herald-Post*, 23 April 1936.
90 This stereotype can also be interpreted more radically. See Bernd Hausberger, "*¡Viva Villa!* Cómo Hollywood se apoderó de un héroe y el mundo se lo quitó," *Historia Mexicana*, Vol. 62/4, No. 248 (2013), 1495-1547.

Celia's was just beginning.[91] It was noted with satisfaction that her performance was without resentment towards the United States, while she sang "cheerful Mexican and Spanish songs—none of them revolutionary."[92]

CONCLUSION

When in 1934 Celia Villa was taken to the United States, her life changed forever. She achieved social status as a representative of a constructed imaginary. All of it began with a fictional film. Although initially put to the service of M-G-M's business, she soon had to manage her own life. Celia commercialized the symbolic value derived from her father, her country of origin, and the revolution. She could do this only by interpreting her Mexicanness, as conceived North of the Río Grande. For this reason, it is almost impossible to know who the "true" Celia Villa was. She represented the eroticized and tamed Latina woman, and therefore also symbolized the containment of Mexico and its revolution. In public, she never managed to emancipate herself from that role, perhaps because she was aware that the attention paid to her depended on it, even though she repeatedly expressed the desire to tell the truth, at least, about her father. In Mexico, her life had a very different meaning. The legacy of Pancho Villa was too grave to connect it sentimentally and erotically to a young singer. Some despised Villa and others adored him, but none, as the dancer Alicia Ayala, Celia's half-sister, suggested, liked the fact that the revolutionary's daughter showed her legs.[93]

---

91 George Ross, "New York," *Albany Evening News*, 21 April 1936.

92 Don O'Malley, "New York inside out," *The Citizen Advertiser*, Auburn, NY, 24 April 1936. See also "Night Club Notes," *New York Times*, 18 April 1936, and "Celia Villa," *New York Post*, 24 April 1936.

93 "Daughter of Villa says he had 13 wives," *Hope Star*, Hope, AR, 13 May 1946.

Berta Singerman, star of *Nada más que una mujer* (1934, Harry Lachman), with cinematographer Rudolph Maté, left, and Lachman. Courtesy of Alejandra Espasande.

Bibliography

Agramonte, Arturo and Luciano Castillo. *Cronología del Cine Cubano I (1897-1936)*. La Habana: Ediciones ICAIC, 2011.

Agramonte, Arturo and Luciano Castillo. *Cronología del Cine Cubano II (1937-1944)*. La Habana: Ediciones ICAIC, 2012.

Agramonte, Arturo and Luciano Castillo. *Cronología del Cine Cubano III (1945-1952)*. La Habana: Ediciones ICAIC, 2013.

Agrasánchez Jr., Rogelio. *Mexican Movies in the United States. A History of the Film Theaters and Audiences: 1920-1960*. Jefferson, N.C.: McFarland & Company, 2006.

Agrasánchez Jr., Rogelio. *Guillermo Calles: A Biography of the Actor and Mexican Cinema Pioneer*. Jefferson, N.C.: McFarland & Company, 2010.

Aguilar, Santiago. "Conchita Montenegro en Madrid: La estrella, su mamá y su marido." in: *Cinegramas,* No. 55, 29, September 1935, n.p.

Álvarez, José Rogelio (ed.). *Enciclopedia de México*. México, D.F.: Enciclopedia de México, 1999. 14 vols.

Amador, María Luisa and Jorge Ayala Blanco. *Cartelera Cinematográfica 1930-1939*. México, D.F.: UNAM, 1980.

The American Film Institute Catalog of Motion Pictures Produced in the United States. Feature Films: 1931-1940. Berkeley: University of California Press, 1971-1999, available online as *AFI Catalogue of Feature Films. The First 100 Years, 1893-1993*: https://catalog.afi.com/Catalog/Showcase

Armero, Álvaro (ed.). *Una aventura americana. Españoles en Hollywood*. Madrid: Compañía Literaria, 1995.

Arnold, Mario. "Conchita Montenegro es morena y sevillana," in: *Popular Film,* No. 248, 14 May 1931, 4-5.

Arnold, Mario. "Conchita Montenegro no quiere ser española," in: *Popular Film,* No. 296, 14 April 1932, n.p.

Barnard, Tim (ed.). *Argentine Cinema*. Toronto: Nightwood Editions, 1986.

Bernstein, Matthew and Gaylyn Studlar (eds.). *Vision of the East. Orientalism in Film*. New Brunswick, N.J.: Rutgers University Press, 1997.

Bethell, Leslie (ed.). *A Cultural History of Latin America: Literature, Music and the Visual Arts*. Cambridge: Cambridge University Press, 1998.

Beylie, Claude. "Biofilmographie de Carlos Gardel," in: *L'Avant-Scene Cinema*, Nos. 377/378, Jan/Feb 1989, 148.

Binder, Michael. *A Light Affliction: A History of Film Preservation and Restoration*. Raleigh, N.C.: Lulu, 2014.

Borcosque Carlos. Disc recordings, Margaret Herrick Library, Academy of Motion Picture Arts and Sciences, Beverly Hills, California.

Borcosque, Carlos. Ancestry.com, accessed at http://search.ancestry.com/cgi-bin/sse.dll?gl=allgs&gsfn=Carlos%20F&gsln=Borcosque&gss=seo&ghc=20

Bordwell, David, Janet Staiger and Kristin Thompson. *The Classical Hollywood Cinema: Film Style and Mode of Production to 1960*. London: Routledge, 1988.

Brenez, Nicole. "Retos disciplinares, políticos y ontológicos del gesto: poética del actor," in: Benavente, Fran, and Glòria Salvadó (eds.), *Poéticas del gesto en el cine europeo contemporáneo*. Barcelona: Intermedio, 2013.

Caneto, Guillermo. *Historia de los primeros años del cine en la Argentina*. Buenos Aires: Fundación Cinemateca Argentina, 1996.

Cine y Audiovisuales. Spanish Cinema database, accessed at: http://www.mcu.es/bbddpeliculas/cargarFiltro.do?layout=bbddpeliculas&cache=init&language=es

"Conchita Montenegro," in: *Picture Play*. Vol. XXXIV, No. 1, March 1931, n.p.

"Conchita Montenegro," in: *Popular Film* 243, 9 April 1931, 1.

"Conchita Montenegro," in: *The New Movie Magazine*. Vol. IV, No. 6, December 1931, 54.

"Conchita Montenegro," in: *Picture Play*. Vol. XXXVI, No. 1, March 1932, Cover.

"Conchita Montenegro ha ido a Paris a casarse y a rodar una película," in: *Cinegramas,* No. 54, 22 September 1935, n.p.

Córdova, Arnaldo. *La Revolución en crisis. La aventura del maximato*. Mexico, D.F.: Editorial Cal y Arena, 1995.

de la Vega Alfaro, Eduardo. *Fernando Méndez (1908-1966)*. Jalisco: Universidad de Guadalajara, 1995.

de la Vega Alfaro, Eduardo. *La Revolución traicionada. Dos ensayos sobre literatura, cine y censura*. Mexico, D.F.: UNAM, 2012.

de Paco, José. *José Crespo. Memorias de un actor*. Murcia: Filmoteca de Murcia, 1994.

"Desde Hollywood: Las próximas películas de Ramón Novarro," in: *La Vanguardia*, 18 March 1931, 12.

Di Núbila, Domingo. *La época de oro. Historia del cine argentino 1.* Revised edition. Buenos Aires, Ediciones del Jilguero, 1998.

España, Claudio. *Argentina Sono Film. Medio siglo de cine.* Buenos Aires: Editorial Abril, 1984.

Espina Rawson, Enrique and Alfredo Echániz. *Archivo Carlos Gardes.* Buenos Aires: Editorial Proa, 2013.

Finkielman, Jorge. *The Film Industry in Argentina: An Illustrated Cultural History.* Jefferson, N.C.: McFarland & Company, 2004.

Flores Montenegro, Rafael. *Gardel y el Tango, Repertorio de Recuerdos.* Buenos Aires: Ediciones de la Tierra, 2001.

Ford, Charles and Jeanne René. *Histoire Encyclopédique du Cinéma: Le Cinéma Français 1895-1929.* Vol. 1. Paris: Robert Laffont, 1947.

Gámez, Silvia Isabel. "Comparte cine la crisis de Cuba," in: *Reforma* (México, D.F.), June 11, 1994.

García Carrión, Marta. *Por un cine patrio: Cultura cinematográfica y nacionalismo español (1926-1936).* Valencia: Universidad de Valencia PUV, 2013.

García de Dueñas, Jesús. ¡*Nos vamos a Hollywood* ! Madrid: Nickel Odeon, 1993.

García Riera, Emilio. *Historia documental del cine mexicano, 1929-1937.* Guadalajara: Universidad de Guadalajara, 1992.

García Riera, Emilio. *Breve historia del cine mexicano. Primer siglo, 1897-1997.* México, D.F.: Ediciones Mapa, 1998.

Gilbert, Liette. *Decolonizing the City: The Construction of Social and Spatial Consciousness of Mexicans in Los Angeles,* M.A. Thesis, UCLA, 1995.

Goity, Elena. "Cine policial. Claroscuro y político," in: Claudio España (ed), *Cine argentino, 1933-1956.* Buenos Aires: Fondo Nacional de las Artes, 2000, 422-425.

González, Reynaldo. "Drácula resucitó en La Habana." Program notes. La Habana: Aula de Cultura ARABA, 1991.

Gubern, Román. *El cine sonoro en la II República (1929-1936).* Barcelona: Lumen, 1977.

Gubern, Román and Paul Hammond. *Luis Buñuel. The Red Years, 1929-1939.* Madison, WI: University of Wisconsin Press, 2012.

Gunckel, Colin. "The War of the Accents: Spanish Language Hollywood Films in Mexican Los Angeles," in: *Film History,* Vol. 20, No. 3, 2008.

Gunckel, Colin. *Mexico on Main Street. Transnational Film Culture in Los Angeles before World War II.* New Brunswick, N.J.: Rutgers University Press, 2015.

Gunckel, Colin, Jan-Christopher Horak, Lisa Jarvinen (eds). *Cinema Between Latin America and Los Angeles. Origins to 1960.* New Brunswick, N.J.: Rutgers University Press, 2019

Hadley-García, George. *Hispanic Hollywood.* New York: Carol Publishing Group, 1990.

Hammerlindl, Carlos Ferrer, "Jardiel en Hollywood," in: *Revista de Aula de Letras, Humanidades y Enseñanza,* No. 1, 1 July 2002.

Heinink, Juan B. and Robert G. Dickson. *Cita en Hollywood. Antología de las películas norteamericanas habladas en español.* Bilbao, España: Mensajero, 1990.

Hernández Girbal, Florentino. *Los que pasaron por Hollywood.* Edición de Juan B. Heinink. Madrid: Verdoux, 1992.

Hernández Girbal, Florentino, Juan B. Heinink and Robert G. Dickson. "Romualdo Tirado" in: *Los que pasaron por Hollywood,* accessed at: http://www.cervantesvirtual.com/obra-visor/los-que-pasaron-por-hollywood-0/html/ff1c4606-82b1-11df-acc7-002185ce6064_109.htm

Hershfield, Joanne, and David R. Maciel (eds.). *Mexico's Cinema: A Century of Film and Filmmakers.* Wilmington, DE: Scholarly Resources, 1999.

Hershfield, Joanne. *The Invention of Dolores del Río.* Minneapolis and London: University of Minnesota Press, 2000. H.T.S. "At the Teatro Hispano," in: *The New York Times,* May 21, 1938.

Jarvinen, Lisa. *The Rise of Spanish-Language Filmmaking. Out from Hollywood's Shadow, 1929-1939.* New Brunswick, N.J.: Rutgers University Press, 2012.

Kanellos, Nikolás. *A History of Hispanic Theatre in the United States.* Austin: University of Texas Press, 1990.

Katz, Friedrich. *The Life and Times of Pancho Villa.* Stanford: Stanford University Press, 1998.

King, John. *Magical Reels: A History of Cinema in Latin America.* New edition. New York: Verso, 2000.

Kohner, Pancho. *Lupita Tovar. La novia de México*. Pepe Romay, 2012.
English edition: *Lupita Tovar, The Sweetheart of Mexico*. XLibris Corporation, 2011.

López, Ana M. "Early Cinema and Modernity in Latin America,"
in: *Cinema Journal*, Vol. 40, No. 1, 2000, 48-78.

Manrupe, Raúl, and María Alejandra Portela. *Un diccionario de filmes argentinos*.
Buenos Aires: Corregidor, 1995.

Maranghello, César. *Breve historia del cine argentino*. Buenos Aires, Laertes, 2004.

McCarthy, Todd. "Through a Lens Darkly: The Life and Films of John Alton,"
in: John Alton, *Painting with light*. Los Angeles: University of California Press, 2013.

Medin, Tzvi. *El minimato presidencial: Historia política del Maximato, 1928-1935*.
Mexico, D.F.: Editorial Era, 1982.

Melville, Annette, and Scott Simmon. *Film Preservation 1993: A Study of the Current State of American Film Preservation*, Vol. 1. Washington, D.C.: Library of Congress, 1993.

Mendoza López, Margarita. *El Teatro de Ayer en Mis recuerdos*.
Mexico: Editorial Porrúa, 1985.

México bautismos, 1560-1950. Family Search database,
accessed at: https://familysearch.org/ark:/61903/1:1:V1SN-LMT

Miquel, Ángel. *Crónica de un encuentro: El cine mexicano en España, 1933-1848*.
Mexico, D.F.: UNAM, 2016.

Mojica, José. *Yo pecador*. México, D.F.: Editorial Jus, 1956.

Monteagudo, Luciano and Verónica Bucich. *Carlos Gardel y el primer cine sonoro argentino*. Huesca: Festival del Cine de Huesca, 2001.

Mora, Carl J. *Mexican Cinema: Reflections of a Society, 1896-2004*.
Berkeley, CA: University of California Press, 2012.

Muñoz Unsaín, Alfredo. "Drácula en Cuba," in: *AFP* (La Habana), April 22, 1991.

"Never the Twain Shall Meet," in: *Motion Picture Review*, Vol. II, No. 6, June 1931, 6.

Nieto, Pepe. *Mi vida*. Madrid: Ediciones Astros, 1943.

Noriega Hope, Carlos. *El mundo de las sombras*. Mexico, D.F.: Ediciones Botas, 1920.

Núñez Gorritti. Violeta, *Cartelera Cinematográfica Peruana 1930-1939*.
Lima: Universidad de Lima- Fondo de Desarrollo Editorial, 1998.

Oroz, Silvia. La "Época de Oro" del cine latinoamericano: el momento nacionalista,,», in : Edgar Soberón Torchía (ed.), *Los cines de América Latina y el Caribe. Parte 1: 1890-1969*. La Habana: Escuela Internacional de Cine y Televisión, 2012.

Pareyón, Gabriel. *Diccionario Enciclopédico de Música en México*. México, D.F.: Universidad Panamericana, 2006.

Pearson, Roberta E. *Eloquent Gestures: The Transformation of Performance Style in the Griffith Biograph Films*. Berkeley: University of California Press, 1992.

Pérez Bowie, José Antonio. *Materiales para un sueño: En torno a la recepción del cine en España 1896-1936*. Salamanca: Librería Cervantes, 1996.

Phillips, Alastair and Ginette Vincendeau (eds.). *Journeys of Desire: European Actors in Hollywood*. London: British Film Institute, 2007.

Pierce, David. *The Survival of American Silent Feature Films: 1912–1929*. Washington, D.C.: Library of Congress, 2013.

Pitts, Michael R. *Poverty Row Studios, 1929-1940. An Illustrated History of 53 Independent Film Companies, with a Filmography for Each*. Jefferson, N.C.: McFarland & Company, 1997.

Posadas, Abel, Mónica Landro and Marta Speroni (eds.). *Cine sonoro argentino 1933-1943*. Vol. 1. Buenos Aires: El Calafate Editores, 2005.

Posadas, Abel, Mónica Landro, Marta Speroni and Raúl Campodonico (eds.). *Cine sonoro argentino, 1933-1943*. Vol. 2 . Buenos Aires: El Calafate editores, 2006.

Ramírez Berg, Charles. *Latino Images in Film: Stereotypes, Subversion, and Resistance*. Austin, TX: University of Texas Press, 2002.

Rodríguez, Clara E. *Heroes, Lovers, and Others: The Story of Latinos in Hollywood*. New York: Oxford University Press, 2004.

Rotellar, Manuel. *Cine español de la República*. San Sebastián: Festival Internacional de Cine, 1977.

Sánchez, George J. *Becoming Mexican American. Ethnicity, Culture, and Identity in Chicano Los Angeles, 1900-1945*. New York: Oxford University Press, 1993.

Saratsola, Osvaldo. *Cinestrenos. El cine en Montevideo*. Database accessed at: http://www.uruguaytotal.com/estrenos/

Skal, David J. *Hollywood Gothic: The Tangled Web of Dracula from Novel to Stage to Screen*. New York: Faber and Faber, 2004.

Skretvedt, Randy. "Catching Up with Laurel & Hardy in Spanish," accessed at: www.cinema.ucla.edu/support/laurel-hardy-spanish

Slide, Anthony. *Nitrate Won't Wait: A History of Film Preservation in the United States.* Jefferson, N.C.: McFarland & Company, 1992.

Soila, Tytti (ed.). *Stellar Encounters: Stardom in Popular European Cinema.* New Barnet, North London: John Libbey Publishing, and Bloomington, IN: Indiana University Press, 2009.

Solomon, Aubrey. *The Fox Film Corporation, 1915-1935. A History and Filmography.* Jefferson, N.C.: McFarland & Company, 2011.

Taibo II, Paco Ignacio. *Pancho Villa: una biografía narrativa*. México, D.F.: Planeta, 2006.

Tortolero Villaseñor, Alejandro. *De la coa a la máquina de vapor. Actividad agrícola e innovación tecnológica en las haciendas mexicanas: 1880-1914.* México, D.F.: Siglo Veintiuno Editores - Colegio Mexiquense, 1995.

"Una española en pleno triunfo," in: *Popular Film,* No. 417, 9 August 1934, n.p.

Vasey, Ruth. *The World According to Hollywood, 1918-1939.* Madison, WI: University of Wisconsin Press, 1997.

Vázquez Bernal, María Esperanza, and Xóchitl Fernández. *Gabriel García Moreno: hombre de cine.* Harlington, TX: Tres Piedras Publishers, forthcoming.

Waldman, Harry. *Hollywood and the Foreign Touch. A Dictionary of Foreign Filmmakers and Their Films from America, 1910-1995.* Lanham, MD, and London: Scarecrow Press, 1996.

Yepez Pottier, Arturo. *La lágrima en la garganta. La fascinante vida y extraordinaria vigencia de Carlos Gardel.* San Juan, Puerto Rico: Producciones El Copihue, 2017.

Zúñiga, Ángel. *Una historia del cine*. Vol 1. Barcelona: Ediciones Destino, 1948.

Spanish-language Films Made in Hollywood (1929-1939)

The following titles are those featured in *Cita en Hollywood*, by Juan B. Heinink and Robert G. Dickson (Bilbao, Spain: Mensajero, 1990). This list comprises 175 features and shorts, and two titles—the feature *Sesenta segundos de vida* (1937) and the short *El caballero alegre* (1930)—discovered after the book's publication.

Excluded from this list are one-reelers, documentaries, and shorts with musical numbers. In the book there are as complete credits as were available at the time of publication; and the authors also provide a wealth of production information culled from newspapers and magazines of the 1920s and 1930s, from Spain, Latin America and the U.S., catalogues, books and articles. An immense labor of love, this thorough compilation work was done before the Internet era.

Only the title [alternative titles], year of release, and the title of any original English-language version are included here. Complete credits for the Spanish-language feature films can be consulted in *Cita en Hollywood*, and are also available at the *AFI Catalog of Feature Films. The First 100 Years, 1893-1993* (https://catalog.afi.com/Catalog/Showcase), courtesy of Juan B. Heinink and Robert G. Dickson.

- *Sombras habaneras* [aka *Bajo el cielo de La Habana, Noches habaneras*] (1929)
- *Sombras de gloria* (1929), *Blaze O' Glory* (1929)
- *Ladrones* (1930), *Night Owls* (1930)
- *Los pequeños papás* [aka *Jugando a papás*](1930), *The First Seven Years* (1930)
- *Charros, gauchos y manolas* [aka *Revista musical Cugat*] (1930)
- *Un fotógrafo distraído* (1930)
- *La estación de gasolina* [aka *La gran patada, El puesto de gasolina*] (1930), *The Big Kick* (1930)
- *La vida nocturna* (1930), *Blotto* (1930)
- *Los fantasmas* (1930), *When the Wind Blows* (1930)
- *La rosa de fuego* (1930)
- *¡Pobre infeliz!* [aka *El infeliz*] (1930), *The Shrimp* (1930)
- *Los cazadores de osos* (1930), *Bear Shooters* (1930)
- *El jugador de golf* (1930), *All Teed Up* (1930)
- *Así es la vida* [aka *Cosas de la vida*] (1930), *What a Man* (1930)
- *Alma de gaucho* [aka *Alma gaucha, Amor argentino*] (1930)
- *Tiembla y titubea* [aka *Tiembla y vacila*] (1930), *Below Zero* (1930)

- *El cuerpo del delito* [aka *Juego, amor y sangre*] (1930), *The Benson Murder Case* (1930)
- *Estrellados* (1930), *Free and Easy* (1930)
- *La fuerza del querer* [aka *La gran pelea*] (1930), *The Big Fight* (1930)
- *Radiomanía* (1930), *Hog Wild* (1930)
- *El caballero alegre* (1930), *The Snappy Caballero* (1930)
- *Un hombre de suerte* [aka *Un trou dans le mur, El tesoro de los Menda*] (1930)
- *Monsieur Le Fox* [aka *El Zorro*] (1930), *Men of the North* (1930)
- *El precio de un beso* [aka *Un beso apasionado, La canción del beso*] (1930), *One Mad Kiss* (1930)
- *Amor audaz* (1930), *Slightly Scarlet* (1930)
- *La jaula de los leones* [aka *La tragedia del circo*] (1930)
- *Locuras de amor* (1930) [aka ¡*Ay amor, cómo me has puesto!*] (1930), *Fast Work* (1930)
- *Galas de la Paramount* [aka *Paramount de gala*] (1930), *Paramount on Parade* (1930)
- *El hombre malo* (1930), *The Bad Man* (1930)
- ¡*Huye, faldas!* (1930), *Girl Shock* (1930)
- *Noche de duendes* [aka *Deudos y duendes*] (1930), *The Laurel-Hardy Murder Case* (1930)
- *El rey del jazz* (1930), *The King of Jazz* (1930)
- *Doña Mentira* [aka *Las morenas*] (1930), *The Lady Lies* (1929)
- *Cascarrabias* (1930), *Grumpy* (1930)
- *El secreto del doctor* [aka *Media hora*] (1930), *The Doctor's Secret* (1929)
- *Olimpia [aka Si el emperador lo supiera*] (1930), *His Glorious Night* (1929)
- *Del mismo barro* [aka *Arcilla, Barreras sociales*] (1930), *Common Clay* (1930)
- ¡De *frente, marchen!* (1930), *Doughboys* (1930)
- *El nombre de la amistad* (1930), *Friendship* (1929)
- *Cupido chauffeur* [aka *Amor en la frontera*] (1930)
- *El príncipe del dólar* (1930), *Dollar Dizzy* (1930)
- *El* último *de los Vargas* (1930), The *Last of the Duanes* (1930)
- *Entre platos y notas* (1930)
- *La voluntad del muerto* [aka *La heredera de Mr. West, El gato y el canario*] (1930), *The Cat Creeps* (1930)

- *El valiente* [aka *El patíbulo*] (1930), *The Valiant* (1929)
- *Las campanas de Capistrano* [aka *Amor y sacrificio*] (1930)
- *Wu Li Chang* (1930), *Mr. Wu* (1927)
- *Toda una vida* [aka Corazones de plomo] (1930), *Sarah and Son* (1930)
- *El dios del mar* (1930), *The Sea God* (1930)
- *La carta* (1930), *The Letter* (1929)
- *Los que danzan* [aka *Pájaros de cuenta, Fin de fiesta*] (1930), *Those Who Dance* (1930)
- *El presidio* (1930), *The Big House* (1930)
- *Oriente y Occidente* [*El barco del amor*] (1930), *East is West* (1930)
- *Sevilla de mis amores* [aka *La Sevillana, El cantante de Sevilla*] (1930), *Call of the Flesh* (1930)
- *Una cana al aire* (1930), *Looser than Loose* (1930)
- *Cuando el amor ríe* [aka *Ladrón de amor, El domador de mujeres, Por una apuesta*] (1930), *The Love Gambler* (1922)
- *La fiesta del diablo* (1930), *The Devil's Holiday* (1930)
- *Parlez vous?* (1930), *Parlez vous?* (1930)
- *El barbero de Napoleón* (1930), *Napoleon's Barber* (1928)
- *Regeneración* [aka *La mujer que supo amar*] (1930)
- *La llama sagrada* [aka *Amor contra amor*] (1931), *The Sacred Flame* (1929)
- *Desconcierto matrimonial* [aka *Desconcierto conyugal, Desacuerdo matrimonial*] (1930)
- *A media noche* [aka *Evidencia*] (1930)
- *¡Salga de la cocina!* [aka *Suegra para dos, Dulce como la miel*] (1930), *Honey* (1930)
- *Oui, oui, Marie* [aka *Sí, sí, María*] (1930), *We! We! Marie!* (1930)
- *La cautivadora* [aka *Corazones de acero, El triunfo de una mujer vencida*] (1930)
- *El alma de la fiesta* (1931), *Thundering Tenors* (1931)
- *Drácula* (1931), *Dracula* (1931)
- *Su última noche* [aka *Toto*] (1931), *The Gay Deceiver* (1926)
- *Sombras del circo* [aka *En mitad del camino del cielo*] (1931), *Half Way to Heaven* (1929)
- *¡Hola, Rusia!* (1930), *Hello, Russia!* (1930)

- *De bote en bote* [aka *Los presidiarios*] (1931), *Pardon Us* (1931)
- *La dama atrevida* (1931), *The Lady Who Dared* (1931)
- *En cada puerto un amor* [aka ¡Paso al *marino!*, *La ruta del marino*] (1931), *Way for a Sailor* (1930)
- *La gran jornada* [aka *Horizontes nuevos*] (1931), *The Big Trail* (1930)
- *Don Juan diplomático* [aka *Diplomático de salón*] (1931), *The Boudoir Diplomat* (1930)
- *Resurrección* [aka *El príncipe y la aldeana*] (1931), *Resurrection* (1931)
- *Los calaveras* (1931), *Be Big* (1930) and *Laughing Gravy* (1931)
- *El código penal* (1931), *The Criminal Code* (1931)
- *La fruta amarga* [aka *Estrella negra*] (1931), *Min and Bill* (1930)
- *La señorita de Chicago* (1931), *The Pip from Pittsburgh* (1931)
- *La mujer X* (1931), *Madame X* (1929)
- *La incorregible* [aka *La homicida*] (1931), *Manslaughter* (1930)
- *Del infierno al cielo* [aka *Camino del infierno, Regeneración*] (1931), *The Man Who Came Back* (1931)
- *Politiquerías* (1931), *Chickens Come Home* (1931)
- *Gente alegre* [aka *¡Arriba el telón!*] (1931)
- *Monerías* (1931), *Rough Seas* (1931)
- *El tenorio del harem* [aka *Caballeros árabes*] (1931), *Arabian Knights* (1931)
- *Cheri-Bibi* (1931), *The Phantom of Paris* (1931)
- *Su noche de bodas* (1931), *Her Wedding Night* (1930)
- *El impostor* [aka *La mujer del otro*] (1931), *Scotland Yard* (1930)
- *Carne de cabaret* [aka *El triunfo de un amor, El torbellino del jazz*] (1931), *Ten Cents a Dance* (1931)
- *El príncipe gondolero* (1931), *Honeymoon Hate* (1927)
- *Entre noche y día* [aka *La casa del terror*] (1931), *77 Park Lane* (1931)
- *El proceso de Mary Dugan* (1931), *The Trial of Mary Dugan* (1929)
- *Estamos en París* (1931), *Parisian Gaieties* (1931)
- *Lo mejor es reír* (1931), *Laughter* (1930)
- *El comediante* (1931)
- *Cuerpo y alma* [aka *Escuadrones*] (1931), *Body and Soul* (1931)
- *Un caballero de frac* (1931), *Evening Clothes* (1927)

- *Esclavas de la moda* [aka *Sobre su espalda*] (1931), *On Your Back* (1930)
- *Hay que casar al príncipe* [aka *Príncipe de amor*] (1931), *Paid to Love* (1927)
- *Soñadores de la gloria* (1931)
- *El pasado acusa* (1931), *The Good Bad Girl* (1931)
- *Las luces de Buenos Aires* (1931)
- *El hombre que asesinó* (1931), *Stamboul* (1931)
- *¿Conoces a tu mujer?* (1931), *Don't Bet on Women* (1931)
- *La ley del harem* [aka *En brazos de ella, El hijo del desierto*] (1931), *Fazil* (1928)
- *La pura verdad* (1931), *Nothing but the Truth* (1929)
- *Eran trece* (1931), *Charlie Chan Carries On* (1931)
- *Mamá* (1931)
- ¿Cuándo te suicidas? (1931), *Quand te tues-tu?* (1931)
- *El cliente seductor* (1931)
- *Mi* último *amor* [aka *Su* último *amor, Momento loco*] (1931), *Their Mad Moment* (1931)
- *Hollywood, ciudad de ensueño* [aka *Bajo el cielo de Hollywood*] (1931)
- *Marido y mujer* (1932), *Bad Girl* (1931)
- *Hombres en mi vida* (1932), *Men in Her Life* (1931)
- *El caballero de la noche* [aka *Dick Turpin, Tu amor o la vida*] (1932), *Dick Turpin* (1925)
- *El* último *varón sobre la tierra* (1932) [aka *El* último *de su sexo, Espérame*] (1933), *The Last Man on Earth* (1924)
- *Melodía de arrabal* (1933)
- *La casa es seria* (1933)
- *Buenos días* (1933)
- *Primavera en otoño* (1933)
- *El rey de los gitanos* [aka *El zíngaro vagabundo*] (1933)
- *Dos noches* [aka *Amante y traidora*] (1933), *Revenge at Monte Carlo* (1933)
- *Una viuda romántica* (1933)
- *La melodía prohibida* [aka *La canción prohibida*] (1933)
- *No dejes la puerta abierta* [aka *Viaje de placer, ¿Dónde has pasado la noche?*] (1933), *Pleasure Cruise* (1933)
- *Yo, tú y ella* [aka *Mujer, Triángulo*] (1933)

- *La cruz y la espada* [aka *Oro de California*] (1934)
- *La ciudad de cartón* [aka *Hollywood, la ciudad de cartón*] (1934)
- *Amor que vuelve* (1934)
- *Granaderos del amor* [aka *Mascarada*] (1934)
- *La buenaventura* (1934)
- *Un capitán de cosacos* [aka *El centauro, Cosacos, Entre dos fuegos*] (1934)
- *Cuesta abajo* (1934)
- *Dos más uno, dos* [aka *¡Ojo, solteros!, ¡No te cases!, Deshabillé*] (1934), *Don't Marry* (1928)
- *Las fronteras del amor* [aka *¡Viva mi tierra!, En alas del amor, El vuelo del amor*] (1934)
- *El tango en Broadway* [aka *El amor entre rascacielos*] (1934)
- *Tres amores* (1934), *Bachelor Mother* (1933)
- *Nada más que una mujer* [aka *La llama blanca, La venda en los ojos*] (1934), *Pursued* (1934)
- *El cantante de Nápoles* (1934)
- *Señora casada necesita marido* [aka *Mi segunda mujer*] (1934)
- *¡Asegure a su mujer!* (1934)
- *Julieta compra un hijo* (1935)
- *Angelina o el honor de un brigadier* (1935)
- *El día que me quieras* (1935)
- *El Diablo del mar* (1935), *Devil Monster* (1935)
- *Tango Bar* (1935)
- *Contra la corriente* (1935)
- *Te quiero con locura* (1935)
- *Piernas de seda* (1935), *Silk Legs* (1927)
- *Milagroso Hollywood* [aka *Hollywood milagroso*] (1935)
- *Un hombre peligroso* (1935)
- *La última cita* (1935)
- *Rosa de Francia* (1935)
- *Alas sobre el Chaco* [aka *Tempestad sobre los Andes*] (1935), *Storm over the Andes* (1935)
- *No matarás* [aka *Mi hermano es un gangster*] (1935)

- *El crimen de media noche* [aka *El fantasma de media noche*] (1935), *The Midnight Phantom* (1935)
- *De la sartén al fuego* [aka *La legión extranjera*] (1935), *We're in the Legion Now* [aka *The Rest Cure*] (1935)
- *El capitán Tormenta* (1936), *Captain Calamity* [aka *Captain Hurricane*] (1936)
- *El carnaval del diablo* [aka *El diablo se divierte, La canción de los Andes*] (1936), *The Devil on Horseback* (1936)
- *Tengo fe en tí* (1937/40)
- *La vida bohemia* [aka *Tragedias de la vida bohemia*] (1937)
- *Sesenta segundos de vida* (1937)
- *Castillos en el aire* (1938)
- *Verbena trágica* (1938)
- *Mis dos amores* [aka *Mi primer amor*] (1938)
- *Di que me quieres* (1938)
- *El trovador de la radio* (1938)
- *Papá soltero* (1939)
- *Los hijos mandan* (1939)
- *El otro soy yo* [aka *El vagabundo, La vuelta del hijo pródigo*] (1939)
- *Cuando canta la ley* [aka *El rancho del pinar, El charro cantor*] (1939)
- *El milagro de la Calle Mayor* [aka *Quiso ser madre*](1939), *Miracle on Main Street* (1939)
- *La Inmaculada* (1939)

Author Biographies

Rogelio Agrasánchez Jr. was born into a family related to the Mexican film industry. He has lived in Texas since the middle 1970s and holds an M.A. in Latin American Studies from University of Texas, Austin. Rogelio is the Agrasánchez Archive's founder, co-chair and curator, as well as a researcher focused on Hispanic film pioneers and on Mexican cinema as distributed and exhibited in the United States. Besides, he has been involved in collecting and studying Mexican film publicity for three decades. He is also engaged in film preservation projects and has ten books and numerous articles and essays published. Among his books are: *Poster Art from the Golden Age of Mexican Cinema; Mexican Movies in the United States, 1920-1960; Guillermo Calles: A Biography of the Actor and Mexican Cinema Pioneer;* and *Viaje Redondo: Cine mudo mexicano en Estados Unidos, 1900-1930.*

Núria Bou (Barcelona, 1967) is a tenured lecturer for undergraduates in Audiovisual Communication at Pompeu Fabra University. Currently she heads the MA in Contemporary Film and Audiovisual Studies. She is the author of *La mirada en el temps. Mite i passió en el cinema de Hollywood* (Ed. 62, 1996), translated into Italian by Editori Riuniti. She is also the author of *Plano/Contraplano* (Ed. Biblioteca Nueva, 2002) and *Diosas y tumbas. Mitos femeninos en el cine de Hollywood* (Ed. Icaria, 2004). She has participated in several books and journals on the topic of the actress, such as *Les dives: mites i celebritats* (Ed. 3 i 4, 2007), "Modernism Born Out of Classical Cinema: the Body of Marlene Dietrich" (*L'Atalante*, 19, 2015) and "Lois Weber: female thinking in movement" (*Cinema Comparat/ive*, 8, 2016). She is the main researcher of the Spanish Ministry of Culture's R+D project "El cuerpo erótico de la actriz bajo los fascismos: España, Italia y Alemania (1939-45)."

Luciano Castillo (Camagüey, Cuba, 1955) is a film critic and historian. He has a Master's degree in Latin American Culture. Member of the Union of Writers and Film Artists of Cuba, and the Cuban Film Press Association, affiliated with FIPRESCI. He writes for many specialized magazines and journals. He participates in weekly radio and television shows on Cuban cinema. He is a frequent lecturer in universities and cultural institutions in several countries, and has been a juror at film festivals, including Valladolid, Mar del Plata, New York, Havana, Cartagena, Lima, Guadalajara and Huelva. Among his publications are: *La verdad 24 veces x Segundo; Concierto en imágenes; Con la locura de los sentidos; Ramón Peón, el hombre de los glóbulos negros; Entre el vivir y el sonar; Pioneros del cine cubano;* the definitive edition in four volumes of *Cronología del cine cubano*, with Arturo Agramonte; *Conversaciones con Jean-Claude Carrière*, with Javier Espada; *Carpentier en el reino de la imagen; El cine cubano a contraluz; Apostillas para una historia del cine en Camagüey; El cine es cortar*, with editor Nelson Rodríguez; *Trenes en la noche; Retrato de grupo sin cámara*, and *La biblia del cinéfilo*. He was the coordinator and writer in *Diccionario del cine iberoamericano: España, Portugal, América* (Madrid, 2011). He is a programming advisor for the Havana Film Festival in New York. The Cuban Ministry of Culture awarded him the National Cultural Prize in 2013. He directed the film library "André Bazin" of the International School of Film and Television in San Antonio de los Baños (1995-2014), and he is currently the director of the Cinemateca de Cuba.

María Elena de las Carreras is a Fulbright scholar from Argentina, living in Los Angeles, California, since 1987. A lecturer in film studies at UCLA and Cal State Northridge, she is a regular collaborator of the Latin American Cinemateca of Los Angeles and an accredited journalist at the Berlin Film Festival since 1986. In 2017 she co-curated the UCLA Film & Television Archive series "Recuerdos de un cine en español: Latin American cinema in Los Angeles, 1930-1960." Since 2014 she has been a researcher and interviewer for the Academy of Motion Picture Arts and Sciences' Visual History Program. Publications include "A case of entente cordiale between State and Church," chapter in *Moralizing Cinema* (2014); "The 'Setentista' discourse in recent Argentine political documentaries," in *Arctic Antarctic*, vol. 6 no. 6, 2012; "Luis Buñuel's quarrel with the Catholic Church," in *Buñuel*, siglo XXI. Spain: Instituto Fernando el Católico, 2004; "The Catholic Vision in Hollywood," in *Film History*, 14, 2, 2002; "El control de cine en la Argentina: 1968-1984," and "El control del cine en la Argentina: 1984-1991," in *Foro Político, Revista del Instituto de Ciencias Políticas*, Buenos Aires: Universidad del Museo Social Argentino, XIX.

Eduardo de la Vega Alfaro (Mexico City, 1954). Doctor in History of Cinema from the Autonomous University of Madrid. He is a full professor-researcher in the Department of Sociology of the University of Guadalajara, where he teaches courses on film topics at the undergraduate and graduate levels. He has published a critique and essay on various cinematographic aspects in newspapers, magazines and books published in Mexico and abroad and is also the author or co-author of monographs on the life and work of Mexican filmmakers and actors. He has carried out dissemination tasks among which the organization of the nine editions of the National Colloquium on the History of Regional Cinema, and the research work for several documentaries on cinematographic art stand out. Winner of the "Premio Nacional de Crítica de Artes Plásticas Luis Cardoza y Aragón" (1995), he is also a member of the National System of Researchers (Level III).

Mar Díaz Martínez. A Spanish journalist, she has worked for 22 years in Spanish public television, TVE, on film programs. She became interested in Spanish actor Antonio Moreno and his long Hollywood career, and her 13-year research became the feature documentary *The Spanish Dancer* (2015), with research in Spain, the U.S.A. and Mexico. It won the first prize at the 2016 Festival of Memory in Morelos, Mexico. She has since directed the documentary *José Luis Gómez: La máscara y la palabra* for the TVE series *Imprescindibles*. She is currently curating an exhibit on Antonio Moreno and working on his biography.

Robert G. Dickson was born and educated in Scotland, and has lived in Los Angeles for more than fifty-five years. He has photographed, and frequently produced, close to two hundred educational and documentary films. He has also filmed for the BBC's Natural History Unit, CBC, Disney, the United Nations, and UCLA. He has worked throughout the United States as well as in Canada, Zaire, Thailand, and Central America. He has contributed to many publications on film history and has written a comprehensive study of the Spanish-language films made by Laurel and Hardy. He has also written hundreds of records for the American Film Institute's Catalog of Feature Films, and works as an archival processor in Special Collections at the Margaret Herrick Library of the Academy of Motion Picture Arts and Sciences. His special interest is film preservation, and he has supplied funding for making prints and subtitles of two Spanish-language versions made by Fox Film Corp., *No dejes la puerta abierta* (1933) and *Nada más que una mujer* (1934).

He has also funded preservation activities in Mexico and Scotland. With Juan G. Heinink he wrote *Cita en Hollywood* (Bilbao, Spain, 1990), the first and most comprehensive catalogue of Spanish-language films made in the U.S. between 1929 and 1939.

Alejandra Espasande Bouza works at the Academy Film Archive at the Academy of Motion Picture Arts and Sciences. She received her Masters from the Moving Image Archive Studies Program at UCLA. She is co-curator of the Getty-funded exhibition, "Recuerdos de un cine en español: Latin American cinema in Los Angeles, 1930-1960."

Xóchitl Fernández was born in Mexico, where she had experience in teaching, training, and business consultancy. She has lived in Texas since 1999, when she married Rogelio Agrasánchez Jr. Xóchitl is now the Agrasánchez Film Archive co-chair, in charge of its iconographic holdings, administration, and acquisitions. She is the author of *Invicta Luz: Carlos Peinador, artista y republicano*. Her research focuses on the work of Mexican film technicians in Hollywood, especially inventor and filmmaker Gabriel García Moreno.

César Fratantoni is a resident of Los Angeles, born in Argentina. While studying business administration in his home country, he was the editor of *La Jirafa*, a magazine dedicated to local culture. Interested in the film industry, he came to Los Angeles for an MBA degree. He works for the City of Los Angeles, and is active in community events. He has investigated and written in *El Suplemento*, a local magazine, about the careers of Argentine film actors who succeeded in Hollywood, such as Fernando Lamas, Linda Cristal, Barry Norton, Mona Maris, and Alejandro Rey. Two years ago, he began the blog *Mundo Gardeliano* about tango legend Carlos Gardel. He is an expert on Gardel's film-related activities in the United States.

Roberto Green Quintana was born in Spain. He received his Master's degree from the Moving Image Archive Studies Program at UCLA. He worked for two years at the UCLA Film & Television Archive as an assistant on the project, "Recuerdos de un cine en español: Latin American cinema in Los Angeles, 1930-1960."

Bernd Hausberger (Austria, 1960) received his PhD in History from the University of Vienna and was Assistant Professor at the Institute of Latin American Studies at the Free University of Berlin. Since 2006 he is Professor of History at the Center for Historical Studies at El Colegio de México. His works focus on Latin American colonial history, global history and the relationship between history and cinema. His last publications include: *La Revolución Mexicana en el cine. Un acercamiento a partir de la mirada* ítaloeuropea (México, El Colegio de México, 2013), which he edited with Raffaele Moro; "*¡Viva Villa!* Cómo Hollywood se apoderó de un héroe y el mundo se le quitó," in *Historia Mexicana* 62 (2013); "La Revolución mexicana en los cine de Roma de la posguerra," in *Tzintzun. Revista de Estudios Históricos* 64 (2016); and *Historia mínima de la temprana globalización* (México, El Colegio de México, 2018).

Juan B. Heinink, born in Bilbao Spain, in 1949, began his professional career in the late 1960s publishing articles and film reviews, while also working in radio shows, music and designing record covers. Between 1977 and 1984 he produced and directed several experimental films for Heiga Filmeak, including *Ikurriñaz Filmea, Criss Cross & deskarga* *batzuk, Gerla eta maitasun gertakaria*. In 1986 he published *Catálogo de las películas estrenadas en Bizkaia: 1929-1937*. He has researched since then other areas of film history. He is a member of the Asociación española de historiadores de cine, and the Association Française de Recherche sur l'Histoire du Cinéma. With Robert G. Dickson he wrote *Cita en Hollywood* (Bilbao, Spain, 1990), the first and most extensive catalogue of Spanish-language films made in the U.S. between 1929 and 1939.

Jan-Christopher Horak is Director of the UCLA Film & Television Archive and Professor for Critical Studies. He received his PhD from the Westfählische Wilhelms-Universät in Münster, Germany. He previously held directorships at George Eastman Museum, the Munich Filmmuseum, Universal Studios Archives & Collections, and was curator of the Hollywood Entertainment Museum. He has previously taught at the University of Rochester and the University of Salzburg. He has published over 300 articles and reviews. His book publications include: *Film and Photo in the 1920s* (1979), *Anti-Nazi-Films Made by German Jewish Refugees in Hollywood* (1985), *The Dream Merchants: Making and Selling Films in Hollywood's Golden Age* (1989), *Lovers of Cinema. The First American Film Avant-Garde 1919-1945* (1995), *Saul Bass. Anatomy of Film Design* (2014). He was named an Academy Scholar in 2007. He is co-editor of *L.A. Rebellion: Creating a New Black Cinema* (University of California Press, 2015), which won the SCMS Best Edited Collection Award, and the Andor Kraszna-Kraus Film Book Award. Forthcoming is *Cinema Between Latin America and Los Angeles. Origins to 1960,* ed. by Colin Gunckel, Jan-Christopher Horak, and Lisa Jarvinen (New Brunswick, NJ: Rutgers University Press).

Violeta Núñez Gorriti is a filmmaker, film historian and former professor. Her work as a historian resulted in a series of books, including *The Golden Age of Peruvian Cinema 1936-1950* (Colmillo Blanco Ed., 1990); *Peruvian Cinema Billboard 1930-1939* (Universidad de Lima, 1998); *Peruvian Cinema Billboard 1940-1949* (Lima, 2006); *The cinema in Lima 1897-1929* (Lima, 2011) and editor of the book *When the Cinema was a party: the production of Law 19327* (Lima, 2013) as well as articles in various media. She has directed the documentary *Cinema, history of a passion* (Casablanca Latinfilms, 2004). She has participated in International Film Colloquiums such as "El arribo del cine to America "(Guadalajara, 1994), "Silent Cinema in Ibero-America: nations, narrations, centenarians" (UNAM, Mexico, 2010); she is a member of the Organizing Committee and speaker of the Colloquium "Las rutas de cine en América 1896-1910" (UNAM, Mexico, 2011). She has been a juror in several festivals, including Festivals of the Peruvian Filmmakers Association (Lima, 1991), Guadalajara FICG 2002, Los Angeles Latino International Film Festival - LALIFF 2013, Guadalajara International Film Festival in LA 1914. She is currently preparing "The cinema in Lima 1930-1969", "Jorge Vignati: a camera his combat weapon"; "Between two laws: Peruvian films 1960-2000".

Esteve Riambau is Professor of Audiovisual Communication at the Universitat Autònoma de Barcelona. He has been the director of the Filmoteca de Catalunya since 2010 and a member of FIAF's Executive Committee since 2011. Along with Elisabet Cabeza, he has co-directed the feature films *La doble vida del faquir/The Magicians* (2005) and *Màscares/Masks* (2009). The author of some thirty books on the History of Cinema and a renowned specialist on Orson Welles, he has written four monographs on him, the script of the documentary *Orson Welles en el país de Don Quijote* (2000), as well as the adaptation and direction of the play *Obediently Yours: Orson Welles* (2008). In 2013, he organized a Symposium and an Exhibition about Multiversions at the 69th FIAF Congress in Barcelona.

Esperanza Vázquez Bernal was born and lives in Mexico City. She is an independent researcher and film historian. She has participated in several projects at the Filmoteca de la UNAM between 1977 and 2017, among them, the editorial restoration of three Mexican feature films: *Santa* (1918), *El tren fantasma* (1926), and *El puño de hierro* (1927). Esperanza is also Gabriel García Moreno's authorized biographer. She has co-authored with her husband, Ph.D. Federico Dávalos Orozco, two published books, *Filmografía general del cine mexicano (1906-1931)* and *Carlos Villatoro: pasajes en la vida de un hombre de cine*, and several articles and essays. Besides her work on Mexican silent cinema, she has ventured into research and writing on the history of Mexican film studios.

Rosario Vidal Bonifaz, born in Chiapa de Corzo, Chiapas, is a Doctor in Human Development Sciences, in the area of Cultural Studies, Member of the National System of Researchers, level I and Prodep Profile. She is currently tenured Professor "C" in the Department of Sociology at the University of Guadalajara. She has written several essays and book chapters about the history of Mexican and Latin American cinema, she has worked as an executive producer in several documentaries; she is a member of selection committees and jury of several film festivals, as well as advising and curating various exhibitions on the history and aesthetics of Mexican cinema. She is the author of the books *Surgimiento de la industria cinematográfica y el papel del Estado en México (1895-1940)* (Editorial Miguel Ángel Porrúa, 1ª reimpresión, México 2011); *Cinematográfica Marte. Historia de una empresa fílmica sui géneris* (Secretaría de Cultura-Cineteca Nacional, México, 2017).

Index

Acknowledgements

This publication was born from the FIAF Symposium *Hollywood Goes Latin: Spanish-Language Cinema in Los Angeles / Hollywood Goes Latin: Cine en español en Los Ángeles (o Cine hispanohablante en Los Ángeles)*, held at the Linwood Dunn Theater of the Academy Film Archive on April 29-30, 2017. A publication of this scope involves a lot of work by many different people, which the Editors are happy to acknowledge.

First and foremost, we would like to thank the team at the Academy Film Archive, who handled the lion's share of the organizational work for both the 73rd Congress of the International Federation of Film Archives and the Symposium: Randy Haberkamp, May Haduong, Josef Lindner, Dan Faltz, and Michael Pogorzelski.

We would also like to thank the members of the curatorial team for the *Pacific Standard Time: LA /LA* project, *Recuerdos de un cine en español/ Latin American Cinema in Los Angeles,* Colin Gunckel, María Elena de las Carreras, Alejandra Espasande Bouza, and Jan-Christopher Horak, as well as Symposium funders The Getty Foundation, the Academy of Motion Picture Arts & Sciences, and the UCLA Film & Television Archive.

Finally, we would like to thank the FIAF Executive Committee for proposing a partnership between FIAF and the UCLA Film & Television Archive for the publication of this volume, and all those who were involved in its final preparation—especially Christophe Dupin and Christine Maes at the FIAF Secretariat, and Catherine A. Surowiec (proofreading and copyediting) and Lara Denil (layout)—for their hard work on its production.

The Editors